Single State of the Union

Single State of the Union
Single Women Speak Out on Life, Love, and the Pursuit of Happiness

"I Am Getting Married" is excerpted from "Family Values," in *I Have Chosen to Stay and Fight* by Margaret Cho, © 2005 by Soundball International, Inc. Used by permission of Riverhead Books, an imprint of Penguin Group (USA) Inc.

"The Speech" is excerpted from *The Idiot Girls' Action-Adventure Club* by Laurie Notaro, © 2002 by Laurie Notaro. Used by permission of Villard Books, a division of Random House, Inc.

"THUNDER" is excerpted from *My Horizontal Life: A Collection of One Night Stands* by Chelsea Handler, © 2005 by Chelsea Handler. Reprinted by permission of Bloomsbury USA.

"Marriage Ain't Prozac" is excerpted from *Kiss My Tiara* by Susan Jane Gilman, © 2001 by Susan Jane Gilman. Used by permission of Warner Books, Inc.

"Doctor, Donor, Desperado" is republished with permission of Crossroad Publishing Company from Margaret Smith's *What Was I Thinking? How being a Stand-Up Did Nothing to Prepare Me to Become a Single Mother,* copyright 2005, permission conveyed through Copyright Clearance Center, Inc.

"Life After Death" by Genevieve Davis Ginsburg originally appeared in *The New York Times Magazine* (December 2, 1990). Reprinted by permission of Paul Ginsburg.

"Cinderella" is excerpted from *Pretty is Hard: Poems About Shoes, Chocolate, and Best Friends* by Veronica Markey, copyright 2004. Used by permission of Arundel Books.

"How I Dodged a Reality Show Bullet" by Sasha Cagan, © 2006 Sasha Cagan.

 Published by
Seal Press
An Imprint of Avalon Publishing Group, Incorporated
1400 65th Street, Suite 250, Emeryville, CA 94608

Library of Congress Cataloging-in-Publication Data
Single state of the union : single women speak out on life, love, and the pursuit of happiness / [compiled by] Diane Mapes.
    p.˜cm.
ISBN-13: 978-1-58005-202-3
ISBN-10: 1-58005-202-9
    1. Single women—United States–Social life and customs—21st century.
    2. Single women—United States. I. Mapes, Diane.

HQ800.4.U6S547 2007
306.81'530973090511—dc22
2006038582

Art Direction by Kate Basart/Union Pageworks
Cover design by Traci Daberko
Interior design by Kate Basart/Union Pageworks
Printed in the United States of America

SINGLE
State of the Union

SINGLE WOMEN SPEAK OUT ON
LIFE, LOVE, AND THE
PURSUIT OF HAPPINESS

EDITED BY DIANE MAPES

SEAL PRESS

To SINGLE WOMEN EVERYWHERE:
YOU'RE GREAT—JUST AS YOU ARE.

CINDERELLA

A POEM

I don't know,

if it were me,

I'd have gone back

for that shoe.

———

—VERONICA MARKEY, AGE 5
Pretty is Hard: Poems About Shoes, Chocolate and Best Friends

Contents

Introduction: Greetings from Spinster Island

★

by DIANE MAPES

I was sitting at the bar of my favorite neighborhood restaurant not too long ago, futzing with the table of contents for this very book, when a man next to me struck up a conversation. He was six-tyish, alone, perhaps a wee bit inebriated. Like others before him, he was curious about what a fortysomething woman could possibly be up to sitting all by herself with only a manuscript and a plate of food for companionship. To me, it seemed apparent—I believe it's called a working dinner—but I needed a break so I played along.

"Well, I'm a writer," I told him. "But at the moment, I'm working on an anthology called *Single State of the Union.*"

"Single state of the whah?" he asked, and I realized he was well past the wee point.

"It's a collection of essays by single women," I explained. "Stories about all the different aspects of a single woman's life."

"A single woman," he said, and appeared flummoxed. "But . . . but . . . that's unnatural."

"Unnatural?" I said, noticing that *he* didn't happen to be wearing a wedding ring.

"Yeah, unnatural." He shook his head as if it were surrounded by tiny bees. Aunt Bees perhaps, from *The Andy Griffith Show,* each one trying to fill up her sad, useless life with heaping platters of fried chicken and scraps of tossed-off affection. "No woman *wants* to be single."

We've all been there. Endured the snide remarks from strangers and relatives, the endless queries from coworkers, the "helpful" nudges from friends: When are you going to settle down, get serious, get married? When are you going to stop fooling around and *get a real life?* Sure, singles have made a few strides these last few years, thanks to advocacy groups like Quirkyalone, Leather Spinsters, and Single Mothers by Choice (not to mention the less mancentric episodes of *Sex and the City*). But the myth of the insignificant incomplete single is still being held firmly in place by gigantic cultural pushpins labeled *The Rules* and *How to Get the Guy.*

Who cares if you're the head of a billion dollar corporation and so famous you don't need a last name (I'm talking to you, Oprah)— if you're not married, there's something *wrong* with you. You're too selfish. You're too picky. You're immature or commitment-phobic or maybe gay but you just won't admit it.

For whatever reason, single women just seem to drive people a little nuts.

Back in 1912, a Colorado minister by the name of Elmer V. Huffner preached a sermon in which he suggested that every old maid in America be shipped off to a barren island as a "waste product." Unmarried women were a "detriment and a menace to society," he thundered from his pulpit. "No woman has done her duty to the world until she has borne children."

Sadly, Elmer's whole waste-management message hasn't changed much through the years. Sure, the sermon's been refined a bit here and there, but we're still being bombarded with what seems to be a universally accepted "truth": A single life is an unhappy, unfulfilled, *unnatural* life.

In fact, some have argued it's a *perverse* life.

Take Dr. Walter C. Brown, for instance. In 1961, Dr. Brown published *The Single Girl,* "a medical doctor's intimate report on the problems of the unmarried female in our contemporary society," in which he asserts the single girl is an abnormal entity racked by a host of behavioral problems. She may *tell* you she's happy with her career or single only because she hasn't met the right guy just yet, but truth be told, she's a lonely, troubled soul whose only chance for true happiness is to quit dawdling and embrace a "normal" existence—i.e., become a wife and mother—and fast.

"From the twin standpoints of psychology and physiology, the most wholly suitable life for a woman in our society is that life afforded by a permanent and fulfilling marriage to one man," he writes. Fail to marry, and you're risking a life of "lesbianism, alcoholism, frigidity, sadomasochism, mental illness, nymphomania, and bisexualism."

And we wonder where those weird single girl stereotypes come from: the crazy cat lady, the boozy slattern, the priggish plain Jane who'd sooner die than have sex—even with herself. Who could forget mousy librarian Mary Hatch without George Bailey around to "save" her in *It's A Wonderful Life?* Or sniveling spinster Michelle Pfeiffer before she went all black vinyl as Catwoman?

As it happens, these oh-so-flattering depictions started in France, according to *Bachelor Girl* author Betsy Israel, set in motion when Molière created the world's first "proto-spinster" in his 1672 play *Les Femmes savantes*. Since that time, the desperate and deluded single gal has become a mainstay of popular culture, branching off to form new cartoonish stereotypes with every generation (much like the Republican Party). From the skinny, schizophrenic Olive Oyl (portrayed as both wheedling old maid and commitment-phobic vixen) to the mannish and man-crazed Miss Jane of *Beverly Hillbillies* (apparently even pseudo-lesbians were dying to get married in the '60s) to the knife-wielding nutcase in *Fatal Attraction* (driven mad by her desperate need for a man) to Flavor Flav's bitch-slapping, backstabbing harem of reality TV hos ("I don't need no BFF, I need Flav!"), single women have had the dubious honor of seeing themselves depicted as lonely, lazy, querulous, crazy, career obsessed, cat possessed, marriage mad, scantily clad, shoe crazed, sexually depraved, biologically clocked, and perpetually stalked.

In other words, anything and everything but happy, whole, and well-adjusted human beings with, you know, normal lives. But take a look at recent studies, and it's pretty obvious single women aren't exactly hyperventilating every time they get near a Ben Bridge or weeping quietly into the spit-up blankets of their married sister's babies.

In March 2006, a study by the Pew Internet and American Life Project found some "55 percent of singles report no active interest in seeking a romantic partner," a circumstance that was "especially true for women." As for the 16 percent of Americans who *were* actually looking for love (or something like it)—single men in search of a committed relationship outnumbered single women looking for the same thing by a margin of 2.5 to 1.

But maybe Pew didn't pose the question correctly. Or perhaps the researchers were too distracted by the loud ticking sounds emanating from all those single gals' biological clocks. Except that ticking has quieted down considerably these last few years as single women have figured out a way to beat the clock by having babies on their own—either through adoption, with the help of a bed buddy (or "basting buddy"), or by tapping their friendly neighborhood sperm banks.

0In the March 2006 issue of *The New York Times Magazine,* Jennifer Egan reports that the National Center for Human Statistics found that "between 1999 and 2003, there was an almost 17 percent jump in the number of babies born to unmarried women between ages thirty and forty-four in America," a figure that doesn't even take into account the number of single women who are adopting children.

Single women are doing just fine in the white-picket-fence department, as well (although some have grown weary of seeing the word "spinster" or some other musty throwback on their mortgage documents). In 2005, the National Association of Realtors found that 21 percent of all homes were purchased by single women, a number that's more than doubled since 1981. My guess is vibrator sales are right up there as well (at least in states where such things are still legal).

What does all this mean? Well, for starters, somebody needs to bury those old stereotypes—they're really starting to stink up the joint. But that's easier said than done.

In a *Salon* interview in December 2005, sociologist E. Kay Trimberger described what she called the "new single woman," based on a ten-year study involving a group of single, middle-class, over-thirty-five females. Trimberger's study—and subsequent book, entitled *The New Single Woman*—found that while many of the women were open to romance, none of them were miserable as singles, and all of them were "appreciative of the choices they had," as well as the idea that "there are more ways to find passion in life than through a soulmate."

What was the response?

"I suppose there's something to be said for transforming the dreary and tragic into an uplifting narrative about progress," a reader posted in one of many sour follow-ups.

"I accept the fact that more and more women are single," wrote another, "[but] isn't it also true that more and more women are being treated for depression?"

In other words, sure, you may be a sociology professor with decades of research and statistics to back up your findings, but *we* know better. Conventional wisdom (not to mention Dr. Brown and those lunkheads who keep churning out cheesy reality dating shows) holds that single women are nothing more than a bunch of lonely, troubled souls desperately trying to get *Hitched*—and fast. Or they're abnormal entities racked by depression and/or a host of intimacy issues. Or maybe they're just a bunch of lesbians who refuse to admit it (I'm sorry, but who *doesn't* come out in this day and age, for crying out loud?).

And so it goes. For every upbeat article proclaiming we're "Single, Female, and Desperate No More," there are twenty-five anguished interviews with hapless *Desperate Housewives* star Teri Hatcher, a tragic figure not for the sexual abuse she suffered as a child, but for her perpetual single status. For every AARP study that determines 81 percent of single women *aren't* overly concerned about the prospect of growing old alone, there are hundreds of self-help books telling us we'd better hurry up if we want to *Find a Husband After 35.*

At times it almost seems as if single women *have* been relegated to Rev. Elmer's mythic island of spinsters, a metaphorical rock in the midst of the ever-choppy Sea of Love, where the only thing to wash ashore with any regularity are vapid articles on how to downplay your pesky doctorate degree in order to meet Mr. Right. So much of what society sees, reads, and slogs through on a daily basis concerns the pitiful plight of the single woman: her desperate search for love, her pathetically empty womb, her despair over romance gone wrong (Jen dumped! Jessica divorced! How will they *ever* endure ten whole minutes of singledom? Next up on *ET!*). Is it any wonder that our friends and families and coworkers paint our lives as so bleak and black and meaningless when practically every magazine, television show, and movie within spitting distance reaffirms the notion that a single woman's overarching need for love outweighs all other concerns (save that of her need to lose weight and create a kicky new holiday hairstyle)?

These days, love not only conquers all, it pounds the living daylights out of anything in its path.

Do single women not have dying parents or sick pets or the occasional termite problem? Do we not have careers that fascinate us, friends that aggravate us, gods to grapple with, sexual personas to explore, preludes to learn, hoodies to knit, dogs to train, hogs to ride, corn to hoe, children to raise, and, now and again, a backed-up toilet to fix? Are we truly so vacant, so one-dimensional, so shallow and predictable that our *only* concern is figuring out which online dating service we'll log on to tonight and/or which pair of strappy sandals we'll wear on our exciting date with Dirk from accounting?

Hardly. It's just that, for many members of society and the media (for instance, the people responsible for promos like, "Up next, when the party begins, the women compete for the bachelor's attention—and for a pair of diamond earrings!"), that's their story and they're sticking to it. Whether single women like it or not, we're going to have our feet crammed into a pair of tiny glass slippers and sent stumbling off in the general direction of a ball. And for many, present company included, the toes on those little glass suckers are really starting to pinch.

"As a single, childless woman, it seems like all I get is either dating advice or warnings about how my life must be empty and meaningless," one reader emailed in response to *Salon*'s piece on 'The New Single Woman'. "No one seems to consider that I might be happy alone."

"It's so refreshing to read an article regarding single women that doesn't make us all sound like neurotic, desperate spinsters who look back on our lives as nothing but lost opportunities and relationships," penned another. "I am single both by choice and circumstance."

Are single women happy individualists? Marriage-crazed manzillas? Commitment-phobic thrill-seekers? Lovable but loopy singletons ricocheting from one dysfunctional relationship to the next? Are we confused or content? Bitter or better off? Lonely or living la dolce vita? None or all of the above?

That's the question of the hour. In fact, more than ever we seem to be at a cultural crossroads as social arbiters try to figure out if the new single woman is a card-carrying member of the Quirkyalone movement or if she's mincing about in a strapless prom dress, making cow eyes at *The Bachelor.*

Back in 1961, good old Dr. Brown asked three burning questions: "Who is the single girl? How does she live? How did she *get* that way?" I'd say it's time to ask those questions again, to take a careful measure of our current Single State of the Union.

Only this time, let's ask the "single girl" herself.

Part 1

How Come a Nice Girl Like You Isn't Married?

Living alone is an abnormal state for a woman.

—*HOW TO PICK A MATE: THE GUIDE TO A HAPPY MARRIAGE*
(E. P. DUTTON & CO. 1946)

Single-Minded

★

by SUSAN SHAPIRO

I just met a new man!" I told my mother long-distance a while back. "He's cute and funny and just my type."

"Your type is neurotic, self-destructive, and not interested in you," she said. "What's wrong with this one?"

"Nothing," I answered. "I mean, well, he's not quite divorced yet."

My mother hung up.

Her impatience with my relationships was understandable, given the circumstances. For fifteen years, she had accompanied me through the frenzied and frustrating New York City dating scene, a scene she never had to contend with.

In a way, my mother had it easy. At nineteen, she married a New York Jewish doctor. This was in the 1950s, when that sort of thing was still fashionable. She quit her job, moved to a big white house in West Bloomfield, Michigan, and had four children. I was sixteen years older than she was at her wedding, and she could not fathom why I would rather be making books than babies.

When I moved to New York after college, I rebelled against her chauvinist, suburban-married mentality, in which the men work and play God and the women stay home, do the laundry, and change diapers. I still liked Jewish men. But I rejected doctors, MBAs, accountants, attorneys, and basically any man in a business suit who made money, seemed closed-minded, and wanted a wife to stay home and raise children. I wrote passionately, and between pages I dated Jewish poets, professors, painters, and documentary filmmakers.

Lucky for me, I was best friends at the time with Monica, whose father was a poor but critically acclaimed fiction writer. Having grown up in the city with a bunch of bohemians, Monica had rebelled, too. She sneered at the sight of a man in jeans reading the *New York Review of Books*. Monica and I were the perfect man-hunting team. Any male in a suit was hers. Any schlep with indications of a tormented soul was my territory.

Then Monica met my brother the surgeon, moved to the Midwest suburbs, had four kids in six years like my mother did, and became the daughter my mother always wanted. I was still alone in the big city, tied only to my computer.

During those years, I struggled constantly with my editors, my muse, and my mother. She couldn't understand why a master's degree in English, psychoanalysis, my weekly writing workshop, and a freelance career were essential to my existence.

"It's Saturday night!" my mother yelled into the receiver. "Why aren't you out?"

"I'm on deadline," I said.

"You work too much. It's not healthy."

"The last two magazines haven't paid me yet," I told her. "It's been four months."

"I'll send you money," she promised. "Just go out and have fun while you're still young."

"How do they expect someone to stay in business if they never pay on time?" I asked.

"Who cares? For god's sake, go get yourself a man!"

I tried, and I did find a few. They were usually artsy intellectuals who politically professed a penchant for feminism but at the same time expected dinner on the table and the creation of their clones. Their woman's work always took a back seat to their own. Finally, I met Ira, a true feminist and freethinker.

"Mom! I met a new man, Ira Cohen! Really smart," I told her. "And Jewish!" (As if she thought Ira Cohen was Irish.)

"What's this Ira of yours do?" she skeptically asked.

"He's a poet. He wrote a brilliant book called *Nightmare of Pain*."

"That and a token will get you on the subway," she said, "which, by the way, you shouldn't take alone at night. . . . So, how old is this manic depressive of yours, anyway?"

"Fifty-seven," I said.

She hung up again.

Ira and I had a great time going to book parties, doing *The New York Times* crossword puzzle together on Saturday nights, and reading Sylvia Plath in bed. But soon I was editing through *Nightmares of Pain, Volume II,* and playing Ira's confidante, mother, and shrink. He would do the cooking and cleaning, but I had to listen for hours on end to his self-obsessed, repetitious Freudian tirades. When Knopf rejected his manuscript, Ira had a nervous breakdown and moved out of the country. I gave up on men.

My writing career was satisfying enough. I published book reviews, personal essays, and humor pieces.

"Do you have to win a Pulitzer Prize before you get yourself a husband?" my mother asked.

"Don't be ridiculous," I said. But when I broke into *The New York Times Book Review,* I started dating again.

By my midthirties, I was getting cynical. Most of my friends were married, and the others were dropping like flies. To my younger brothers' kids, and my Michigan cronies, I was known as "Aunt Susie."

I met a lot of creeps, all of whom wanted to move in with me, immediately. The seemingly decent ones were either taken or called back three months later, saying, "Hey, how's it going?" as if we'd last spoken yesterday.

Finally, a friend fixed me up with Aaron, a workaholic TV comedy writer who had picked up some cool credits and made money along the way to our blind date. He was a judge's son who'd grown up in the Westchester version of my family and actually liked getting dressed up.

"You're sweet," I told him. "But I can't sleep with someone who wears a suit."

He offered to take off the suit. I politely declined.

A week later he barged into my apartment unshaven, wearing torn Levi's, and quoting Bob Dylan's *Blood on the Tracks*.

Now we're in love. Our idea of a good time is critiquing rough drafts of each other's prose while ordering in sushi at midnight. For some reason, it's working.

In the meantime, my mother got bored waiting to plan my wedding and gave up on me. When my youngest brother went away to college, she decided to start her own business. Though I'd been telling her to go back to work for years, I was suddenly upset when she didn't have the time to phone me every day. I assumed she no longer cared.

"Hey, Mom, I'm seeing a great guy named Aaron," I told her. "I want you to meet him. Can I bring him home for Passover?"

"Bad time," my mother said. "I'm not making it this year. Too busy. . . . Oh, by the way, I liked that last essay of yours. Nice twist at the end. Good use of quotes."

"Thanks. But Mom, listen. This is serious."

"You want to know what's serious?" she said. "My main client owes me $3,000. It's been four months and the jerk still hasn't paid."

"Send him a second invoice and mail one to his accounting department with a 'Past Due' notice on it," I told her. ". . . So anyway, Mom. Aaron is smart, tall, really cute, funny, Jewish, and together. His family is just like our family—"

"How do they expect someone to stay in business if they don't pay their bills on time?" she went on.

"Mother! Please hear what I'm saying. I'm in love with a fantastic guy! You would approve of this one! I might even marry him!"

"So what's the big hurry?" she said.

How I Dodged a
Reality Show Bullet

★

by SASHA CAGEN

I t was midnight, the day after Thanksgiving, and I had just arrived back at my mother's house after gorging on leftovers at a friend's place, when I plopped down in front of the family computer and checked my email. I always have high expectations for email. In the back of my mind, there's an irrational, tiny, monstrous feeling that today might be the day for the email that will change my life. Every so often, I'm not disappointed.

This potentially life-changing email arrived in my MySpace account from someone named Kat. The subject line: "Let me know what you think."

> Hey—I am working on a show called *Single Minded.* This is NOT a typical dating show. There is no competition, no elimination, and nothing to lose. The show will be *Sex and the City* meets *Bridget Jones,* a light-hearted, real-life romantic comedy following a group of successful, smart, and funny single girls trying to find "the one" in San

Francisco. The producers are the same guys that do *Queer Eye for the Straight Guy*. Check out the website www.scoutvision.com, and write back ASAP if you are interested.

I was in a food coma, but suddenly, the idea of being on a reality show brought me back to life. *Me, you want me to be on your dating show? My struggle, my drama, my love life, all filmed for national TV!* The rush was enormous. But in addition to feeling flattered, I also felt confused. Was I just one in the vast sea of San Francisco thirtysomethings Kat had spammed because my pictures were so irresistibly cute, or was Kat more sophisticated than that? Had she contacted me because she knew I was a singles expert?

You see, I am not just a single woman in San Francisco. I am a *professional* single woman, a writer who has achieved minor celebrity status by writing about an emerging trend of people who prefer to be single rather than settle. By coining a new term— 'quirkyalone'—to describe these ultraromantic, independent types, then writing a book about them, then starting a movement to bring them together, I've become an accidental pundit to whom the media often turn for the "happy single" perspective. I've bantered with Anderson Cooper and in countless international versions of *Cosmo* to combat the tyranny of coupledom—the idea that people need to be in a relationship at all times in order to be happy.

So although my calling card is about being single, I am not your typical candidate for a dating show. In fact, you could even say I've served as the voice of those who *hate* reality dating shows. I told *USA Today* that people like me "don't want dating turned into a job, [or] pressure from the online dating industry and . . . the reality dating TV shows where people are desperate to find someone."

But hey, I'm also all for irony, for saying yes rather than no, a lesson I learned in a comedy improv class. Being invited to interview for a reality dating show was so deliciously ironic that I had to sit and smile, stunned in front of the glow of the computer screen. Maybe I could infiltrate. Maybe, my mind twisted beyond all recognizable logic, I would find the love of my life.

I told my family and friends about the email over the rest of my Thanksgiving trip, and everyone loved the publicity possibilities, the fun of having a relative on TV. They thought I should follow up, but I wasn't so sure. Hadn't I publicly maligned these shows as a conspiracy against self-respecting single women? Besides, my personality was much more suited to writing than performance. I have insomnia. I need solitude. If cameras were following me around every day, I might never calm down enough to sleep. I could have a mental breakdown.

But then, back at work in early December in the daily grind of my proofreading job, my quite-real concerns dissolved as boredom got the best of me. The office environment can have a distorting effect on one's judgment. I started to think about movies in which authors proclaim the advantages of being single and then find themselves undone once they get on television. *Down with Love* came to mind. Best-selling female advice author (Renée Zellweger) has all the answers until a sly journalist playboy (Ewan McGregor) starts asking the questions and they fall in love. I wondered if that could be me.

I told myself to stop, that these were sick thoughts, the product of watching too many romantic comedies, and then I downloaded the PDF outlining the qualifications for the show: "Each participant must be able to continue her day-to-day life, including her current job, throughout the production period, and allow her daily life (including causing her workplace to allow) access for production of the Program." How weird. They would want to come to my proofreading job. That would be thrilling footage. The program would be taped over approximately eleven weeks. There was no prize and no compensation. None of it made sense. But as they say about love, if it doesn't make sense, trust it.

I walked into a conference room, shut the door, and called Kat.

I asked, "I'm just wondering why you contacted me. Was it because of my book, or were you just contacting people on MySpace?" She said, "Well, we were looking on MySpace for girls over twenty-five, who were cute and had interesting profiles. . . . The show is really fun. It's about women who are looking for Mr. Right, who are ready to settle down." She wanted to know if I wanted to come in for an interview. We settled on Monday at 5:30 PM at Hotel Monaco, a luxury hotel a few blocks from San Francisco's shopping district.

Over the next few nights, I shared the details with friends and even recruited one of them, Halo, for the show. We were out at karaoke and analyzed the appeal over drinks. My rationale for auditioning was to write about the process, but I had to admit, there was a thrill in being considered. Halo thought it would be fun for everyone from her past to come out of the woodwork to say, "Hey, I saw you on TV." She also thought *Single Minded* could be a path to dating Joaquin Phoenix.

I wasn't so convinced. For me, the appeal felt like a delusion: the delayed prom-queen complex. By that, I mean, a secret part of me wanted to be chosen, recognized as the heroine I am. My life is *Sex and the City,* a romantic comedy; it's just that *I'm* the only one watching. If I were on the show, everyone else would be able to appreciate my highs, my lows, my dramas, my neuroses, my universal pain. Let's admit it: It's hard not to want to be universally adored by America. And don't tell me. I know what *really* happens on reality TV: Contestants are humiliated or are just a blip across the screen. But there was a small part of me that thought I could rise above everyone else's fate and become the less self-loathing Bridget Jones, the real Carrie Bradshaw who wears flats instead of heels. That was the dream, anyway.

As I got dressed that Monday, the more analytical part of my brain recognized that the whole thing could be a ruse. They might be looking for Plain Janes to humiliate. Maybe the real name of the show would be *Old Maid*. This thought didn't stop me from trying on multiple outfits. I settled on a maroon Ann Taylor sweater, the same jeans that I wear every day, and brown boots. The winning part of my ensemble: definitely the bright orange coat with a fur-trim hood. I borrowed my sister's hair-shine spray to make my hair shiny and straight, even though my latest communication from *Single Minded* informed me they wanted "real women" and not "glam dolls."

After work, I took the bus over to the Monaco, obsessing the whole time about how to present myself—as a participant or expert? The payoff for being a participant: voyeurism, to see how they treat me and how I respond, to go as deep as possible and write about the journey. The payoff of spinning myself as an expert: Maybe they would hire me as a consultant, writer, coach, or expert.

Cash!

I arrived at the Monaco, where the lobby contained no information about *Single Minded*. I had to ask the young, handsome, bald black man at the desk where to go. It was vaguely humiliating. "Hi, I am here for a reality dating show." Momentarily confused, he pointed me to the lobby, where the casting ladies—or "girls," as I learned they called themselves and all the applicants, just like the hosts on *The Bachelor* do—sat by a table next to a Christmas tree.

Young and blond, casually dressed in jeans and yoga pants, the casting girls looked mildly war-torn, as if they had been camped out in the hotel for weeks. They were in their early to midtwenties, low on the totem pole, probably. Pointing me to the free champagne in the lobby, one woman handed me a stack of paperwork. There were hundreds of questions on the questionnaire, but she told me I didn't have to fill them all out; they wouldn't read all the answers. The questions were just designed to get me thinking.

Apparently, they had been interviewing all week—seventeen interviews on the day I came, the most in a day so far—and they had only found one "girl" the producers liked. They were looking for someone fun, sarcastic, hot, and successful, someone in her thirties who had it all and could laugh at the situation *How is it that I'm still single?* They wanted the show to be positive, not bitter, with contestants who were quirky and inspiring, whose personalities would read immediately on-screen within fifteen seconds. The producers had chosen San Francisco because they had been here interviewing for *Queer Eye* and met so many "hot professional women" who were having a hard time finding someone to date.

"Think funny," Kat called out as I left with my stack. "Funny, funny, funny, funny!"

As I read through the questionnaire, I started to feel sick. It was far worse than filling out an online dating profile. The survey went on for pages, huge life questions with mere centimeters for responses. "What has been your highest moment as an individual? Your lowest?" "What's the craziest thing you have ever done?" "How is your sex life? Has it changed over time?" "Explain your dating/love history. Where has it been and where do you see it going?" "Describe your biggest heartbreak." "Do you fall for the wrong guys? Why?" "Have you ever been treated for depression?"

I started to feel a protest sweep through my body. I was there of my own free will, but it was becoming clear that I couldn't carry on the charade of being a real applicant. I'm used to revealing myself in print and had written about "the best sex of my life"; being deeply, persistently single; my inability to floss; my love of hanging out in the self-help section of bookstores. But I controlled those words; the confessions were in service of something that had larger meaning for me.

There was no way I could sign a contract that gave producers a right to do an STD test and disseminate the results any way they saw fit. Or sign off on "dissemination of material or record-ings that may be unfavorable, humiliating, embarrassing, deroga-tory, or portray her in a false light" (although I found it extremely amusing that they covered both embarrassing and humiliating). Of course there was a confidentiality agreement. The power disparity couldn't have been clearer. The producers could say anything they wanted about me, but I had to remain absolutely mum.

I came back with meager answers and handed them to the young casting director. And then hours passed. Well, an hour and a half. With no time to eat after work, hunger started to vibrate throughout my body. My blood sugar dropped to a terrible low, and I thought I might have to disappear into the night for a banana at the deli next door, when my time finally came to meet Kat. She was up on the third floor and had set up a mini-studio in a hotel room, complete with bright lights, a camera, and a computer attached to stream the interviews to the producers, "Dave" and "Dave," in Los Angeles.

I asked Kat for food, but all she had was a bag of sour cream and onion potato chips and an Emergen-C packet, which I sucked down in a glass of water. First Kat asked me if I was dating. I wondered about an appropriate response. *Dating, what does that mean? Actively engaged in the search? Currently seeing someone?* They didn't want me to be currently seeing someone. The contract spelled out that I couldn't be. I answered with the truth: I had just ended a relationship. How long did it last? "Three months." How did it end? "He went off into the woods."

I realized that I had exactly the funny story they wanted. My latest relationship had ended suddenly when my boyfriend, a Slo-venian computer scientist, got stressed out by the possibility of los-ing his job (and therefore being deported) and disappeared into the woods for a weeklong hike. "Went off into the woods?" Kat looked aghast. Yes, well, a week later he sent me an email. There were more tragicomic details—he didn't have a cell phone, or any phone, except for his work line, so there was no way for me to contact him, and I thought he might be dead. He wore pajama-like pants to work, he didn't know what call waiting or The Gap were. I could have gone on and on. Was this really the kind of thing I wanted to share with America? All of a sudden it was clear. My personal travails were not going to make sense to a mainstream audience. They wanted quirky. I sounded weird.

I silenced the potential reality show star in me and switched over to dating-expert self. Yes, despite dating people who wear pajama pants to work, I was a dating expert. "Really, I'm coming at this from a different angle. I'm an expert. I've written this book about being single," I said, and handed her a copy of *Quirkyalone.*

And thus it died, this nightmare-fantasy of me as participant on *Single Minded.*

Kat said they might need guest experts, and we did a fifteen-minute interview. I explained quirkyalone and International Quirkyalone Day, an alternative holiday I started on February 14 as a celebration of all forms of love, for singles and couples. She asked for dating advice. She wanted specific tips, but as a proponent of quirkyness (and therefore authenticity), I kept my advice simple: Be yourself. They're going to find out about the real you eventually anyway.

Many months passed, and there were no further life-changing communications from Kat. I figured I was too San Francisco, too affirming and positive; they probably wanted someone with firm rules. I felt a little disappointed, but more than anything, I felt curious about whatever had happened to the show.

Then, one serendipitous day in June, I walked outside to get lunch and ran into my friend Jonathon. He practically grabbed me and asked, "Did you see that show last night? *How to Get the Guy?* Four single women looking for love . . . it's set in San Francisco!" I instantly realized that *Single Minded* had been renamed, and although offensive, *How to Get the Guy* was a more accurate title. This was never a show about being single. It was about finding a man, any man.

I couldn't wait until Monday night to watch the first episode. But quickly, anticipation turned to shock. Despite all my public dissing of dating reality shows to the press, I was secretly a fan. I love a bad reality dating show—it makes me feel more justified for sitting at home not dating.

This show—I don't know how to express this. Somehow *How to Get the Guy* managed to be bad, not in a fun way, but in an excruciating way. Not enjoyable bad, not *Glitter* bad, not cult bad, *HTGTG* was so bad—so humiliating to all involved—that it was painful to watch for more than fifteen minutes. The fact that the producers referred to the four women on the show with archetypes like "the party girl," "the career girl," "the girl next door," and "the dreamer" was one clue that the women wouldn't be left with any dignity or individuality. But much worse than the women were the plastic love coaches they hired. Their only qualifications seemed to be the fact that they'd "found love."

The show was structured around giving the four women advice for their man hunt. But the advice sounded like it came out of the pages of a teen magazine: If you want a guy to kiss you, casually caress his collar before saying goodbye; if you want to meet someone, stare at him for four seconds straight; if you want to get intimate on a dinner date, share your food and eat—men love it when women eat! The show was in love with rules. A first date must end with a kiss. If not, it's just an appointment! Each show ended with a montage of the four women writing in their diaries, with a voice-over of them reading aloud the epiphanies of their love search. "Cheesy" is not nearly strong enough a word for this cringe-inducing show.

My shock, of course, quickly turned into relief that I was never publicly associated with such a disaster. I went to bed feeling almost blissfully calm. *Good decision-making, Sasha, you really dodged a bullet!* I refrained from watching for a few weeks, and then, just when I thought I could stomach another episode, an even greater surprise: After airing four episodes, ABC axed *How to Get the Guy* in favor of additional repeats of *Supernanny*. The tragedy deepened. We never found out if anybody "got the guy."

In retrospect, I find it scary, naive, and admirable that I seriously considered being on such a hideous show. But I understand why I did it. For better or worse, I'm an optimist. I've been moved by television before. *Ally McBeal* and *Sex and the City* were revolutionary for me in that they presented single characters I could relate to. They helped inform my ideas around quirkyalone and provided confirmation that I wasn't the only one with a deeply single orientation.

Now that the pendulum has swung the other way, and we're seeing so much *Desperate Housewives* and the *Real Housewives of Orange County* and other celebrations of traditional femininity, I want to again see something original on television about single women's lives. I wanted to be part of the process. I'll also admit a part of me, like everyone, wanted to be famous—the cute girl on TV whom everyone is rooting for. Alas, I now recognize the utter delusion of this fantasy and will refuse all requests for a show centered entirely on *me*. You hear that, Hollywood? It's over!

To be frank, I already have enough fame. I'm famous for putting a positive spin on being single. And that kind of recognition makes me proud. The idea of being famous for being on that train-wreck program, on the other hand, gives me hives. They say all publicity is good publicity, but I'm happy to have my dignity intact.

It's far better to be famous for being happily single, rather than single and desperate.

Coda: Just in case you are wondering, I never signed their confidentiality agreement.

An Open Letter to Mom, Deana, Mary, and the Folks at Work

★

by AMY THOMAS

T o answer your (unspoken) questions: No, I haven't met anyone lately. I haven't been on any dates, and there's no one
"special" in my life that I'm holding out on you. Of course I want
to meet someone. Naturally, I'm making efforts to put myself out
there. And no, I'm not being stubborn or holding my standards
unreasonably high. Yes, I want a life partner. Yes, I want to meet
someone and fall madly, deeply, truly in love. And yes, I know my
clock is ticking, and that does make me nervous.

So there you have it. It's that straightforward.

This outwardly strong, independent woman with the over-
flowing to-do list and jam-packed social calendar does indeed
have babies on the brain. How could I not, when all the friends I
grew up with are pushing strollers by day and passing out in bed
by eight at night? When every magazine on every newsstand on
every corner of the city is cooing about the onesie wardrobe of

some celebrity's baby? Truly, how could I *not* be considering my own thirty-three-and-single situation? What kind of freak do you think I am?

But since we're being candid, let me ask you some questions: Why are you evaluating my life in terms of breeding? Why is giving birth the ultimate benchmark of success? And with everything that's available in this city, this world, and in my life, why should I limit my desires to pairing off and procreating? Whatever happened to the things we used to ponder, like creative fulfillment, professional challenges, and personal growth? Are travels abroad, philosophical debates, and current events suddenly less important than creating a family unit?

It seems to me we're ignoring the fact that children are just one facet of life. Sure, I grew up believing I wanted kids, and chances are I still do. But there's so much more that's important—at least to me. And you don't seem to get that.

I'd be lying if I said it didn't hurt that you *never* ask me about my everyday (single) life. That your eyes glaze over whenever I talk about the crappy state of company politics or the frustrations of trolling fabulous new bars filled with less-than-fabulous people. It bothers the hell out of me that you never ask about my writing assignments—never mind that you don't ask if and when you can read them, or talk to me about them after you have read them of your own volition.

I've looked at hundreds—if not thousands—of photos of your kids. And they're adorable, really. But would it kill you to see something of mine in return? Just because my stories aren't dressed up in hand-knit sweaters or cute pumpkin costumes doesn't mean they're any less worthy. After all, maybe if you read my work once in a while, you would grow curious and subsequently interested in this aspect of my life—sort of like I did when your baby first cut a front tooth or pooped in a pot. And please forgive my bluntness, but maybe if you read some of my work, it might spark some new interests and passions in your life other than the Wiggles' latest DVD.

And while we're on the subject, how do you think it feels to lose my friends to two-year-olds? To come to the painful realization that I can no longer talk to you about movies (you don't have the time to see them) or books (the last one you read was *The Perfect Baby Name*) or restaurants (you haven't been out since your birthday—it's too expensive to hire a sitter) or dating (it's been eight years since you attempted it). Yes, you inquire if I've met anyone, but the path I have to stumble down to meet "the one" doesn't seem worthy of your time. You grow bored when I tell you that the bars are filled with losers, that work is all married men, that the online world has more than its fair share of geriatrics and psycho killers. I'll share the sting and humiliation of being dumped by someone I didn't even like, and all you can come up with is that thanks to your adorable little one, you no longer have to deal with *that* drama. You lob me that age-old pacifier (pun intended), "Don't worry, you'll meet someone soon." Well, that's *one* way to end the conversation.

Yet you're forgiven for your disinterest, your distractions, your disingenuousness, while I'm expected to simply accept the fact that things have changed and learn to become rabidly curious about your baby's bowel movements, sleeping patterns, and sock puppets.

Don't get me wrong. I appreciate how you've limited yourself to asking if I've met anyone or if I'm anxious about having kids to a mere two or three times when we *do* manage to talk. Truly, I know these burning questions have been bubbling beneath the surface ever since you got a ring on your finger and started down your path of happily ever after: Is Amy *ever* going to meet anyone? Doesn't she *want* to have babies? Doesn't she know she doesn't have *forever?*

Well, nobody has forever. For anything. Particularly not for creating the life they want to create which is exactly what I'm trying to do. It may not be the picture-perfect life we grew up believing was waiting for each of us, but it's my life and I like it just fine— lame dates, exhausting colleagues, and frustrating signs of aging included.

And by the way, since I *am* flying solo, the whole baby thing is moot. Sure, I'm aware that I'm approaching that scary age when biological challenges increase by the hour and I "should" be thinking about whether I want kids and what I'm going to do about it. And yes, Mom, I know you'd love a couple more grandkids to dote on. But what exactly are my options? Settle for the wrong guy just for the sake of having babies? Fall victim to the next player who gushes about how crazy he is for his nieces and nephews? Simply grab a turkey baster and some bum off the street?

If you figure it out, let me know.

And while you're at it, maybe you can tell me when I stopped being a human being—a friend or daughter or coworker, a creative mind or curious globe-trotter—and suddenly turned into an empty womb. Maybe you can tell me when my life, my choices, and my varied accomplishments suddenly became insignificant.

At least in your married-with-kids eyes.

Is it asking too much to want you to exhibit the same excite- ment for *my* birthday parties as I do for your one-year-old's? The same admiration for my first home-buying experience as I did for your first labor experience? Am I wrong for wishing that once, just once, you'd send me a card congratulating me on selling a great piece of writing, the way I've done the countless times you've announced a new addition to your family? If you did, then maybe I wouldn't feel the need to ponder motherhood so much, to wonder if I've made the right decision, to question my motives, my belief system, my worth.

Because maybe it's not some overwhelming internal desire to be a mother, but a simple yearning to maintain a close relationship with you, that keeps me fascinated with the minutiae of your life. And I just wish you'd see that. And help me feel that I'm not slipping into irrelevance simply because I don't battle the same breast-pump and solid-food crises that you do.

But for now, don't worry.

I promise you'll be the first to know when I've met someone. I'll respond in kind and tell you all about how wonderful he is, how happy I am, and how much we look forward to having babies of our own. And until then, I'll continue indulging you by attending showers, looking at photos, enduring interrupted phone conversations, and even busting out the baby talk when I'm in the company of your adorable love child.

All I ask is that you stop with the questions, spoken and otherwise. Yes, I have moments of uncertainty, but I'm not becoming that crazy cat lady. Instead, I'm becoming something else, something that doesn't come with neat little labels like "wife" and "mother." And until I do join you on your side of holy matrimony, try to remember that I'm more than content with the answers I've found so far. And the process of discovering the rest of them is a singularly fabulous experience.

Yours in full disclosure, I am,
Amy

P.S. If you happen to have George Clooney's phone number, just fork it over and we can call things even.

I Am Getting Married

★

by MARGARET CHO

I am getting married. I had stopped thinking about it as a possibility for a long time. I got very used to the delicious dream of spinsterhood, independence in solitude, gardening and animal rescue, a varied and lengthy succession of lovers, rejection of the Cinderella fantasies of my peers, looking at settling down like a kind of slow and not all that painful but more just an annoying death, more like a degenerative disease than a stroke. Most of my friends already had a divorce or two under their belts. My fiancé is on his third trip down the aisle.

Marriage for my generation has been a disappointment, for the most part. There is the heady rush of first love, the backlash against the free lovin', swinging '70s key-party antics of our parents, this desire for stability and the pressure to conform. Getting hitched was the emotional part of the American Dream, the pursuit of happiness clause, the completion and reward for the trials of adolescence. The Reagan era gave most of us our values, as we were most impressionable during the reign of Molly Ringwald and the whitewashed vision of John Hughes. The entire Hughes oeuvre maintained that suburban white culture was the true world, the way things really were, how we all wanted them to be. Its power over my generation cannot be ignored or trivialized. Hughes presented to us a tricky nirvana, one in which, if you play by the rules, you will win—and win big—forever and ever. There were characters written into the thin and uninteresting plots to serve as warnings of the pitfalls in life: individuality, personality, originality, ethnicity. Like eccentric old maid Annie Potts in *Pretty in Pink,* living in the "ethnic" neighborhood Chinatown in order to telegraph her insanity to the viewing audience. She wears thrift store clothes and works at a record store, well beyond her youth, in a futile attempt to deny the inevitable, the fact that she must be married in order to move on, like the unfortunate ghosts of the unjustly murdered and unavenged angry spirits of the dead that must be shown the light, the portal to the other side, so that they might be guided to the afterworld and be released from their bondage here on earth. She warns Molly Ringwald of the dangers of not going to the prom in a cautionary tale about a woman who denied herself the high school ritual and spent the rest of her days compulsively looking for shoes, keys, subway tokens, finding them all or finding nothing—all the while knowing that she is really lacking nothing, has lost nothing, but that she, for not going along with the traditions and rites of the American teenager, she herself is what is missing. She is incomplete.

In the end, Molly goes to the prom, and Annie Potts puts on a business suit, with a crest sewn onto the breast pocket, and goes on a blind date with an accountant, finally giving in to the "reality" of womanhood, the true purpose of us all. Completion, surrender, giving in, and giving up.

In *The Breakfast Club,* goth-before-her-time Ally Sheedy stops making art out of her own dandruff and allows herself to be made over by Molly Ringwald, capturing the attention of jocky cock Emilio Estevez and finding out that she has beauty, which will eventually, God willing, lead to her "completion." The title song of this film, "Don't You (Forget About Me)," was a sickening premonition of the future, in that we remembered. We remembered to get married. We remembered that having a family was the best thing that could happen. We remembered that we needed to be pretty, and not stand out too much, in order to achieve that final goal: Completeness. Wholeness. Whiteness. Matrimony. Suburbia. Babies. Death.

So why am I getting married? Because somebody I love asked me, and I want to. I know I am already complete, because I've had to fight to realize my completeness, to see it when all I was offered was blindness. I had to force myself to see what was not there. So now that I have seen it, I just want to spend a lot of my parents' money and have an embarrassing, semi-Satanic wedding where, instead of wedding vows, we exchange blood. Instead of death, we choose immortality, like vampires. Instead of children, we will have dogs and art.

You Can't Go Home Again

★

by JANE HODGES

I'm not sure what made me decide to go back to my ten-year high school reunion in Richmond, Virginia, but these days I chalk it up to anthropology. Maybe I was feeling confident because my life was starting to finally come together and I felt I had some success to display. It was 1998, and I had spent my post-Dartmouth years living in New York, hopscotching through newspaper and magazine jobs while earning an MFA in creative writing. When the reunion flyer came, I was an editor at a small business magazine, and I had just moved to a Harlem apartment overlooking the Hudson River. I had an older, inappropriate lover whose largely secret existence made me feel sophisticated and complex. And after years of aggressive networking, I was about to publish my first *New York Times* story. I was thrilled that this was my life, and I had come to see its uncertainties positively—as forms of freedom, opportunity, and adulthood itself.

If you knew the kind of upbringing I'd had in the former capital of the Confederacy (read: sheltered), or the kind of social life I'd had at the college known for inspiring *Animal House* (read: terrifying), you'd understand why it was all so exciting. To me, the city was an endless graduate school, full of unlikely professors and characters. The apartment buildings were giant dormitories, the cabs and cafés backdrops for encounters that broadened the mind. Though burdened with student loans and perpetual reminders that I was disobeying the Southern mandate for femininity (my sister: "Ever considered freezing your eggs?"), I was mostly aware that the more time I spent away from home, the richer I became in life experience, and the further I felt from the pressures to bow to a Southern man and then reproduce him.

Oh, what the heck, I thought, as I read the bulletin for my reunion at St. Catherine's School for Girls.

Back then, I may have been the overachieving kid from the screwed-up middle-class family, attending the school for rich girls. But I was a New Yorker now. I'd earned my black shoes and my black humor with life experience. I'd covered the dot-com boom, talking late into the evening about the future of "old media" and web design. I'd worked from a pressroom at Cannes and watched my graduate thesis adviser snort coke off a poetry book. I'd chased a mugger, been in a cab wreck, started a novel, and was currently interviewing to work at *Fortune.* I was officially out in the world now—I'd made it to the Algonquin and was ready to drink the cosmo.

I checked the box next to "I will attend" and slipped the RSVP card in the mail.

St. Catherine's was an Episcopal school, founded in 1890 by Virginia Randolph Elliott to prepare girls for college at a time when doing so was not only progressive, but feminist. The campus is beautiful, its Georgian brick buildings interspersed with magnolia and dogwood trees, lined on several sides by tennis courts and fields for lacrosse and hockey. Class sizes were small, the teachers demanding and eccentric. Getting in was no small feat, and neither was paying the price of admission. Parents have clamored to send their children here for decades, some because of the society angle, but most because the school hammers home the kind of classic curriculum required to get into an excellent college. The school turns out lawyers and doctors and journalists and fashion designers; I knew I was privileged to be an alumna, and was even somewhat proud, despite our oddly slutty Christian alma mater: "What we keep we lose, only what we give remains our own."

By the time we reached high school, ninety-five years had passed since the school's founding. What I noticed even as a student in high school, though, was that we students came in two types: women who would put career first and women who were socialites angling, whether they knew it or not, to marry someone of equal stature. Some would go far beyond their comfort zone, and some would never leave it. There was nothing wrong with either approach, of course. Some people are in fact passionate about living where and how they were raised, or they're close to their families and want to repeat the happiness they knew in childhood. But if you come from a, shall we say, more complicated family and grew up in different economic circumstances than your peers, it's likely that, like me, you'd want to leave town and learn to make a living using your brain.

I shared a birthday with Ben Franklin and, like him, I believed in the very American concept of self-invention and self-determination. I believed it was important to set yourself up in life with your career first and pursue the comforts next. Whether that belief dictated my approach to life or whether economic reality did hardly mattered. I was a middle-class tourist in the world of elite education, and I needed to pay for the trip. So it was that, when I came home a decade after graduating from St. Catherine's, I was still paying my dues in New York—working on my career mostly, hoping to "settle down" one day but not worried about it, and generally happy to live this way.

My choices, as usual, were met with skepticism when I reached my parents' house in Richmond a few days before my reunion. When I crossed their threshold, I entered another world, in which my mother beheld me with anguish, observing the circles under my eyes.

"You've been working too hard again," she said, wringing her hands. Where had she gone wrong? One idea: My mother came of age in 1950s Atlanta and was a firm believer that the three worst fates that could befall a woman were failing to marry, marrying and divorcing, and having a career. (Driving while menstrual was also a very serious misfortune, as was being caught smoking Salem Lights.) My mother considered income-generation beneath her— "man's work"—although occasionally, like a latter-day Scarlett O'Hara, she'd haul our clothes to the Junior League consignment store while we were at school, then gloat about her $20 take for the Esprit minis we'd bought with baby-sitting money.

"Janie, if you keep working like this you'll turn yourself into an old maid!" she said. "I don't know why you've decided to work so hard."

Textbook Mom, I thought, turning down the sheets on my spinster's bed and taking a deep yoga breath. Fortunately, I had gone to a challenging school that had served as a respite and counterpoint to my mother's pre-*Feminine Mystique* mindset. I couldn't blame her, really; she was a product of her times, achingly unhappy but unable to recognize her misery as the result of her adherence to a domestic social norm that was outdated even as she was super-gluing it to her subconscious. She wasn't one for therapy or reading disturbing feminist texts with a basic premise easily summed up in the words of Eleanor Roosevelt: "No one can make you feel inferior without your consent."

Instead she'd pack a bag every now and again and threaten to check in at the Executive Motor Inn on Broad Street, never to return, as some sort of protest against . . . what? She was stuck with us. That she lacked the money to escape her domestic burdens, and that she never did so, seemed less important to her than the ability to threaten us with the idea like some petulant adolescent. *So,* I had always wanted to say, and eventually did say, *do something already.*

I put all this out of my head, as I always do when I am in Richmond. I hadn't come home a few days before the reunion to steep myself in masochistic family combat, but to attend a reading by my high school creative writing teacher, a woman who both embodied and disproved my mother's worst fears. She was divorced and she worked and she was more than happy to combine a life of teaching and writing and publishing provocative poetry books chockablock with references to cocktails and sex, tough calls and regrets. My mother used to call the school when I was in this teacher's evening writing class, demanding that I bring the car home due to various "family emergencies," perhaps not a coincidence given Mom's suspicion of her "lifestyle." I thought my teacher was tough and battle-worn and awesome and probably drove in fifth while menstrual. Her reading was the next night.

The reading was brief and excellent, held in the Virginia Museum, and afterward, I met up with a friend (and former classmate) who also lived in New York. Together, we tucked into the book-signing line so we could pay our teacher our respects. The two of us had been roommates right after college, before she started law school and I'd become equally busy. I admired her: She had always worked hard and, in college at Johns Hopkins, had juggled a weekend catering business and part-time jobs with activities ranging from working as a student counselor to being coordinator of a forum where she invited diplomats and authors to discuss the first amendment.

As I write this, she's defending detainees at U.S. military detention camps in Guantanamo Bay, Cuba.

She's the one who spotted our high school college counselor waving at us from across the room. I hadn't kept up with our college counselor, but she had a daughter who'd been a classmate and who'd gone to Princeton and then on to the Bay Area. Maybe she wanted to tell us how her daughter was doing. Or maybe she wanted to hear about what life had been like for us in New York, after she had shepherded us through to Dartmouth and Johns Hopkins. By sending us to these schools, she could claim a little portion of the journey, I felt—and I was happy to let her. This was what I was thinking of, gratitude for the life I'd begun since college, up until the moment she appeared before us and began talking.

"Girls!" she said exuberantly, leaning in. "How are you two doing now? Where are you living?"

"New York," we said, in unison.

"And are you married?" she asked, her eyes widening hopefully.

I felt the wind knocked out of me. This was the first thing that she of all people, the underwriter of our intellect, wanted to know about *us*.

"Umm, no," my friend said.

I shook my head.

She looked from side to side at each of us, as if beholding a pair of Frankensteins she'd accidentally created. Her face was incredulous.

"Are you even engaged?" she asked, inflecting the word *even*, as if we'd deliberately pushed away a series of suitors in defiance.

"No, not engaged," my friend said, her voice gaining an irritated, high pitch.

I remained speechless. I knew many of my fellow alumnae would be married at this reunion. In Richmond, if you're not married (or at least engaged to be engaged) by the back half of your twenties, you are viewed as a kind of social problem—the girl who talks about business with husbands but can't discuss her children with the wives, the woman destined to mother a cat or an eccentric aging uncle.

Maybe this was an issue for the gals who had stayed in Richmond, but did it truly matter for those of us who had left? I didn't believe that accumulating a pile of achievements and anecdotes from my "Days of Ramen" in Manhattan made me better than anyone else; but it did mean dating, while important, took its place among a series of competing interests that, frankly, were winning the competition. My friend and I had been places and done things. Sure, we'd dated; I was dating a man now, but it wasn't a pre-marital sort of dating. And for our college counselor, of all people, to ask The Richmond Question before any others was a betrayal of Shakespearean proportions.

After an awkward laugh, our former counselor grasped her gaffe and began asking other questions about what else we might be doing other than wedding planning. But I could tell she was disappointed that we weren't married, or *even engaged.* Pull the camera back and cue the big Carrie Bradshaw question: Was a woman's education in general, or just in the South, little more than something to distract her until marriage? I didn't think so. But I had never asked myself this question, because it seemed so completely irrelevant to life in a city where everyone was smart, ambitious, sharp-edged, and didn't even have time to take a partner seriously until they were well into their thirties.

"You girls take care of yourselves," our counselor said, bustling off.

"She's kind of crazy," one of us said, as soon as she was out of earshot. "Did she think we went to Dartmouth and Hopkins to get married?"

Apparently so, we concluded.

Perhaps St. Catherine's preparatory program was a sort of intellectual tease: It's okay to be brainy and have a career, *as long as you get married on time.* It wasn't that a smarter woman would make a better world, but a better wife. Was our school really training us for the "comfortable concentration camp" Betty Friedan wrote of long ago in *The Feminine Mystique,* seducing us with the promise that our education would take us places even as it asked us why we would ever travel to them? (The perverse promise that "work will set you free" comes to mind.) Would the alums of St. Christopher's, our "brother school" a mile away, ever have to defend why they were neither married nor *even engaged?*

I didn't think so.

At the book-signing table, our former creative writing teacher hugged us both and signed our books with a flourish. "You're too young to get married," she'd told me over lunch when I was last in town. I was thankful someone understood the importance of getting some living under your belt, of bringing home the bacon.

Eight years have passed since that reunion weekend, and the rest of the details, whom I saw and what we said to each other in the following days, were overshadowed by both the fleeting encounter with our college counselor and her reinforcement of what I had long considered to be a problematic point of view exclusive to my Southern mother, the notion that marriage is the most important piece in a woman's destiny. But rather than caving to the pressure, it revised my feelings of Ben Franklinesque self-determination and made me even more convinced that before you could be a partner, you had to become your own person.

One thing I had learned as a reporter was to ask a lot of questions, and to ask the right questions. *Have I,* I wondered, *not been asking the right questions?* Or was it the other way around? Were my college adviser, my mother, and the other people of their generation not asking *us* the right questions? It wasn't that I believed I should be married at this point or had anything against marriage. I just didn't understand why, in 1998, the marriage question was the first thing a high-achieving pair of women with master's degrees were asked to discuss by someone familiar with the breadth of their aptitudes.

It's 2006, and now I'm nearing my twenty-year reunion. Much has changed in my life since 1998. I took and left that job at *Fortune*. I moved to Seattle, bought a house, hopscotched through a few more journalism jobs, stopped and started relationships. I have now, long past the age at which people like my mother believed it possible, entered into a good relationship.

But my mother never saw me do this. She died of ovarian cancer, the cells of her femininity perversely turning on her.

I was home in 2001, the summer her diagnosis went terminal. I remember an afternoon shortly before her death when my single status came up in conversation.

"You're going to be an old maid," I remember her telling me.

The late-afternoon hour held a typical Southern languor—it was beautiful outside but brutally humid, and the restlessness I felt knowing each minute I spent with my mother might be her last was like the restlessness of childhood afternoons when boredom led me to bookshelves, to wishing I could be somewhere else more comfortable. We were in her room in an institutional, fluorescently lit hospice, and I was combing her wig—the one we called "The Carol Channing"—and trying to maintain a conversation that didn't reference the future. I was trying not to argue with her, but also trying, one last time perhaps, to defend and explain myself.

"By your definition I already am an old maid," I reminded her.

She straightened her legs beneath the white blankets, careful not to disturb the tubes that now processed her bile. Then she looked out the window into the sun and said a thing that surprised me.

"Well," she said. "Maybe I should have worked, too."

Did she really think that, or was she just trying to make an empathetic leap to where I lived in the world, to where the world, in the twenty-first century, asked us to live? I never found out. She sent me home, saying she wanted to nap. That night, while my father and I slept, she died.

Now, as I look back at where I was ten years ago and where I am today, what I find sad is that my mother didn't get to see the one part of my life she had hoped to see: me secure in a relationship with a man who is kind to me, who is a steady, calming influence and a good partner. I may not have entered this relationship at the age she and many of my peers considered appropriate, but in some ways that makes the relationship feel more distinctly my own. When coupling up ceases to be a social directive uttered at every turn (I found, in my thirties, that people assume your dating days are over and, thankfully, tone down the questions), it becomes more possible. At this point, I could marry him, or continue living with him for a long time. He appreciates my independence, and I appreciate his patience. We are always respectful.

But equally sad is that my mother couldn't live a more independent life for herself, or see my life as anything other than tragic because it lacked a mate. Most of my significant experiences as an adult, up until my early thirties, were discounted by my mother—and by strangers—because I was single when I went through them. Though I dated, I seemed always to be single at pivotal moments: my three graduations and two moves to major cities, my myriad job changes and breakthrough publications, my cross-country drives, my mother's death, the purchase of my first home. I don't think it's tragic that I went through these steps and changes without a partner. But it's unfortunate that these transitions have been sullied, in a way, by people who considered them "unserious" because I was "uncoupled" when they occurred.

Facing big decisions on my own and with resistance from my mother, from her cruelly innocent generation, has shaped me, but not as intended, into a so-called "woman fit for marriage and little else." Instead, being alone for a good long time has made me a person who does not require a partner to fulfill some social mandate, and because of that I can now appreciate the relationship that has materialized in my life but also keep the idea of being "partnered" in perspective.

I wish my mother could have seen how my independent attributes—my single Southern status, if you will—have, in this way, become my assets and not my liabilities.

The distinctions between tragedy and comedy are often slight ones, as is always evident when I spend time in Richmond. The tragedy is not that I have been long single; the tragedy is that people there think my single status—and that of other women's—*is* tragic. The tragedy is that women, in particular, have absorbed this point of view and still inflict its narrative upon one another without stopping to question its logic. And that, over time, people like my college counselor and my mother don't know just how funny they have begun to sound.

Part 2

Marriage Can Wait

I think to be a good wife, you have to be

prepared to sacrifice your self to become one

with another person, and I'm not willing to

do that. I think there is something else I'm

supposed to do, and I want to stay on that road.

—OPRAH WINFREY, *ESSENCE* MAGAZINE INTERVIEW, 1991

Cohabitation Hesitation

★

by JUDY MCGUIRE

A fter living alone for ten years, it was a monumental event when, last year, my boyfriend (who, in my mind, had barely begun boyfriending me) moved in. As we live in New York City and I have that rarest of rarities, a rent-stabilized apartment in a pretty good neighborhood, there was no question about us finding a new place: He was moving into mine.

My apartment, filled with *my* stuff. Yep. He was bringing all his boy crap into my cute little apartment. *Mine.* Or did I mention that already? Though I'd spent the previous decade wishing for a stable relationship, now that one was sitting on my sofa, I was a little nervous. Petrified, really.

Of course, I had every reason in the world to be racked with terror; living with another human is scary. What if it doesn't work out? Who gets to keep the apartment and who has to move? (Okay, I didn't really have to worry about that, but still, evicting someone has only marginally less charm than being evicted.) What about all those CDs we were probably going to buy together? How will we split them up if the inevitable occurs? He snores. Is that going to drive me nuts? Will he notice that I also snore? Will he find my secret stash of old-boyfriend nudie Polaroids? What if he tries to talk to me during *America's Next Top Model?* What then? It's enough to give a girl an ulcer.

I've lived with two—oh, wait, now *three*—men. The first time was when I was nineteen. Paul was a tattooed punk rocker, AWOL from the Navy. As he was on the lam, our (my) apartment was more hideout than love nest. And because the naval police were looking for him, legal employment was a dicey proposition as well. So guess who wound up supporting both of us? That's right—that'd be me.

I was a much younger (and more tolerant) woman then and found the fact that he could, at any moment, be hauled off to the brig rather exciting. That is, until he actually did get hauled off to the brig, and I was left with all the bills and none of the sex.

The next time I lived with a guy was about four years later. I'd started seeing Lou, a much older gentleman who had, among other excesses, an extensive newspaper collection. Stacks and stacks of newspapers that you had to navigate through ever so carefully, lest you accidentally knocked a pile onto yourself and wound up like a Collyer brother. (For those unfamiliar with the notorious Harlem brothers, their desiccated bodies were both found buried under giant bundles of old newspapers.) Lou also "collected" back issues of magazines and copies of every book ever written, but the newspapers were really what hit you.

The first time I went home with him, he suddenly stopped at his apartment door, blocking it so I couldn't go in. I thought he was moving in for a kiss, but instead, he solemnly made me swear up and down that I wouldn't make fun of him. At first, I didn't understand. But as he shoved the door open, for once in my sarcastic life, making fun didn't even occur to me. Fleeing, on the other hand, did. I'd seen shows on cable about people who lived like this.

"But—" I started. Cutting me off, he assured me he was aware that the New York Public Library was well stocked with microfilmed back issues of *The New York Times.* Apparently, he just liked the comfort (and presumably the cancerous dust) the decaying papers provided.

After a few years of dating, I convinced him to get rid of about five year's worth of papers (approximately 1/345th of the total collection) and moved my meager belongings into his cramped, rent-stabilized penthouse (think servant's quarters, not anything Trump-related). After I asked politely ten times and threw a tantrum the eleventh, he even removed the portrait of a long-ago ex that had been hanging over his bed. Lou didn't get rid of anything easily. (Well, except me, but that's another story.)

Probably because even the simplest and most mundane tasks, like going to the bathroom or pouring myself a glass of water, involved negotiating piles of periodicals, I always felt like an intruder. Sure, I did my best to make the place my home, furtively throwing out papers whenever Lou's back was turned and prodding him as to why he needed such an enormous used-plastic-bag collection. (Don't ask.) But the fact that I was never added to the lease, had no space of my own, and was forced to fit my own sad possessions around gigantic stacks of crumbling *Spy* magazines made me feel like an uncomfortable visitor in what was supposed to be *our* home.

Eventually it all turned to shit, and so I had to go.

It took me a year or two to recover my bearings, but words can't express the delight and relief I felt the day I signed my very own lease. It was the first time in a long time that I wouldn't have to deal with testy roommates or boyfriends who didn't love me. I could put my stuff wherever I wanted and paint my kitchen hot pink if I so chose. (I chose!) Nobody but my landlord could kick me out—and she'd have to go to court to do so. My newspapers went straight into recycling when I was done with them, and my plastic-bag supply could remain happily paltry. I suddenly had the freedom to walk around naked and howl along with Madonna if the spirit(s) move me. I could do dishes (or not), and I answered to no one. Though I'd certainly experienced serious bouts of loneliness and depression, living alone for these ten years was one of the better experiences in my life.

Which is why I started getting twitchy when my current Special Naked Friend started making noises about maybe moving in together.

Do you have any idea how hard it is to live with a guy? I'd forgotten. First of all, unless you're dating a midget, man stuff is huge. Shoes the size of ottomans, puffy coats that could easily house a litter of piglets, the inevitable action-figure/computer-game/porn collection. Where are you going to put all that? Asking him to remember to put the toilet seat down was the least of my troubles. How about flushing?

Not that living with a woman was an easy adjustment for him, either. One morning he came out of the shower, complaining that the soap he'd used on his face had left a sandy substance and a residue in his beard.

"That's my ass soap," I shrugged, not guessing for a second that this would send him into a tizzy.

You'd have thought I'd tongue-kissed his mother by the reaction I got. First he let out a wail and then began wildly slapping at his face. He ran back into the bathroom to rewash. I tried to calm him, assuring him that he'd washed his face with "Buffy the Backside Slayer," a Lush product specifically designed to de-bumpify your butt. But even learning that the soap didn't actually go *up* my butt, but *on* it, didn't calm him.

And decorating? Unless you're living with a self-proclaimed metrosexual (a whole other problem), straight dudes are notorious for having either a horrific sense of style—or none whatsoever. Not that that will stop him from littering your apartment with milk crates, neon beer signs, and martial arts movie posters. He'll become adamant about making his mark, no matter how tattered or ugly that mark may be.

Before my new man moved his first pair of pants through the front door, I had to find out where he stood on the decorating spectrum. Turned out he was more of a milk-crates/metro-shelving kind of guy. Also turned out, he had concerns as well. He didn't understand why I had so many books, or my fondness for "old" (hello, that's *vintage!)* furniture.

The more we discussed the logistics of his moving in, the more it seemed like maybe not the best idea. I worried that I'd no longer have any time to sit around in my underpants and stare into space. I fretted about those milk crates. But mostly I spazzed over the fact that it had been so long since I'd lived with another human, I was afraid I wouldn't remember how to behave. Even though I had no doubt that I wanted him, the reality of having a l-l-l-live-in b-b-b-b-boyfriend scared the shit out of me.

So to speak, anyway.

When we were first dating, we'd see each other a couple times a week, which meant we were always on good behavior. Then we spent our first weekend together. After forty-eight hours of nonstop togetherness, I was reminded of the hardest thing about having a boyfriend (and no, it wasn't the incessant hair removal or lugging home the economy-size box of ribbed-for-her-pleasure condoms). Oh, no. Far from it. The most difficult thing about having a new man in my life at all hours was trying to hold in my farts. Oh, and figuring out how to poop without him finding out.

Now, I realized that if I were going to be in a mature, adult, committed relationship—a mature, adult, committed *live-in* relationship—the occasional passing of witnessed wind was bound to occur. But having been in a number of long-term affairs (though none particularly mature or committed), I knew once that inaugural fart hit the air, it was just a hop, skip, and a *pfffft* to nonstop pull-my-finger jokes and Dutch ovens.

It's not that I thought my guy couldn't handle it; I just wanted to eke out a couple more weeks of romance. And so I held it in.

And went about the scary business of living with a new beau. Although perhaps it wasn't all that scary. Though he preferred it, he didn't try to fashion any shelving out of two-by-fours and cinder blocks. And yes, while he replaced my tiny TV with something that took up a quarter of the room, for the most part, things were going pretty smoothly.

But after six months of living together, something had to give. I can't say I recall the exact date or time that the levee broke, but it did, and amazingly enough, it did not completely demolish our feelings for each other.

These days, I no longer hold it in till I'm doubled over. And not surprisingly, Boyfriend looks at my newfound comfort with public tooting as some brave new height in our relationship and not only cuts them himself with impunity, but grants my humble contributions a long, drawn-out "Alllllrrriiiggghhhht" of approval.

And while this is certainly mortifying, for the most part, living with him hasn't turned out to be the terrifying experience I once imagined it would be. He can reach the up-high shelves. I'm starting to appreciate the ginormous TV that came along with him—it's nice to be able to read the credits. Plus, the guy cooks, occasionally cleans, and loves the hell out of me. So I've learned to deal with the occasional gastric disturbances.

I guess you could say our romance isn't dead. It just occasionally smells that way.

Marriage Ain't Prozac

★

by SUSAN JANE GILMAN

Right now, there are two things
in my life that need to be done:
me and my laundry. I want to marry
a man who can do both.

—OPHIRA EDUT

When I was five years old, the one thing I wanted to be more than anything else was a Bride. A girlie-girl of the First Order, I thought brides were the bomb. And since I had an inordinate amount of free time on my hands, I spent a lot of it walking around the house in my mother's white-chiffon nightgown with a doily on my head.

Needless to say, this thrilled my relatives.

"Oh, look! Susie's getting *married!*" they'd coo approvingly. "Who's the groom?"

Groom? What groom?

As far as I was concerned, "bride" was about being fabulous and adored. "Bride" was about having a tiara. "Bride" was about being the center of attention. What did any of this have to do with a *groom?*

But the adults said, "Surely, you can't be a bride if you don't have a groom."

And there you have it.

By age five I had absorbed basically everything that drives ninety-nine percent of all women crazy for the rest of our lives. Little else makes us gals quite so anxious as the issue of "marriage." Whether we're gay or straight, puritan or progressive, we've learned by osmosis that society still considers marriage to be the centerpiece of our lives, the defining achievement for a girl. Between our relatives and *The Rules,* we're under a lot of pressure. Only brides live happily ever after, we're taught: A husband holds the key to our happiness.

In the words of my five-year-old self: *Barf.*

Don't get me wrong. I'm not knocking marriage—for either straight or gay gals. In the early days of the women's movement, some feminists claimed that straight women didn't need men, that we were better off without them. Well, I don't buy *that* fairytale, either. Let me be the first to admit that I'm not one of those lucky autonomous women whose idea of bliss is to go to the movies alone with nobody buggin' her. I've usually been fucking miserable when I've been single. And I'm still walking around with that lace doily on my head. Well, metaphorically, anyway.

But as a progressive prima donna, I certainly don't buy that "every Princess needs a Prince" scenario, either. I mean, hel-lo. This is the twenty-first century. If I decide to ride off into the sunset all by myself, that's just as legit, thank you very much. Ditto for if I decide to ride off with another princess.

Plus, as a member of a generation whose parents divorced in record numbers, I also know that real marriage is *real* complicated.

Those "drive-thru" wedding chapels in Las Vegas are insane. They perpetuate the myth that marriage is a Happy Meal—a quick, easy source of gratification and presents. Excuse me, but a good marriage requires serious effort. The least you can do is get out of your car.

Any honest married person will admit this: Marriage can be joyous, but it's also an out-and-out wrestling match between Romance and Disappointment, Expectation and Compromise. Tellingly, when Ann Landers was once asked what problems plague Americans the most, she replied, "The poor want to be rich, the rich want to be happy, the single want to be married, and the married want to be dead."

That should tell us something right there.

The good news, of course, is that American women today are among the first women in history who don't absolutely have to marry for protection, survival, and acceptance. We have the unprecedented luxury of choice: whether to marry, whom to marry, when to marry, and how to marry. We have power and options—and marriage itself has been legally transformed from the glorified master-and-servant relationship of the past into a more equal partnership.

All of this should be a fabulous thing for females! We finally have some control over our own emotional, sexual, spiritual, and financial destiny! The ability to make smart decisions, to make sure we're well suited to our match! Yippee! Uncork that bubbly. Throw that rice in the air. Tell that polka band from Astoria, Queens, to start playing "Respect."

Unfortunately, however, we gals are so imbued with fantasies about marriage that, too often, we approach wedlock in a state of desperation or delusion.

If we're gay, of course, marriage has been cordoned off with razor wire by sanctimonious morons—so that if we do find somebody we want to live with and care for until death do us part, things are complicated right from the start. The best that lesbians can hope for right now is to cobble together a "domestic partnership" through various legal loopholes, inclusive policies, and progressive places of worship. It's sort of *wedlite* instead of *wedlock*. Better than nothing, I suppose, but still not great for the old blood pressure.

Yet if we're straight, deciding to marry is not exactly a three-tiered cakewalk either.

Thanks to our culture, many of us view marriage through a mindset of scarcity. We're told that if we don't "hurry up" and "find" a husband, all the "good ones" will be "taken." So our search for a partner becomes like hunting for a Prada blouse during a one-day sale at Neiman-Marcus. We race to the store, tear through the racks like maniacs looking for something that "fits," and hope that we'll beat the other shoppers to the best bargain before closing time. The fact that we have to choose one outfit to wear every single day for the rest of our lives just makes us even more insane.

Others of us are so convinced we have to be married that we effectually subject ourselves to a shotgun wedding—except that we're the ones holding the pistol, and often we're holding it to our own head, if not to our boyfriend's. We *will* a marriage to occur just so we can be capital-*M* married.

Still others of us are so blinded by fantasy, so ga-ga over engagement rings and white dresses, that we really can't see past the veil over our heads. We walk down that aisle with great expectations but absolutely no clue.

Most people will agree that the decision to say "I do" should not be made lightly. And yet there is so much pressure on women to say yes automatically—to say yes for the wrong reasons—and to say yes unequivocally. We're rarely encouraged to think rationally about marriage: It's considered antiromantic. Nor are we encouraged to entertain much doubt—or to accept that *Hey, all aspects of life are uncertain. Get used to it.*

In how many fairytales does the princess tell the prince that she needs some "time to think"? That she's not sure she's "really ready"? That she "wants to work out certain issues" before she commits to spending the rest of her life in his castle?

Ideally we gals should commit to someone out of strength and desire—not fantasy or fear. This is difficult, I know. Like I said, I've walked around with that doily on my head. For that matter, I've also gone to sleep alone and teary-eyed, convinced I would never find someone as I listened to the clock tick. And when I finally did meet my Monsieur Right, people put so much pressure on me to get engaged right away, it's a wonder I didn't start producing oil.

But why relinquish our power? As my grandmother used to say, "Any two idiots can get married. And they usually do."

It's marrying well—or deciding not to—that takes real savvy. So let's forget the poufy dresses and glass slippers for a moment and try these words of wisdom on for size instead:

1. Holy matrimony is not the holy grail. Certainly if it does resemble the holy grail, it's closer to the Monty Python movie. After the quest for a life partner is over, life itself continues. And this life has the potential to be just as tumultuous, frustrating, and ridiculous as singlehood.

Marriage won't transform a cleaning lady into a princess or a beast into a prince. "A lot of people think that once they're married, their spouses will change dramatically and all the problems in their relationship will disappear," a marriage counselor told me. "That's just not true. Any problems you have before the wedding will still be there after the honeymoon."

In fact, if "Cinderella" were written to reflect the real deal, her story might go something like this:

After P.C. [Prince Charming] and Cindy got back from their honeymoon, they had an idyllic month at the castle until Cindy's mother-in-law, the queen, announced she was moving in. When Cindy told P.C. that either his mother was leaving or she was, P.C. said that *she* was one to talk, seeing as her own stepmother was quite a piece of work. "Besides," he yelled, "You were nothing but a cleaning lady before you met me!"

After babies, diapers, and years of petty arguments, Cindy had a brief fling with a pharmacist whom she met over the Internet, then got addicted to Percocet. P.C. lost a chunk of money in a Ponzi scheme and survived an unspectacular midlife crisis that included an Alfa Romeo and a bulimic Brazilian debutante. In their later years, the couple discovered in-line skating and Viagra. After Cindy had her hip replaced, they retired to Boca, where they spent the rest of their days hitting the early-bird specials, playing mah-jongg, and driving with their left blinker on.

2. A wedding isn't a marriage. At age five, I perceived marriage as a dress, a party, and a spotlight. Unfortunately, there's a whole industry dedicated to perpetuating this idea for females until we're, oh, fifty.

An entire bridal industry is dedicated to feeding and exploiting our childhood dreams, to helping us obsess about stuff like a dress that makes us look like a giant puff pastry! Ice swans! And getting every female in our wedding party to shell out $400 for a chartreuse taffeta dress and dyed-to-match pumps that will make her look like a giant romaine lettuce and that she will never, ever wear again.

(I'm sorry, but bridesmaid dresses are sadistic. I mean, is that really any way to treat people we love? To stage fascist, expensive photo ops that essentially reduce everyone to a color-coordinated backdrop for our dress? I say: Give our gal pals a break. Tell them to keep their dresses simple and save their money for the presents.)

Most ironically, in these scenarios the groom becomes practically irrelevant. He might as well be a doorknob.

Given all this hoopla over the wedding being "our day," is it any wonder that we can confuse the ritual with the reality?

A few years ago, one of the syndicated talk shows ran a feature called "Women Who Can't Stop Watching Their Wedding Videos." Many of the women on it had grown up believing that their wedding day would be "their day"—the most important day of their life.

The problem was, their wedding day was not just "their day" but "their *only* day." Their wedding was really the one time when they were allowed to run the whole damn show, demand exactly what they wanted, and be the center of attention. After it was over, they were devastated. They were suddenly somebody's traditional, doormatty wife—no longer a bride or a beauty. And so they relived their wedding again and again through the VCR, trying to recapture their moment of dominion and glory.

Weddings are sacred, but hey: Every girl is entitled to more than one special day in her life. Let's make sure everyone doesn't forget this.

3. A husband should suit our personality, not our checklist. Years after I first paraded around as a bride, I had a boyfriend who was gung ho to get married. And if mothers could have wet dreams, let me tell you, girls, this guy was it. The perfect mail-order groom.

He was good-looking, reliable, smart, and financially secure. He was faithful, didn't drink, and actually liked going home to visit his mother each month. He wanted children and a house in the suburbs. He doted on me. He even *liked* doing laundry.

Yet, surprisingly, when he told me that he wanted to "start shopping for a ring," I felt none of the euphoria I'd always dreamed of. Instead, I felt a blood-freezing panic.

Because, while this guy was definitely a "catch," he wasn't the right catch for me. Really, I needed a far more idiosyncratic fish.

I mean, I'm my grandmother's granddaughter—and in her day, my grandmother's idea of a great catch was a communist nymphomaniac who looked like Errol Flynn. As her protégée, I wasn't crazy about spending every other weekend with in-laws in Cleveland and living a staid, traditional family life. Since I grew up in New York City—where you never learn to drive and therefore view all cars as a source of vehicular manslaughter—the mere idea of carpooling kids around in a minivan made me apoplectic. And while I approached the world as a hysterical, all-you-can-eat buffet, this guy ate literally seven foods. The day he tried a scallop, it was such a big deal, you'd think he'd donated a kidney.

Our fundamental values were vastly different, our dreams were vastly different, and we couldn't negotiate any compromise.

So, difficult as it was, I told my boyfriend not to buy the ring. *Me,* the one with the doily on her head! (Interestingly enough, most of our friends assumed that he was the commitment-phobe.)

But it became clear to both of us that it's not enough to marry a list of qualities—a person who looks good on paper or seems like the "type" we're "supposed" to marry. In making a lifelong commitment to someone, we also commit to a Life. Better make sure we share the same vision.

4. Go slow. Funnily enough, the next guy who proposed to me was the complete opposite: a gorgeous actor-turned-gourmet chef who had businesses in Hawaii and New York. "We can spend half our time in Maui, half in Manhattan," he promised. "I can support you while you write your feminist discourse. We'll travel the world together. We'll see the great operas, eat at the greatest restaurants, and you'll have as much excitement as you've ever dreamed of!"

Sounded great.

There was only one problem.

We'd been on exactly two dates.

When I pointed out that we barely knew each other, he cried, "So what? Take a chance! Trust me, you'll love it!"—as if marrying him were akin to taking a quick spin in a Ferrari.

Now, romance is almost, by definition, supposed to be a thing of great speed and spontaneity: a "rush," a "whirlwind" that "sweeps us off our feet" and "carries us away."

But who the fuck has ever really enjoyed being hit by a tornado? And who the hell can think rationally in the middle of one?

If we meet a great guy (or gal), we've got to take the time to really get to know each other and grow together—especially if we're young.

Says my friend, Dale, thirty-two, who's just gotten divorced after ten years, "When you're twenty-one, you have no idea how much you're going to grow and change in the next ten years."

Need proof? Just check out the hairdos in your high school yearbook.

5. Keepin' it real. Is there anybody, among all our friends, relatives, siblings, roommates, coworkers, teachers, and lovers whom we could honestly be with 24/7 for the next fifty-eight years, who would not, on occasion, annoy the hell out of us?

Besides, for some people, finding a partner is a matter not of locking eyes with a stranger across a dance floor, but of real estate: Location, location, location is everything. It's a matter of where they are in their lives, where they are in their heads, and where they both want to take things after they meet.

6. Marriage ain't for everyone. As Mae West once put it, "Marriage is a great institution. But I'm not ready for an institution yet."

7. And finally, this advice from the marrieds . . .

- Try to find in-laws who live in Tibet. Better yet, marry an orphan.

- Only register for gifts at stores that will give you cash back.

- Don't build a marriage solely on sexual chemistry. Sure, fireworks are spectacular, but look what happens to them. Fifteen seconds and *poof!*

- Whether you hit city hall or rent out the Ritz, plan your nuptials together. Frankly, any couple that can survive planning a wedding really deserves to be together for the rest of their lives.

Can a Single Woman Really Be Happy Without a Soulmate?

by E. KAY TRIMBERGER

I sigh, tossing the Sunday paper into the recycle bin. Another one of those columns by a midlife single woman, one of those "I'm happy with my single life, but deep down I have to admit that I want a partner" essays. This time, the author is a forty-one-year-old single woman who doesn't want to compromise, who proclaims that she deserves to find someone who will love her deeply, and that she'll love him back equally. And it's in my favorite "Modern Love" column in the *Times!*

I respect my single friends who say they want the daily closeness, the touching and routine of life as a couple, or those who would like a regular sex partner, or who could afford to buy a house if only they had a partner. But I have less regard for an essayist who expresses some vague longing for egalitarian love, for a soulmate.

I shouldn't be so critical, I tell myself. After all, it took me almost forty years to give up the search for a soulmate. Perhaps that long search for a specter is precisely why I *am* critical, though.

When I was seventeen, I announced to my mother that I would never have a wedding. I didn't mean that I would be single, certainly not a spinster, but I did not want her conventional life as a housewife. My mom was an excellent cook and seamstress. She made clothes for her three children, gardened, canned, and played bridge with her friends. But she was always negative. Constantly criticizing my father for not being home, she also nagged me to get my nose out of a book and condemned my unruly long hair and unfeminine style. She even put herself down, saying she wasn't smart like other housewives in the university town where we lived.

My father, by contrast, loved his professorial work. When he was home, his laughter and warmth made him much more fun than my mother. His life seemed preferable to me. I realized then that I wanted a career, although when I came of age in the late 1950s and early 1960s, I knew no woman whose life I could emulate.

I read about a few, however.

French feminist Simone de Beauvoir provided an appealing alternative. Refusing to marry or cohabit, she had a great love relationship and intellectual partnership with the philosopher Jean-Paul Sartre. Drawing on her example, I and other second-wave feminists became early advocates of a philosophy that is now widespread. Rather than a husband and wife being sexually attracted by their differences, and content with distinct roles in the family, we emphasized the importance of deep, intimate sharing with a partner (male or female) to whom we were attracted by our similarities.

Although we didn't use the term in the 1970s, we sought a *soulmate.*

With disillusionment, I later learned from biographies, especially Deirdre Bair's *Simone de Beauvoir,* how unequal, conflicted and unsatisfying de Beauvoir's relationship with Sartre truly was. And I, too, was thwarted in my several attempts to form unconventional relationships with soulmates. Cohabiting with one in my early thirties was a huge disappointment. I learned that the merging encouraged by the soulmate ideal could lead to emotional and physical abuse in a relationship in which one's partner is older and psychologically more powerful. But I didn't want to return to the only alternative ideal of partnership—the conventional and unequal marriage. Only in my fifties, through a dialogue with other long-term single women, did I come to terms with the inadequacies of the soulmate ideal and see single life as the right option for me.

While I told myself I was waiting for "the one," I made a home for myself, found interesting work that sustained me economically, came to terms with my sexuality in different ways as I matured, strengthened my ties to extended family, discovered a supportive community, and, most important, created a large network of friends who met my needs for intimacy, support, and fun.

I still felt, however, that I would be happier coupled.

Even when I decided at age thirty-seven to parent a child on my own—and when at forty I adopted a baby boy—I didn't reject the soulmate search. With my desire for children and family out of the way, I thought that I could focus on finding the perfect mate. I hadn't anticipated the emotional intimacy of parenting, or the time involved. But while completely absorbed by the daily satisfactions and stresses of life as a single mother, I still held on to the ideal.

I remember the occasion in my midfifties when I realized that while clinging to this vague, high-minded goal of finding a soulmate, I had built a life that I actually preferred.

I was going to the Midwest, for both a celebration of my parents' fiftieth wedding anniversary and a reunion with my large extended family. I decided to look up an old boyfriend who, while not a soulmate, would have been a good husband and father. Had I made a mistake in rejecting him twenty-five years earlier while I pursued my elusive life partner?

Since I would be passing through his city, I called in advance and arranged to meet him. While two aunts took my seven-year-old son to a natural history museum, I met the *good husband* for coffee.

As it turned out, he had married another lawyer, who'd become his partner in a law firm, and together they'd raised her children from a previous marriage. In the intervening years, he'd participated in politics and held elective office, something he'd envisioned back when I knew him in his early thirties. He had achieved many of his aspirations and created a satisfying life.

But despite his success, I sensed I'd been right to reject the life of a politician's wife. I remembered a recurring nightmare I'd had in my twenties and thirties: I was sucked back into suburbia, unable to resist the temptations of family and children, and pulled against my will into a life that would make me miserable.

I realized that I had not had the nightmare for many years, and although I *was* a soccer mom, I was not the one that I dreaded.

As I told him about my very different life, I became aware—perhaps for the first time—that I really liked it. I had created a life that suited me. I was a homeowner and a homemaker, living in a university town, but in a very different context from my mother's. Yes, I was raising a child, but I was not replicating my mother's life. I had a full-time career. I was a professor, like my father, but a professor of women's studies. Bohemia had merged with and transformed suburbia. For the first time, I had a vision that this was a life I might live on a permanent basis.

I have not chosen consciously to be ever single. Who would in a culture that so denigrates older single women? But the choices I have made led me—although not inevitably—to a single life. I am glad that I live in an era (shaped by feminism) and in circumstances (middle class) where I had these choices.

However, when I began to articulate to others that I liked being single, that I thought I'd be happy always being so, I received many skeptical responses. Even close friends didn't believe me. They saw this as a new rationalization, one less acceptable, it seemed, than continuing the search for "that special someone to love," like the woman in the "Modern Love" column.

Through time, I've become bolder in defending the single life and rejecting the cultural imperative that tells us that finding a partner, preferably a soulmate, is absolutely necessary for our happiness. I disavow *not* the coupled life, but the idea that it is the only and best way to live.

Singleness, I believe, must also be seen as a satisfying life path, one with many variations and with its own demands and rewards. I have discovered that life outside a couple, life without a soulmate, is not one to lament, but is a life that can be lived with love, dignity, respect, purpose, spirituality, and joy.

Solitary Refinement

★

by M. SUSAN WILSON

P erhaps I should have seen it coming. Like countless women of my generation, my formative years took shape under the crest of the 1970s divorce wave. Mom was one of those women who, in her late thirties, found herself suddenly single—with two kids. Lacking a college degree—she'd grown up in a time and a social class that encouraged high school girls to favor shorthand and typing courses over college prep—she filled the gap between support payments and expenses by taking a job doing basic house renovations and roofing. It was an unforgiving gig in the Florida summer sun; I remember her coming home sunburned through her T-shirt.

Meanwhile, I indulged in the rich terrain of fantasy that to this day runs through my head—a luxury, perhaps, of the oft-single gal (we have the time and space to imagine our lives and the worlds around us in extraordinary ways). While most little girls were playing house, I was playing "Young Divorcée Living in a Tiny New York Apartment." My dolls were all single moms. The only male presence in my imaginary life was a plastic soldier, passed down from my older brother. And I was constantly losing it in the hurricane of toys, shoes, socks, and underpants that was the floor of my room. (The on-again/off-again mate of this footloose fellow, a stoic, blond horse trainer who lived with her one-armed sister and two daughters, always took her lover's long, unexplained absences with dignity.)

Therapists, I know, could write volumes.

But, the thing is, it's not a sad story. Singledom isn't something that necessarily needs a remedy. Ultimately, we choose our lives, and I've spent most of my adult life unattached. At thirty-seven, for the first time in many years, I am living with a man, but I'm still quite happily forgoing marriage.

Okay, yes, my life has been lonely at times. That's only natural. We're social creatures in need of the comfort of companionship. But ultimately, during my single years, I came to love the freedom that comes from having a space in my life where there are no witnesses—the serenity of anonymity when I wanted it, to be free and unobserved in my own private world. The exquisite pleasure of an uncomplicated happiness.

A few days after I moved in with David, he came home to find me under the covers crying. As happy as I was, I knew how profoundly I would miss my solitary years: the pure, incomparable joy of coming home to your own place at the end of a workday with a greasy lamb gyro and a bucket of fries roughly the size of a compact SUV—the sort of meal you'd be obliged to eat with your head in a utility closet if anyone were around to see. The unadulterated pleasure of sitting on the floor and surrendering to a minor storm of ecstasy with every bite—washing it all down with long swigs directly from the wine bottle. The wholly liberating decision to screw the idea of washing that tower of dirty dishes in the sink in favor of simply placing them in the refrigerator so they won't smell and raise the concern of neighbors, who, frankly, already think you're weird. The unmatched delight of hosting a minor, private concert from your bathtub (sung with unapologetic disregard for tone or pitch). The quirky, largely undiscovered fun of vacuuming in the nude. The twisted satisfaction of picking up the phone when telemarketers call, then pretending to cry and refusing to let them hang up (all right, so I never actually did that, but—oh!—imagine the fun). The peace of falling asleep on your sofa under the weight of a thick book or in the blue light of some trashy late-night movie. The unsung bliss of waking up to the dawn, fixing yourself a cup of coffee as dark and bitter as Dick Cheney's soul, and just sitting alone in your window, spying on the city below as it shakes off the night and begins the business of another day.

Of course, anyone who stays single long enough knows: There are moments of doubt, of asking yourself, *Am I making the right choices with my life?* And there's the guilt born of concern that you're worrying your friends and family. Getting beyond that takes some emotional fortitude. Because, let's face it: It's scary when you sense that other people feel sorry for you. Do they know something I don't? Do they see some disastrous outcome to my life that I've somehow yet to mine from the more hyperbolic recesses of my single-girl imagination? Truly, what awaits me?

On my deathbed, will I raise a knobby-knuckled arthritic hand, pull off my oxygen mask, tug on my home-healthcare attendant's sleeve, and cough out the words, "I. Regret. Never. Marrryyyyiiiiing." [Flatline.]?

Will I, at some point in my middle years, bump into a former lover on the street and suddenly succumb to a bizarre but irresistible urge to wrap my arms around his ankles while screaming, "I can still look good in white, given the right lighting. Please, for god's sake, man, help me!"

Will I make an unfettered ass of myself at my nieces' and nephews' weddings by diving over my walker—support hose and prescription shoes trailing behind me—as I make a desperate play for the bouquet toss? Or allow myself to be duped into a green-card marriage by a smarmy, over-the-hill ballroom-dance instructor named Rico who calls me his "special lady"? Will I write fan letters to television evangelicals? Bequeath my remaining worldly possessions to the last in a line of tiny dogs I will have lived with for the preceding thirty years, naming each one something like Mr. Dibbles, dressing them in hand-knit cardigans and matching hats, and taking them on an annual cruise?

And if so, so what?

I can only choose to do each day what makes me happiest. And whatever the future holds—marriage, living in sin, babies, single motherhood, renovating roofs, or sharing vacation memories with a dangerously overgroomed Chihuahua—I know I'll find my way through it. Even though I'm partnered now, there's a mighty strong single gal with a fierce sense of fun inside of me. And if she emerges again in this life, I suspect we'll take it all in stride together—and have a blast along the way.

Part 3

The Single Girl

Here is a book which examines

[the single girl's] problems—lesbianism,

bisexualism, alcoholism, frigidity, nymphomania,

narcissism, sadomasochism, or asexualism—and

seeks to gain some measure of understanding

of the various types of girls who get

trapped by so-called single blessedness.

—FROM DR. WALTER C. BROWN'S *THE SINGLE GIRL:*
A MEDICAL DOCTOR'S INTIMATE REPORT ON THE PROBLEMS OF THE
UNMARRIED FEMALE IN OUR CONTEMPORARY SOCIETY
(MONARCH BOOKS, 1961)

Faux Boyfriends

⭐

by JANE GANAHL

More than a decade ago, when I divorced for the second time and found myself single at forty, I was a dithering mess. Every time my car coughed, or the vacuum cleaner belt broke, or I felt lonely at night, I thought the world was caving in.

That was all before I decided to go for a second occupation at midlife; before I became a Career Single Woman.

This is different from a *single career woman,* which defines pretty much any female who is unmarried and working in a profession. No, I'm talking about taking single life and turning it into a career unto itself, with the same set of challenges and joys of accomplishment. And its own skill set. I've learned to do all kinds of handy things around the house, from changing a vacuum cleaner belt to gardening, painting touch-ups to taking out the trash.

I am Career Single Woman! Hear me tinker!

Okay, it doesn't pay a red cent, but oh—the sense of satisfaction at the end of the day. To know you're paying your own bills and calling your own shots, without the benefit of the male species!

Well, most of the time.

I've also learned this important lesson about being a Career Single Woman: No one can do it alone. You need emotional support from friends and family, a sturdy pet to smother with kisses when loneliness invades, as it occasionally will. And a quiver of faux boyfriends. These are men who are supportive, true blue—and provide some kind of vital service in your life—without expecting husband's rights in exchange.

In fact, when you think about it, becoming a skilled Career Single Woman means slowly eliminating the need to have a man at your side—at least for nonromantic reasons. (We all still need romance occasionally, *n'est-ce pas?*) But as skilled as a woman can become, there are still those times when one wants to pitch a fit and wail about something one cannot fix alone. Those times can feel lonely indeed. Unless you have done as I have and put faux boyfriends in line to help. It took me a long time to line them up, but since I have, I feel that there's nothing I can't do with one of them by my side.

In fact, it's from one of them that I recently learned the true meaning of male-female commitment.

I was two hundred miles from home, in Southern California, when my car broke down on the freeway in an unfamiliar town. (Call it one of a single woman's greatest nightmares, up there with finding a python in her toilet.) I managed to limp off the freeway to a service station, where they told me the transmission was blown and would have to be replaced. Of course, I was frustrated and upset—I was due to visit a friend in Carmel on my way home and would have to cancel and figure out how the hell to get home.

But I was also fuming that just six months earlier, this very same problem had been fixed—or so I thought—by my local car genius, Guido (a.k.a. Faux Boyfriend #1). I called him on his cell (what does it say about my car's lemon status that I have his cell phone number?) and spared no words.

"I thought you fixed this!" I said accusingly. He felt terrible, as I should have known he would. I am his friend—but also one of his best customers. (Based on how many times the family cars have been in his shop, he ought to have retired to Tahiti by now.)

"I'll come and tow it home," he said without hesitation.

"Guido, I'm in *Santa Barbara!*"

"Is that farther than L.A.?" he asked.

"No," I rolled my eyes at his lack of geographic awareness. "It's about ninety miles north. Forget it—that's ridiculous."

"Piece of cake," he said, ignoring my protestations. "I can leave in the morning. Can you rent a car one way to get home?" And then he told me about a company that offered good one-way rates.

Immediately, I felt my anxiety begin to dissipate and realized this situation, while annoying, was definitely not cancer or the end of the world. I felt soothed and cared for. Almost as if I had a real boyfriend/husband/lover who was stepping in to . . . not *rescue* me, exactly, but help facilitate a solution. And help me not feel alone.

My automotive crisis hasn't been my only one in recent months; something must be in the stars. When my home email burped and ate my entire outbox—five years' worth of emails— Don the computer dweeb (Faux Boyfriend #2) fielded my hysterical phone call.

"Don! I've just erased half my life!" I wailed.

My techie is a young guy (aren't they all?), but he has a great computer-side manner: a reassuring voice and sweet smile. When he shows up at my front door in his checkered Vans, I know things are going to be okay.

Or at least he'll die trying to make them so. When he couldn't figure out the source of the gremlin invasion, he spent hours researching the problem online. And when no fix-it attempts yielded fruit, he took my iMac with him and left me a loaner laptop. Finally, he, like Guido, cut me a break on the bill. Having heard me whine about my constant state of writerly privation, Don never seems to charge me the going rate. And he could. Without my email, my technology, I am nothing.

Then again, without my handyman, Brian, I'd have no finger-nails left.

Brian (Faux Boyfriend #3) is a guru of home repair sent to guide me through the mysteries of home ownership. With men like him in the world, Career Single Women don't need to feel that they have to become experts in everything from lawn seed to load-bearing walls. When I got a note from my condo association remind-ing me that I was responsible for the yearly staining and sealing of my wood deck (Whaddaya mean, it could collapse beneath my feet?), I called in the cavalry.

Together, we went to the hardware store to pick the stain color (an errand that could likely have ended in an argument with a lover), then he spent a few hours spreading the goop—all the while explaining to me how rain and sun take a toll on wood. And *voilà!* I didn't have to get my hands dirty, and I learned a few things in the process.

Brian isn't infallible. But just as I've continued to love boy-friends or husbands when they come up short, so do I stick with my handyman. Sure, complicated plumbing issues elude him. When my sink backed up and threatened to drown my house in brown ooze, no amount of suctioning or chemical enemas would undo the clog. Brian brought in the snake (no phallic jokes, please), and I held my breath while he snaked away, praying that I'd be able to get by with paying him his usual $50 an hour, rather than the king's ransom demanded by the guys in the white truck (i.e., actual plumbers).

It didn't work, but I now have another faux boyfriend, whose name is on a magnet on my refrigerator. Unfortunately, this new faux boyfriend is too expensive: He only wants me for my money.

So, for the time being, I'll stick with Guido, Don, and Brian; after all, a woman can only juggle so many men. And they do demand attention, despite their nonlover status. Right now, I have to go to the bakery to get Guido some cookies. Would you believe he drove his tow truck all the way to Santa Barbara to get my car, fixed it in a day, and didn't charge me a penny?

Greater love hath no real boyfriend.

The Taming of the Shrew

★

by JESSICA VALENTI

There's something about unmarried women that gets the media all hot and bothered. And not in a good way.

In the skewed lens of the mainstream media, single women aren't actually autonomous people with lives and careers—they're anomalies, albeit "sexy" ones. If we're not itching to get married, we're itching to par-tay! In the eyes of the media, all single women are looking for men (lesbians don't really exist), and the sluttiest of us are looking for *yours*.

Or we're exotic creatures, diligently profiled in stories that recall *National Geographic* covering some Amazon tribe. Actually, the word "Amazon" is used too much for my comfort level, as are other, more animal-like references.

Take for example the office piranha. This terrifying breed of single woman hasn't gotten a job to make a career for herself—oh no. As the *Financial Times* reports, the goal of the office piranha is to snag a "high-earning, high-flying, high-virility man." Usually one who's already married. Finally, a way to put that degree to good use!

Then, of course, there are women who have no desire to get married right away—they're parasites. According to *The Washington Post,* young Japanese women who put off marriage in favor of going out and living it up are "parasite singles." Because clearly, living life for your own enjoyment is selfish and parasitic.

And for those women who lived the married life only to have gotten divorced? Well, they're "cougars": older, sexually charged women who are out on the prowl for younger men. In fact, the term "cougar" has become so popular that there's a website dedicated to these sex-crazed beasts, a cougar book, and talk of a movie with Susan Sarandon.

Now, I'm all for the media exploring the wonderful world of unmarried gals, but are single women so anomalous that we can't even be talked about as, well, *people?*

I understand that there's something catchy and funny about trend pieces with silly nomenclature (I mean, really, how many times have you seen the term "catfight" lately?), but the cartoonish image of single women in the media isn't limited to fluffy lifestyle pieces.

In the 2004 presidential election, single women—who were being touted as the "must-get" demographic—were referred to as *Sex and the City* voters. You would think that a group of people who had the potential to change the fate of a country could be called something that brought to mind politics and agency instead of fucking and Manolos. But that is our media fate, I suppose. While men remain "bachelors" and "unmarried," we're stuck with "single," "spinster," and a bevy of subhuman nicknames.

And when the names aren't enough to put us back in our place, there are always the scare tactics.

According to recent articles and "studies," your chances of getting married go down if you're too successful (scares the men away), you're too educated (you won't find an equally educated man), or you're too old (as in, like, twenty-eight).

Even über-successful *New York Times* columnist Maureen Dowd has fallen for the single-gal backlash. In a 2005 *New York Times Magazine* piece, she frets that her professional status keeps all the eligible menfolk away. Dowd describes running into an acquaintance who tells her he always wanted to ask her out, but found her job as a *Times* columnist "too intimidating" and noted that men "prefer women who seem malleable and awed."

Never mind that this particular gentleman was, perhaps, an asshole, Dowd takes her personal thesis to the next level, claiming that a new trend is men's taking up young women in caretaker positions: "their secretaries, assistants, nannies, caterers, flight attendants, researchers, and fact-checkers."

But, I ask you, if a man just wants a mommy, why should a single woman really be itching to have him anyway?

Then, of course, if you're a fan of being educated, you'd better watch out. No man for you! *New York Times* columnist John Tierney wrote in a recent article about the "boys crisis" in education that "advocates for women have been so effective politically that high schools and colleges are still focusing on supposed discrimination against women. . . . You could think of this as a victory for women's rights, but many of the victors will end up celebrating alone."

The idea is that men aren't getting education and women don't "date down." Choose one, ladies—diploma or mate. *(Forbes* magazine's running an article titled 'Don't Marry a Career Woman' doesn't exactly help, either.)

So apparently the secret to landing a man is to stay uneducated, and unsuccessful, and never get old. You don't have to look far for articles reminding you that once you're past your midtwenties, you're no longer desirable—to men or as a vessel for those babies you'll so desperately want.

Of course, the funniest/saddest thing about all of these scare tactics is that they assume single women's main goal in life is to be married. You may remember that the Centers for Disease Control and Prevention (CDC) issued federal guidelines asking all women of reproductive age to treat themselves as "pre-pregnant." You know, no smoking, no drinking, taking folic acid—all in preparation for the mighty fetus.

Much in the same way that the CDC expects women to be caring for themselves in anticipation of a baby, the media seem to want single women to prepare themselves in anticipation of a man. We're not single, we're just pre-married. Or so they hope.

Because the only thing worse than a successful, educated, single woman is a successful, educated, single woman who actually likes being single (by choice!). It's just too much for them to take—hence the unflattering animal names, the fear-ridden labels of bitch, barracuda, she-devil, shrew.

But at the end of the day, the media backlash against single women is really a backlash against women's progress as a whole. Animal names and silly trends aside, the real point that's being made is that women who don't get married are bizarre, and that those who don't want to get married will live to regret it.

And there's nothing funny about that.

What Daughters Do

★

by AMY HUDOCK

H airless people hid under hats, wigs, and scarves, their arms attached to tubes injecting poisons meant to save them. Light flowed in from a wall of windows, reflecting off the polished hardwood floors. The room smelled clean, clear, crisp—seeming to offer no place for cancer to hide.

My mom filled up a seat by the windows, looking out at a collection of trees left behind by surrounding development. A small, untouched wild area. A creek ran through the small valley, and hardwood tree branches made shadows on the fallen leaves on the ground. Mom sat back in her recliner, watching the dark on light.

"Do you need anything?" I asked in my perpetual attempt to do something. Anything.

She reached out her hand to stroke mine, and seemed satisfied with the touch as she smiled her "no."

The cheerful atmosphere of the room belied the reason we all were there. We could be in an airport somewhere, all waiting to step through a doorway to a new place, a new destination. Instead, we fought against open doorways—lighted tunnels—new destinations. This was not a place of departure but of staying, of clinging, of desperation. But no one talked about it.

The nurse came by to check on Mom and gently laid her hand on my mom's arm. Such tenderness. Relatives sat close by their loved ones, watching. I heard women laughing at a joke. A group of nurses cheered for a woman whose last day of chemo was today, drumming, singing, and placing a silly hat on her head. I caught bits of conversations all around me, focusing on anything but the now.

But I could not forget the clear plastic tube that led to a needle stuck into my mother's vein. My eyes couldn't stay away from the *drip drip drip* of the toxins into my mother's body. They offered both life and death—carefully balanced. I watched the drip—did they get it right? Was it balanced well enough? Was this what would save my mom?

I watched the body that gave me life and wondered, *Can I, now, help give her life? Can I do enough? Is anything I can do enough?*

I didn't know what I feared more—the cancer or the chemo. I knew the correct answer was the cancer, but Mom wasn't sick until she started the chemo. Now she was sick.

I thought back to better days, to when I was thirty years old, following Mom through the forest, placing my feet carefully to avoid getting stuck in the mud. Mom and her dog walked ahead with the bear gun while I tried to keep up. I heard her singing to warn the bears of our approach. I was too out of breath to sing. My pack bit into my shoulders. The gun holster pulled me slightly off balance. A .357 Magnum, I learned, is a very heavy gun.

I learned to shoot a gun by the time I was ten years old. I could ride a bucking horse, hike long mountain trails and make my way home in the dark, find clean drinking water in the middle of nowhere, but I could not, right then, keep up with my fifty-four-year-old mother. Though I had followed her through many forests, down many rivers, across many fields, she now walked with a confidence, a solidness, I had never seen in her.

Her life in the lower 48 was like most people's lives—a bit quirky, but recognizable. But when the last child left the house when she was forty-nine years old and she became single again, she sold almost everything she had, stored the rest, and hopped a plane to Alaska. She went to live her dream of being a pioneer. She became a person I didn't know.

When she wasn't out working a contract as a bush nurse for the Native American Health Service, she lived in a log cabin nearly two miles from the nearest road. Across a river. Off the grid. Off the water supply. Off toward the edge of the civilized world. Behind her land stood the wide-open spaces of Denali National Park. I was getting tired of the grandness of it all and wanted to sit.

She turned to me. "Doing okay, city girl?"

I nodded, resentful but knowing she was exactly right. I had become a city girl. Our experiences had grown far apart, and what she was learning, she hadn't been able to teach to me.

We got to the creek, and we could see Mom's cabin up on the bluff across the water. She grabbed the boat, directed me to sit in it, and began rowing us as I sat there, useless.

"I have to start here so that I can angle the boat just right to hit my landing spot," she explained to me. "The water's down, but that was not the way it was a few weeks ago. Melt-off and rain flooded it, and I saw something I thought I would never see. I heard all this thunder, and when I went outside to look, the boulders were rolling. I never thought I would see something so large move like that."

I looked at the truck-size boulders. "You didn't have to cross it, did you?" I said in awe.

"Only once," she admitted. "And that is something I don't want to do every day. I didn't know if I was going to make it. Someday this creek is gonna get me. When I go, it will probably be right here."

As I watched the sure way she guided the boat, I thought, *No, it'll never get her.* We landed and hauled ourselves and our gear up to the cabin.

Once we were settled, Mom took a good look at me and said, "You need a bath." It had been three days, so I didn't argue. Instead, I offered to haul the water.

Warm water hit the back of my head and ran down my face. I took a deep breath and then it came again. I watched the suds from my hair drip off my naked feet and through the wide space between the floorboards. I knew the weeds under the sauna were surprised by the sudden rainfall. My mother, I'm sure, usually didn't use this much water; hauling it makes it too dear. But this was a special day. She was washing my hair.

The eldest woman washing the hair of the newcomer or guest of honor has a long tradition among Alaska's Yupik women. A few Yupik women whom my mother helped through labor once invited her to join them for a sweat. And this was the way they honored her, the eldest washing the hair of the healer. And it was how my mother now honored me, a daughter returned from faraway places. I stood perfectly still, not wanting the moment to end.

Afterward, we sat on the porch, rocking and drinking Tang. The sun moved toward the tops of the mountains in the distance, getting ready to rest just below the horizon for a few hours before coming up again, creating the longest sunset/sunrise I would ever see. Here, at the top of the world, daylight ruled the summer, and darkness was pushed into small moments. The animals would come out to hunt for food under the cover of the long twilight, working swiftly against the coming of the light. We were safe, there on the porch.

Back at the cancer center, we sat watching the fading of the light as cancer stalked us, and as I thought back on her life in Alaska, I wondered, *How can she be ill? How can she die? Ever?*

Later that night, back at home, I woke to a retching sound. I stumbled out of bed. It was 3:00 AM. I went to my daughter's room first, thinking she must be sick. As a single mom, I was the only one there to respond to illness in the night. But my daughter was sleeping peacefully. I turned with a start toward the bathroom door.

I found my mom on the floor, filling the toilet with last night's dinner. Her body was cold and shaking. I wrapped my arms around her, putting my body warmth to hers, and I held her head. She had nothing left. She heaved air.

When she was done, I got her back in bed and she went to sleep. Miles of sleep. She alternated waking and sleeping like a baby for days, never spending much time in either state. When she was awake, her voice sounded weak, small, strangled by nausea. Like I cared for my daughter when she had the flu, I now cared for my mother. I brought her small offerings of tomato soup, crackers, and water. I called the doctor and got her more medicine. I held buckets to catch vomit. I held her as she cried.

With no medical training to give me confidence, I fought my own fear of doing the wrong thing—and acted despite my fear. Because I had to. She had only me. Although I couldn't stand to see this woman who had braved boulders the size of buildings brought so low, I couldn't let her see my feelings. She might see my fear as loss of hope.

So I cried behind the door of my room, muffling the sound with my pillow. I made bad cancer jokes that anyone but my mother would not have found funny, their inappropriateness making us laugh even harder. I kept maniacally busy, organizing Mom's medicines, her supplies, her clothing. And I hovered until Mom looked up at me with the evil eye. "Stop lurking over me!"

The next evening, she finally got up on unsteady legs. She hugged me and said, "Thanks for all of this. But is this too much? Am I asking too much of you by coming to live with you during treatment? We have to do this for six more months."

I sighed and held her closer. "This is what you did for me, so many times. I can't even begin to pay you back, no matter how much I do now."

She countered, "But that is just what mothers do."

I pulled back so she could see my sincerity: "And this is just what daughters do."

The Straight and Nappy

★

by APRIL SINCLAIR

My mother has obsessed most of my life over how I choose to wear my hair. She and I were on the same wavelength, so to speak, until the early 1970s, when I opted to proudly wear my hair natural on a regular basis. Back then, Mama refused to even be seen with me publicly unless I covered my afro. I was still a minor and was forced to abide by my mother's wishes in order to keep the peace. So I would tie a scarf over my head or even occasionally don a wig, just so I wouldn't have to hear it from her.

For decades, my very traditional mother has continued to harp on how long and how straight my hair isn't. I was a single woman of a certain age when I decided that it was finally time for Mama and me to focus on what was really important, before it was too late.

"Mama," I began in a long-distance telephone conversation, "I will be fifty in a few years."

"Fifty! Don't remind me," Mama groaned. "I hate to think that I will have a child that old. I can't imagine being old enough to be Reverend Al Sharpton's mother."

"Well," I swallowed, "I think that it's important that you and I really appreciate each other at this point in our lives. I know that in the past, you've focused on how I wear my hair. But in the scheme of things, that just doesn't seem important. Now that I'm getting up there, and you're really up there in age, it just seems like whatever time we have left is that much more precious. I mean, our love for each other goes way beyond something as superficial as hair.

"When I see you next week," I continued. "I don't want the length or the texture of my hair to be the main topic of discussion. I want us to really enjoy each other's company and savor the time that we spend together. We live two thousand miles apart, for goodness sakes. We don't see each other that often. Our time together is precious. Don't you feel the same way, Mama?"

I paused and noticed the lump in my throat. I even felt a tear forming in my eye. Mama was quiet. I realized that I must've really gotten through to her. Finally, things would be different, after all these years. This was a real breakthrough! Mama and I were about to enter a whole new, wonderful phase of our mother-daughter relationship.

"April."

"Yes, Mama?" I sighed, my heart bursting with love and new-found hope.

"How short is it?"

When I was a little colored girl growing up on the South Side of Chicago, I asked my mother if she was happy. I thought that this was a reasonable question. But I believe that my mother found it irritating, because she sighed before she answered me.

Looking back, I realize that Mama didn't have time to answer philosophical questions about impractical subjects such as happiness. She had clothes to wash on a rub board, cloth diapers to soak in a pail, food to buy, dinner to cook, clothes to starch and iron. And, last but not least, she had hair to straighten with a hot pressing comb (to Mama, short nappy hair was the hair of the have-nots, while long straight hair was the hair of the haves, synonymous with femininity, fairytales, and the status quo). Mama also worked outside the home. And she had an infant, a toddler, and two more kids to take care of.

I was six, the oldest. Mama often needed me to hand her things. And once when she got sick, back when I was only four, she had me stand on a wooden box and wash the dishes. That same time I also went to the store all by myself, even though I had to cross two streets. Times were different back in the early '60s. Children were expected to make themselves useful. And I was a brave little girl; or at least I pretended to be. Because I was the oldest, my role was to be fearless. I was a superwoman in training.

"Nobody is happy all of the time." Mama sniffed, as she changed my baby sister's dirty diaper.

"Happiness comes and goes," she mumbled, the pink plastic top of a safety pin sticking out of her mouth.

I felt disappointed by my mother's answer. It flew in the face of all of the fairytales that I'd heard. Every fairytale that I could think of ended with, "And they lived happily ever after." None ever ended with, "And they were happy sometimes," or, "And their happiness came and went." No, every single fairytale gave the clear message that it was possible to be happy all of the time, forever.

But I feared that it would work my mother's nerves if I pointed out that she was out of step with the brothers Grimm and everybody else's fairytales. Mama would consider it talking back. She'd told me her answer to my question, and that should be it. I decided to take a more roundabout approach.

"Mama, you say that happiness comes and goes." My mother nodded, seemingly relieved that it had sunk into my head. "Well," I asked bravely, "are you happy right now?"

Mama frowned as she cleaned Nina up and rolled the dirty diaper into a heap. "Here, shake this out in the toilet and put it in the pail," she instructed.

Eww. I took the rolled-up diaper and headed for the bathroom. There was no point in repeating the question. It would make me sound stupid. How could Mama be happy at this very moment when she was just done dealing with a dirty diaper?

"When I get a chance, I'm going to have to touch up your kitchen," Mama shouted after me. The "kitchen" referred to the back of one's head. *The heck with happiness,* I thought. Mama was more interested in straightening my hair. I learned early that, in my mother's book, happiness couldn't hold a candle to avoiding nappiness.

I secretly wanted to be happier than my mother appeared to be.

But I could never say that to somebody who worked so hard and who was often stuck in the house with kids. My father could just put his hat and coat on and say, "I'm gone." And even though my father worked at his job, mopped the floors at home, fixed stuff, did carpentry, and painted at times, I couldn't help but feel that he had the better deal. Daddy never washed a dish or changed a diaper. He never bent over a rub board or pushed an iron. He had the louder voice and he got served his dinner. He drove the car, while my mother struggled to hoist her kids onto the bus. Mama seemed stuck to me. I quietly hoped my life would be different—dare I say, better.

My life has been very different from my mother's, all right. But who's to say which life has been better? My mother and I came of age during very different times. I've had more opportunities and have made different choices. But we both have achieved success. My mother went to night school while working and raising four young children. She became a science teacher and retired about a decade ago after teaching special education. I have achieved success as an award-winning, best-selling author, workshop leader, and public speaker.

These days, my parents divide their time between Chicago and Florida. They are retired, still married, and surrounded by children, grandchildren, and other relatives. I live in Berkeley, and I am surrounded by two adorable, stubborn mutts (one just farted), cherished friends, a supportive writing community, natural beauty, and long-distance family love.

My mother, to her credit, has never worried me about getting married or having kids; my siblings have blessed and burdened my parents with grandchildren. My mother has mainly worried me about my hair; I suspect she wouldn't mind if I used "food money," if necessary, to pay to get it straightened.

Sometimes, I wonder about the road not taken. I wonder if I will ultimately regret not having had children. But then I get to lecture one of my nephews, long distance, about getting his life in order, or caution one of my nieces about her boyfriend. And I feel like I do have some of the joys and frustrations of parenting.

Recently, after preaching to one of my nephews about getting his life together, I paused and listened for his reply.

"I have to admit . . . " my nineteen-year-old nephew began. I breathed a sigh of relief, hopeful that he might decide to get a job or go back to junior college. " . . . that 50 percent of what you say makes sense," he continued.

I did not regret not having children at that moment.

Conversely, I had the pleasure of chatting with a young man whom I played a role in parenting. He's college bound now and told me that he wants to write a book. He said he never forgot hearing me read at Borders when he was a child. I was touched, but didn't even recall that he ever came to one of my readings. But I did wonder privately if he remembered giving me a hand-made Mother's Day card one year. I couldn't imagine that he knew how much it meant and still means to me. It's something that I will always cherish. I'm proud to have played a parenting role in his life.

I would no doubt have been a different sort of parent than my mother, but not necessarily a better one. I am in awe of the monumental sacrifices that my parents made to raise their four children. When we were young, my mother did the lion's share of the housework while working a job outside of the home. And there was a stretch when my father worked two full-time jobs in order for our family to achieve the American dream.

Would I have made these kinds of sacrifices?

In addition to her high standards when it came to hair, Mama also held her children to high standards of academic excellence. But in relation to sports, she couldn't have cared less, at least where her girls were concerned. Mama didn't want us to bring home less than a "C" in gym class, but she could sympathize if you weren't one of the first ones picked for kickball, or if you dreaded push-ups or generally lacked coordination. After all, normal girls shouldn't be too good when it came to sports.

Exercise was just not high on most women's lists back when my mother came along. I vaguely remember a guy in tights on a black and white television set leading a group of housewives in jumping jacks. I don't remember my mother actively joining in. But maybe I just don't recall.

Anyway, Mama still cautions me about getting muscles. I've told her that I'm just trying to trim the fat. I know that I will never look like women bodybuilders, nor do I want to. But I'm proud that I'm working out and converting fat into muscle. I'm committed to fitness. And if I can deliver a mean punch when the need arises, so be it.

I recently did the Bay to Breakers race in San Francisco. I had my doubts about my ability to get up the infamous Hayes Street hill and to finish the 7.48-mile course. I'd never done any major walk or run before. I was somewhat toned but still overweight. And I hadn't especially trained for it, just did my usual Curves workout, water aerobics, Berkeley Marina walks, and weekly yoga class. I told myself that if I lasted two and a half miles, took one look at the Hayes Street hill, and hightailed it back to BART to ride home, it would be okay. My self-talk went like this: *You don't have to prove anything to anybody. You're doing more than most middle-aged people you know by just getting up before daylight and showing up. Didn't Woody Allen say that 90 percent of life is just showing up? Okay, then.*

But somehow, when I reached the top of the three-block-long Hayes Street hill, something changed for me. I'd done something that I hadn't really thought I could accomplish. It was a turning point for me, and I became determined to finish. The blaring music, the interesting costumes, the cool weather, and the cheering crowds would all help me complete the course. By the time we entered Golden Gate Park with still more than a few miles to go, and some additional naked bodies to avoid, my feet were on fire. I wasn't sure if I could do it. That's when I realized that the hardest part hadn't been the Hayes Street hill, after all. The hardest part was getting through Golden Gate Park with sore knees and joints and an ankle that had never healed from a break more than twenty-five years before.

When I finally saw the beach in the distance and then the finish line, I knew I had to do it. And, when I did do it, it was one of the proudest and happiest moments of my midlife. Afterward, I hobbled down to the beach and dipped my tired, sore, aching feet into the cool, soothing sand. Then I called my mother on my cell phone.

"Bay to who?" Mama asked. I hadn't even told anyone in my family that I was attempting a footrace. I explained to my mother that I'd walked almost seven and a half miles from the Embarcadero, near the Bay Bridge, all the way to the ocean. I told her that I was sitting there watching the breaking waves as we spoke.

"That's why it's called Bay to Breakers, get it now? Mama, I didn't think that I could do it," I added breathlessly. "But I did it!"

"Well, you won't ever have to do anything like that again, will you?" my mother asked.

I tried to explain that this was one of the most important days of my life. That I'd taken a risk in midlife and had triumphed. It wasn't a big deal on the world stage, but it was significant to me. Mama remained unimpressed, reminding me of the time in my early twenties when I showed off my plough position. I was new to yoga and quite proud of my flexibility.

"Mama, look!" I'd shouted like an exuberant kid. "Look what I can do! In yoga, they call this the plough."

"The who?"

"The plough. Aren't you proud of me?"

"Proud of you?" my mother asked, skeptically. "Why would I be proud of you just because you can put your feet behind your head?"

I felt disappointed by my mother's chilly response then and now, but I wasn't deterred from my desire to continue down the road that she hadn't traveled. I realized that a large part of me just wasn't like my mother and probably never would be.

I could've married my high school sweetheart, raised a family, and lived a more conventional life, but I didn't. Instead, I moved to California without a job, without a permanent place to stay, without knowing a soul. I practiced meditation, the Feldenkrais Method, martial arts, and got Rolfed. I boiled Chinese herbs, soaked in hot springs, placed and answered personals ads, and traveled to the Greek Islands by myself.

The road hasn't always been easy. I wouldn't mind being in a loving, committed, long-term relationship, but I've experienced a reasonable amount of love and lust over the years. And, at present, I have a friend with benefits, plus a powerful vibrator.

As a single woman, I'm hardly pining away. Instead, I'm often juggling activities in order to make time to fit everything in (no pun intended).

I asked to speak to my father so that I could tell him the good news about Bay to Breakers.

"You don't need to talk to him about it right now," my mother said. "You need to save your breath."

The next day, I joked with acquaintances that my mother probably wondered why anyone would walk more than seven miles when they owned a car. She's as pragmatic today as she was back when I was six, grilling her about life's big philosophical questions while she battled dirty diapers

My mother and I don't always agree when it comes to hair, sex, politics, religion, or vigorous exercise for women. But at this point in my life, I agree with her that happiness comes and goes. No one is happy all of the time.

But I'm very happy that I still have her to call.

The Return on My Investment Has Quadrupled

★

by ADELE SLAUGHTER

T he deed to my house reads, "Adele Slaughter, an unmarried woman."

My real estate broker, an openly gay man no doubt sensitized to labels, warned me it was going to read that way. I remember sitting down to sign the papers at a large oval conference table that was too big for the room. I recall kicking the leg of the table and feeling like a second grader.

There it was at the top of the page, in type that seemed larger than the rest of the print. A scarlet letter. I balked. Why did they have to put it like that? Do they write "Joe Blow, an unmarried man?" Hardly.

This "unmarried" branding came at a particularly inopportune time. I was still reeling from my divorce and feeling like a failure. On top of everything else, I was now being cast as "unmarried," as if that meant something, as if "an unmarried woman" couldn't carry a mortgage. Why not call me a "single woman"? Or just label me an "old maid"?

Shrug it off, the mortgage broker (a married man) suggested. *Sure,* I thought. *Easy for you to say.* But in the end, I had too many other things to take care of in my new life to worry about being branded "an un-something" on the deed to my house.

The good news was, I *had* a house. No matter what they called me—single, unmarried, marital misfit—I was a homeowner.

And as such, there were all sorts of new things I had to learn, like how to change the filter in my air-conditioning unit, how to fix my garbage disposal, and how to do the 1,001 other tiny things my husband used to take care of for me. My ex was the kind of man who handled everything from decorating to ditch-digging quickly and efficiently. I, on the other hand, was terrified at the prospect not just of being alone, but of being alone without a clue about how to be an adult. It felt as if my ability to take care of myself had completely atrophied.

But with each small accomplishment, I became slightly more victorious and slightly more single. Until one day, I thought to myself, *I'm good to go. I like waking up alone in the morning. Walking down the oak wood hallway, my bare feet* flap-flap*ping against the floor. I like making myself a cup of Earl Grey and looking out my window at the sky.* Living alone was doable, I realized. Even more than doable, I liked it. And perhaps most of all, I liked being financially independent.

For me, married life had been like playing house. Not only did my husband make all the money (and a good amount of it), he also paid all the bills, handled all the investments, took care of all the insurance (life, health, and car), and managed our retirement funds. He was the materialistic patron and I was the noble poet.

Granted, I wasn't *completely* without resources—I'd earned some money over the years as a poet-in-residence—but during the entire course of our marriage, I never earned more than $15,000 a year. And I resisted the idea of going back to school to earn more at a "real" job (why should I when my husband made so much?). My attitude toward money was immature, my marriage was a life of privilege, and I routinely ignored how much work it took for my husband to provide a live-in nanny, a Volvo, a country club membership, and a five-bedroom house.

All that changed when we were divorced, although it didn't *seem* to change right away. I kept the huge house, maintained custody of our child. Our divorce mediator (whom we used in lieu of lawyers), allowed me seven years of maintenance in order to get me back into the workforce, or as he put it, to *rehabilitate*. I didn't think I needed to be restored to be a productive member of society.

I was naive.

One winter, after the twenty-first snowstorm of the season had me yet again shoveling our long walk and sliding on the ice around my car, I decided it was time to move. I wanted a smaller house. I wanted a lifestyle that fit my single status. And most of all, I wanted to keep my head above water, financially speaking. We sold the marriage house and I used my share to buy a cute little bungalow, my current home. It was the first in a series of decisions I made about money, and it was the most important one—I decided to get serious. My first lesson.

Since then I've had to learn how to find my way through a jungle of IRAs, Keoghs, health insurance, life insurance, checkbooks, Quicken programs, taxes, budgets, and, oh yeah, somehow figure out how to earn enough money to live and then how to earn enough money to live *well.* Lesson number two in the re-education and rehabilitation of Adele was to get a job.

My first job after the divorce was for a Hollywood producer who made inexpensive power yoga videos and trailers for movies that went straight to video. His offices were in Encino (in what

Angelenos sneeringly refer to as "The Valley"), and I was, in a word, his flunky. One afternoon, as I was driving my fourteen-year-old Volvo over the hill from The Valley to Century City to drop off a script at a huge entertainment conglomerate, I began to sob. I had gotten an MFA from Columbia University and here I was, shepherding someone else's script around town like a pizza delivery guy. I hated driving. And I loved writing. What was I doing?

Einstein once said something about how the mind that houses the problem is not the mind that can solve the problem. At that moment, I realized that I could no longer use my way of thinking about money, men, and work. Instead, I needed to become a seeker, to search out a way to live my new life with financial acumen.

So I began to attend seminars and twelve-step programs, to interview CEOs, CFOs, and executive producers, and to watch enough feel-good abundance programs on PBS to be on a first-name basis with Wayne Dyer and Suze Orman. I went through a financial sea change, and, somehow, it worked. Truthfully, some of it had to do with good fortune—my dad left me in the hands of a great insurance company, a friend recommended a good CPA (who all my friends use today), and I played tennis with a woman who turned out to be a crackerjack investment broker. But the rest of it I did on my own. By obsession or divine intervention I managed to make ends meet, even after the spousal maintenance ran its course, even after child support ended.

More than that, I managed to prosper. I've become a single mother who has raised a son successfully and well (his father is paying for Oberlin, a private college in Ohio). And I've done what I never thought I could do—invested money, owned a home (even built on an addition), paid taxes (though not marriage tax), held different jobs, been paid a lot and a little, and somehow survived above the poverty level, which in this day and age is a feat in and of itself.

Recent studies show that after divorce, a huge number of women live at or below the poverty level. In 1998, the median income for all females in the labor force was 73 percent of her male counterpart's ($25,862 per year, as compared to $35,345 per year). For college graduates twenty-five and older, the gap is even wider, with women earning only 71 percent of what men make ($35,408 to $49,982, respectively). Though I do periodically suffer from a fear of homelessness, I have always thought of myself as savvy enough to keep from falling below the invisible demarcation that separates me from poverty, or something close to it.

And after being divorced for thirteen years, I'm doing better than simply keeping the money in the bank account long enough for the check to clear. I'm financially autonomous and have a clear plan for remaining so. Granted, I now share my house with a partner, but I'm still, technically, a single woman.

Lest I forget that fact, I still have my deed to remind me each time I refinance or pay my property tax. My partner is put off by the "unmarried woman" designation as much as I am, but neither one of us cares to change it. With so many broken marriages between us, we both seem to prefer it this way, i.e., if you don't build it, it can't be broken.

Even so, what we have is stronger than anything else either of us has ever had before. We accept each other as is; neither one of us puts money or work before love and art. We are both honest and willing to admit (even to each other) when we are wrong. And ironically, in this partnership *I* am the financier.

All these years and dollars later, I've discovered that I'm good at managing money and getting better with each passing day. More than that, I enjoy making money, and I particularly enjoy the fact that I'm making money doing what I love to do.

T. Harv Eker, author of *Secrets of the Millionaire Mind,* suggests that you reset your financial thermostat. I'm not sure that I have one, but I do know that something has been reset over the past thirteen years. If Harv says it's my thermostat, who am I to argue? Many authors speaking for the New Age suggest that there is unlimited prosperity out there waiting for you. Just walk to the place in the future where you have more than enough money, see yourself having it, see yourself surrounded by it, see yourself bathing in it. Envision a future with loads of dough.

Though this sounds good in theory, it has never worked for me. (I must say, though, that in my mind's eye I look *great* on a bed of greenbacks. Naked. Placing hundred dollar bills *just so.* . . .)

More practically, I've found that if you're willing to *learn* how to manage your money well, you can. And if you do manage your money *well,* you can have more of it than you had before. Call it my third lesson.

The Great Cookie Offering

★

by LITSA DREMOUSIS

I baked chocolate chip cookies for the last guy I slept with. For me, this was a much bigger deal than having fucked him in the first place.

"You must really like him," my friend Tamara said. "Either that, or the sex was phenomenal."

She was right on both counts. He was electrifyingly intelligent, funny as hell, genuinely sweet, all muscle, and prodigiously talented. The sex positively crackled, as did our conversations. I found myself aroused in random and inappropriate places (Kinko's, the pharmacy) and felt grateful that I couldn't sport a telltale hard-on.

So, I baked. As I don't keep a well-stocked cupboard, I drove to the store at midnight, when my creative bouts usually seize. I giddily plucked just the right chocolate chips and organic flour from the shelves. Me, the writer girl, in my look-at-me red leather boots, reading labels on bottles of gourmet vanilla. The novelty of it all. Surely, he would be moved by the depth of my affection.

Back home, I put on Macy Gray and Elvis Costello and had at it. I found an apron on the top shelf of my closet. I excavated the electric mixer my mother gave me years ago, when she still hoped I'd become a girl who gave dinner parties. I meticulously cracked eggs and added baking powder with long-ignored measuring spoons. God help me, I *sifted*.

Two hours later, buzzing from pilfered dough, exhaustion, and love or something like it, I took the final cookie sheet out of the oven. My kitchen and I were both a mess, but I was happy. "The Great Cookie Offering," I called it. If he doesn't love me now, he never will.

Which, as it turns out, was precisely the case. He was touched and appreciated my effort and consumed the entire batch in one sitting. But he didn't love me, and while he said that this could change, I doubted it would.

My heart more bruised than broken, I couldn't help but think that this was a lousy reward for my once-an-election-cycle culinary endeavor. Damn it, I *baked*. I shelled out forty bucks for ingredients, even though I was in between permanent day jobs. I went to my crappy temp job the next day with two hours of sleep and a splitting headache. All so I could be told that he thought I was an amazing, beautiful, intelligent woman to whom he was really attracted, but that it "could be another six months to a year" until he figured out what he wanted from a relationship.

Many years and several men ago, this whole cooking thing was not such a big deal. My college boyfriend and I were together for three years. As a matter of course, I made homemade raspberry cheesecakes and apple-cinnamon pancakes and omelets with smoked gouda. I whisked salad dressings and squeezed fresh lemonade and made gingersnaps—some crunchy and some chewy, because he liked both kinds.

Then he dumped me. Granted, we had problems, and I was the one who suggested seeing other people. But he broke up with me during my first-semester law school finals while my grandfather was dying. During the day, I struggled with the incomprehensible

Federal Rules of Civil Procedure. At night, I visited my heretofore invincible grandfather in intensive care.

This is when Randy tossed me aside for a "younger woman" I had introduced him to. I was all of twenty-two.

As a result, cooking became inextricably linked to feelings of intense vulnerability. Besides, I had seen my mother—my best friend and one of the city's most skilled litigators—wear herself ragged preparing elaborate family dinners for twenty and then fielding late-night calls from detectives scheduled to testify the next day. Cooking was such a stereotypical Greek thing anyway. Who needed it? I was well read, driven, in good shape, and loved sex more than shoes. Fuck it. Men would just have to take me as is.

And take me they do. To newly opened trend-whore restaurants and punk-blaring dives and pastry shops and bars and coffeehouses where I have to repeat my order three times to the still-stoned baristas. But my dirty little secret is that I miss having someone to cook for.

Or, more precisely, I miss having someone who stirs me so much, I don't mind stirring. By all accounts, I'm an excellent cook. But I loathe most things domestic and probably always will. And that, perversely, is what felt good about my sugar-strewn kitchen cacophony: I loved him enough to do something I hated. I balk if someone rearranges my words, but in my wide-awake 3:00 AM moments, I want someone to rearrange my heart, to make the world seem new again.

That's the best we can hope for, isn't it?

I'm thirty-four and long ago learned the difference between love and sex. However, now that the fairy dust has settled, I can't help but think that my recent cookie episode had more to do with longing than with a real belief that this almost-paramour was my soulmate.

I love what I do—in the last two years, I directed and produced three plays, two of which I wrote. And I'm truly blessed with an extraordinary circle of family and friends. I am lucky in so many ways. But the void is wide and the echo is loud, and I've been dating for seventeen years and I haven't met him yet.

Right now, the thought of cooking for another man makes my stomach lurch. Maybe, soon, it won't. Mom just gave me a recipe for devil's food cake.

I'm saving it. Just in case.

Gold Shoes

★

by SUZANNE COPE

I'm the girl in the gold shoes who your boyfriend is looking at. I'm wearing a short black dress that I haven't put on since high school, almost a decade ago. I was just rude to the guy at the pharmacy when I went to pick up my birth control pills, stuffing the unwieldy plastic pastel box into my small evening bag. I wouldn't have used that tone of voice if I had remembered to pick them up after the gym a few hours earlier, sweaty and unremarkable in my shorts and sneakers. Was it because of the way his eyes went from the birth control, then slowly up the length of my outfit, as if to say, "I know what you're all about"? Was I rude because I knew I could be and his leering grin wouldn't disappear?

Admittedly, it's too early in the day to be wearing gold sling-back sandals and a silk cocktail dress to run an errand and take public transportation. As soon as I left my house, I could feel people watching me walk down the sidewalk, out of place on a warm June afternoon. The stares and the shoes are becoming uncomfortable. I'm taking the subway to a bachelorette party downtown because with my small graduate student budget I'd rather spend the twenty bucks for a taxi on drinks. The judgmental stare of the pharmacist has reminded me, though, that I am not ashamed of my choices, and by the time I am clicking my heels down the train platform, I feel confident again.

On the half-filled car I choose to sit one seat away from the innocent-looking group of college boys so as to give myself room between the narrow seats to be able to cross my legs as demurely as possible with such a short hemline. And maybe I want them to notice me. Instead, an eccentric, fortysomething man sits down in the empty seat and talks to me all the way to Park Street, grilling me with questions about my vocation, my neighborhood. I answer curtly while trying to send him a message with my body language: *I am not public property.* No one comes to my rescue.

I look down and see that my feet are already swelling from the tight straps of my sandals and wonder if anyone else can see this imperfection. We approach the subway stop and he gives me his card, which I toss into a trash can as soon as he is out of sight. Most days I would have blended into the crowd with a copy of *The New Yorker* stashed in an unstylish tote bag, but not tonight. The tiny leather clutch I'm carrying matches my shoes.

As I walk down the platform, I try to ignore the looks the fresh-faced women in jeans and Red Sox T-shirts give me, or how they squeeze their boyfriend's hand a little tighter while both sets of eyes look me over as they hurry to catch the Green Line to Fenway for tonight's game. *Of course I would hit Red Sox traffic,* I think, not slowing my strut or dropping my posture at the stares of the people around me. I feel both empowered and embarrassed at this attention, but you can't slink into the background if you are wearing gold shoes.

On any other day, I would be that girlfriend watching her boyfriend watch the tramp in the short dress walk by. I would look that woman up and down and decide what, if anything, she had on me besides a confident walk and a good pair of heels. Thinking, *Sure, she may not be as pretty as me, but her thighs are thinner. She has nice hair too, but so do I.* Giving unnecessary thought to what the truth may be about this scenario: *Is she really a whore, or does she just like to wear revealing outfits? Or is her real story somewhere in between?*

Like my story today. I'm not a prostitute or an exhibitionist, just a girl going to a party—but no one knows that. They are left to make up their own scenario about me. I know I would have given my boyfriend a dirty look for bothering to ogle the girl in the gold shoes. And I know I would have looked too, feeling confident knowing that I had more class than her; that I would have at least waited until *after dark* to wear my sexiest shoes and my shortest black dress.

I meet my group of girlfriends for drinks, then dinner, then dancing. We are less conspicuous as a group, my gold shoes blending in with their diamond jewelry, bright skirts, and my one friend's legs that go on forever. Finally the sun is going down. We toast love and marriage and sex and commitment. Taking the last train home, I don't quite get the stares I did eight hours earlier. My smudged mascara, drooping eyes, and slightly drunk swagger match most everyone's on the train; but I do get a few slurred catcalls and innuendos. I slip into bed that night in just my panties—my feet aching from those damn heels—and caress my hipbone, cup my own naked breast, and feel sexy.

Fast-forward eighteen hours to me shaking uncontrollably. I feel powerless over my voice, my hands, my legs, and my body. I have found evidence that my boyfriend has engaged in a shameless flirtation whose details I can only imagine. My boyfriend who is on tour in Europe for two weeks, due home in three days. My boyfriend who is moving in with me when he returns. My boyfriend whom I cannot call. So I call my girlfriends, one right after another, until someone picks up the phone.

Waiting for Jessica to come over, I put on a Bob Dylan record, one of the few that I own. I have set up a turntable in the last few days as a surprise for my musician boyfriend who grew up listening to records. It all seems ironic now, when I have to keep getting up to move the needle with my shaking hands to keep repeating the song whose lyrics I now realize are my life: "Now I know how it feels to be on my own. There are no more secrets . . . I know how it feels."

I let the record play straight through when my friend arrives with a pack of cigarettes. She mixes me a strong gin and tonic and before long, half the pack is gone and the record is making only hissing sounds. I'm in jeans and the first shirt I found on the floor of my room. My eyes are red and puffy, and my breath stinks of smoke. I am decidedly not sexy. My friend and I decide that, given the evidence (an ongoing email exchange between my boyfriend and his ex), there is a best-case and worst-case scenario, and that the truth likely lies somewhere in the middle. I cry anew, now because I am drunk and also so thankful that I have friends who will mix me cocktails and promise to leave their cell phones on all night when I am at my lowest. Yesterday I was setting up a home, missing my love, and feeling like I could conquer the world in my sexiest black dress. Today I cannot imagine how I could ever feel that way again. Despite the alcohol, I don't think I will sleep at all tonight.

"I know the truth," I tell him when he calls the next morning. What truth? He wants to know. He swears it is not as it seems. "What does she have that I don't?" I yell into the tinny connection. Is she his girl with gold shoes? Am I the clutching, needy girlfriend in the T-shirt and ball cap?

"It was only words," he claims. One last vicarious dalliance before we move in together. It was stupid, he was immature, he openly admits. He wants to be with me, commit to me. He can see our future, and it is beautiful and full of children and marriage and happiness.

He comes home two days later, and I meet him wearing flip-flops. We cry and embrace and decide to forge ahead. I am twenty-seven, after all, and he is older than me. We've been together three good, fun years. My heart wants to forgive him, believe him. My head sleeps with one eye open, dissects the phone bill line by line. It will not be fooled again.

Life goes on, with lazy candlelight dinners spent listening to the summer sounds of the city. Sirens and distant fireworks, the new baby next door crying, and the deep roar of jet planes flying overhead become our daily patchwork of sound. Every day feels a little more normal between us, a little more comfortable. Once, I even slip on my gold sling-backs for a special dinner out on the town and I feel sexy and strong again.

Trust is a funny thing in that you can choose it, just like you choose what pair of shoes to wear for the day. Most days I look into my boyfriend's eyes and smile, happy that we both put the past where it should be. Some days it's not so easy. I have a breakdown and call my gin-and-cigarettes friend, who originally advised me to break it off with my boyfriend. Now she says, "You chose to believe him and move forward, so now you have to do it wholeheartedly."

Every day I choose—believe those illicit words that still echo in my head, or believe my boyfriend. Choose to scroll through received and dialed calls on his cell phone, or choose to leave it sitting there. Choose to look through his wallet or . . . I choose to look through his wallet.

I can't help it. A newspaper clipping has been tucked inside the billfold for a few weeks now. What will I find this time? An ad for an apartment he plans to move into? A woman's phone number? With that familiar shaking-hands feeling, I unfold the fragile paper and turn it over a few times, wondering if this is truly what he has been keeping all these weeks. It's a picture of a handsome, young male nurse diapering a round-bottomed baby. The caption indicates that it was taken at a Romanian orphanage. Is this the best-case scenario? What does it mean?

I know I could ask him in our new, more honest relationship, but I choose not to. I like wondering what about this photo inspires him, compels him to keep it tucked away in his back pocket. I like to think that he is choosing to see himself in a new, more nurturing and settled role. Yet, like life, things are not so obvious. There's a best- and worst-case scenario, and the truth often lies somewhere in between.

I went shoe shopping today and couldn't decide what pair I liked. I almost bought a new pair of heels—in red this time—but instead opted for the sensible pair I could wear to work. When I add them to my pile in the closet next to my boyfriend's meager collection, I consider how far I have come. Am I the girl in the gold shoes or the girl crying on the couch, swilling a gin and tonic? Does the other woman wear gold shoes, or is she clutching a cigarette and bemoaning a lost love? The answer to everything is sometimes. Sometimes you choose the gold shoes, sometimes you choose something more comfortable.

Part 4

Sex and the Single Girl

"Please don't hurt me," I whimpered.

"Oh no," she said. "We are definitely

going to hurt you. We are single

women, and we hurt people."

—FROM NEAL POLLACK'S "A REPORT ON THE HABITS OF THE SEXUALLY
RAVENOUS SINGLE WOMEN OF NEW YORK, WHO ALSO HAVE JOBS,"
MCSWEENEY'S

Victoria's True Secret

★

by DANA ROZIER

I knew I'd stepped into a different world when the first display that caught my eye was a pink and green sign exhorting me to WEAR CUTE UNDERWEAR! A full-size stuffed dalmatian with large pink spots stood next to the sign. Both presided over a table piled with pink thongs printed with tennis rackets, multicolored polka-dot hipsters, white string bikinis with lavender hearts.

I contemplated my own blue cotton briefs. Practical, yes. Long-wearing, yes. But *cute?* Definitely not.

Across the aisle, a round table draped in cream-colored silk held bottles of shampoo. GET SUPERMODEL-SEXY HAIR!

My short brown pageboy did not tumble down my back in tousled waves of blond like the woman's hair on the advertisement. Perhaps the shampoo contained transformative powers. The supermodel seemed poised to transform herself. With one tug on her black lace panties, she'd be buck naked, conceivably ready to revel in bacchanalian festivities. Her parted red lips exposed sharp white teeth. The table next to her sold fragrances with names of alcoholic beverages: Gin and Tonic, Cosmopolitan, Kamikaze, Mojito.

I had never ventured into a Victoria's Secret before. And wouldn't be here now except that on a recent trip to New York, a seven-foot-high poster advertising the NEW! WIRELESS IPEX in the window of a Victoria's Secret seized my attention. The shape of the bra's smooth, round cups and its delicate pink color called to me in a language that was unrecognizable to my external ear. In my mind, I heard only a practical voice reminding me that my old bras were wearing out. Once I returned home, I told myself, I'd need to replace them.

I buy most of my clothes out of catalogs, and my bras from Title 9 Sports, a company named after the 1972 legislation mandating that schools spend as much money on girls' sports as they do on boys'. From my couch, I can flip through pages and pick out which bra I like, which will offer me the support I need. Barbell icons act as a handy reference guide. A one-barbell bra provides the least support; a five-beller, the most. I own a couple of the Double Dry Concealers, one in white and one in buff, a two-bell bra noted in the catalog for its comfort and ability to wick away sweat.

Practical fabrics are big where I come from. A single mom, I live in a university town in the Pacific Northwest where fleece, raingear, and hiking boots are staples in everyone's closet. Casualness, as a style, is *in*. Only when I travel to places like Manhattan or Boston do I realize how utilitarian my wardrobe has become. I *do* own one little black dress, but for the past two years, it's been encased in a dry-cleaning bag in the back of my closet.

For the past couple of years, I've been encased in grad school, working on my MFA in writing. And when I'm not writing, I'm making lunches for my two kids, shuttling them to violin or soccer practice, supervising homework, or mowing the lawn, activities that do not call for formal attire.

This semester, my head has been immersed in the world of Apollo and Dionysus, in Nietzsche's *The Birth of Tragedy*—research for a lengthy critical paper. Apollo, the sun god, symbolizes order and control. Dionysus, the god of wine, represents wildness, sexual abandonment, creativity. Nietzsche argues in his book that art consists of Apollonian and Dionysian forces. If the wild side is overlooked or forgotten, art becomes stagnant, incapable of generating fresh ideas.

I wondered what Nietzsche would have thought of the WEAR CUTE UNDERWEAR! sign in front of me.

I'd always pooh-poohed Victoria's Secret, rolled my eyes at its advertisements, its come-hither hype. Didn't women have anything better to do than shop for sexy lingerie? And in whose eyes did they want to look sexy? Surely not their own.

But here I was.

Looking around, I wondered what the other customers were doing here. Wondered what I was doing here. Two middle-aged sisters dressed in ski parkas and jeans stood in the cute-underwear section. One held up an ivy-covered string bikini for her sister's approval. Yes? A black-haired woman who looked as if she smoked too many packs of cigarettes announced to the nearest saleswoman, "I need a pretty green bra!" Pairs of teenage girls in ponytails and low-slung pants sorted through a rack of spaghetti-strap tank tops.

Color was everywhere. Pink polka-dot wallpaper. Sky-blue tiny T-shirts. Apple-green silk pajamas. Lemon-yellow tank tops. The candy colors tinted the store with a festive atmosphere, and I began to feel more at home. On a whim, I plucked a bottle of Mojito from the fragrance display and spritzed the perfume behind my ear. The faint smell of rum made me feel slightly intoxicated.

I remembered I'd come in search of the Ipex and ventured into another room. The cheerful colors were replaced by a montage of pink and black. Lots of black. Black corsets and black merry widows with long garters hanging down like tentacles. Black bustiers that laced up the front. I thought of my little black dress. I'd always considered it elegant, and black *is* elegant, at least in a dress. Black lingerie, however, appeared slightly ominous, especially contrasted with the pink. The pink was spun sugar. *Sugar and spice and every-thing nice, that's what little girls are made of.* Or maybe not.

I moved into the third room, where the hues changed again. Rows of tangerine, light yellow, mint-green, pink, and pale-blue Ipex bras hung in neat rows against the back wall. I had never seen bras in those colors before. Something about their shape seemed familiar. Those round cups . . . those pastel colors . . . *eggs!* They reminded me of the Easter eggs my kids and I had dyed the week before.

A saleswoman in her twenties, dressed in a black pullover sweater, black pants, and black pointy-toed shoes came over and stood beside me.

"If you want to try on anything, just let me know."

"I'd like to try on one of these." My eyes pointed to the Ipexes.

"What size do you wear?"

"34 B."

"Have you tried on bras here before?"

I shook my head.

"Then you might like this. Follow me."

I followed her to an area by the dressing rooms where wooden drawers were stacked as tall as she was. The saleswoman pulled out drawer 34 B and handed it to me. Folded neatly inside were at least a dozen black bras representing all the styles Victoria's Secret carried.

"If I want cleavage," the saleswoman told me, "I like to wear this bra." She pulled out Secret Embrace from the drawer. "For extra padding, this one's good." She held up The Miracle Bra. "And if you want a push-up, try Infinity Edge. And here's the Ipex. The wireless version has been really popular."

I took my box and stepped into the changing room with its mauve walls, thick burgundy carpet, and full-length mirror, then closed the plum damask curtains and began to strip. Off came my fleece top, my buff Champion Double Dry, my jeans. On my body went the Ipex.

I turned and faced the mirror.

An image reflected back: a black satin bra full of breasts; blue cotton briefs; a violin curve of waist and hips; muscular arms and legs; smooth stomach; lined face. As my eyes scanned my body, noting the contradictory images of sexy and plain, male and female, youth and middle age, I thought of Dionysus with his dual nature. He represented both sexual abandonment and danger. The god of wine gave civilization the power to loosen control over itself, yet with this power came the possibility of destruction. I thought of the mixed messages in Victoria's Secret. On one hand, sex was fun—Wear cute underwear! On the other, it was slightly dangerous—don a black merry widow while wearing Kamikaze perfume, and let's just see what happens.

I looked at the pile of fleece and denim on the floor at my feet and Nietzsche's argument came back to me. If the Dionysian side is overlooked or forgotten, art becomes stagnant.

A person's life could become stagnant, too. Especially if she were a single mom, a grad student, a person who spent a good portion of the day holed up in her house in front of a computer screen. A woman who had hardly dated since her divorce three years ago. A woman who would *like* to sleep with a man but, between being a full-time student, parent, and homeowner, found little time to buy new underwear, let alone go on a date. Or even *look* for a date.

I wondered if some ancient impulse—and not the poster along Broadway back in New York—was the true force compelling me into Victoria's Secret. Sure, I *thought* I was in search of a new bra, but maybe I was in search of something else. I pictured the other customers in the store. None of us—at least outwardly—resembled the woman on the advertisement selling Supermodel-Sexy Hair. None of us would look dynamite in a string bikini. What brought us in?

Perhaps the store called to us, even if we couldn't hear its voice, to remember our Dionysian side, that part of us that so often gets hidden away, buried beneath work and chores and relentless obligations. It's easy to forget your wild side when the dishwasher needs loading and unloading, when the library books are overdue, when, the day before school starts, you discover your twelve-year-old has lice.

Perhaps this ancient call was Victoria's *true* secret.

Two thousand years ago, Euripides wrote *The Bacchae,* a story about a group of women who abdicated their roles as mothers, wives, and daughters in order to worship Dionysus. Banding together, they twined wreaths of ivy into their hair, traveled into the forest to territory beyond the safe confines of their village, and there honored this god. Men from their town tried to capture these wild women, but the Bacchae easily routed them. The women's wands of fennel stalk inflicted wounds, while the men's metal spears drew no blood.

Pentheus, king of the village, became furious at Dionysus for exerting such force over women and commanded his troops to capture this man masquerading as a god. The soldiers tried to convince Pentheus that Dionysus *was* some kind of supernatural being. They had witnessed the power of the Bacchae. Pentheus, however, refused to believe that Dionysus could be a part of the divine nature and chained him in prison. In the play, Dionysus broke free, of course, because he *was* a god. His divine nature could not be restrained.

As I stood in the dressing room of Victoria's Secret, gazing at myself in the silky black Ipex, I could sense the chain links loosening and knew that my divine nature could not be restrained either. An ancient voice urged me on. *Have a glass of wine when you get*

*home. Call that man who gave you his phone number last week. Go
ahead, buy some cute underwear.*

A few minutes later, I was in line purchasing two Ipex bras—
one in pink and one in black. A woman in front of me clutched
several pairs of cute underwear. We nodded to each other, ivy
wreathed in our hair.

The Streak

★

by SUZANNE SCHLOSBERG

T rue story: In my early thirties, I went 1,358 days without sex. To save you the calculations, that's three years, eight months, and twenty-three days—longer than the combined length of J.Lo's first two marriages *plus* the number of days that Lisa Marie Presley was married to Michael Jackson *and* Nicholas Cage. It's 278 days longer than the duration of the Kennedy administration.

Don't get the wrong idea: I am not especially virtuous. In my twenties, I'd always been able to nip my dry spells in the bud—a fling with a snuff-dipping sportswriter, a spur-of-the-moment tryst with a coworker in my Honda on company property. When, at age thirty, I dumped my commitment-phobic boyfriend, I assumed there'd be plenty more before I found the man of my dreams. While searching for Mr. Right, I figured why not go for a test drive or two with Mr. Remote Possibility?

But what started out as a normal dry spell somehow evolved into a drought of epic proportions. Eventually, around Day 600, I even gave it a name: The Streak. No, I didn't keep a daily tally, like Ted Koppel during the Iran Hostage Crisis, but on my birthday and holidays—those benchmarks that remind you that you're older and still single—I'd instinctively do a recalculation.

For a while, I used The Streak whenever I was in need of a little sympathy from friends, and the strategy worked. The number made an impression on people, eliciting both shock and condolences. But then, as it entered high triple digits, The Streak began to backfire. Sentiment started to shift from "Gee, that's really awful" to "Gee, Suzanne, what's your problem?"

It was a fair question. The statistics alone suggested something more was at play than simple misfortune. By this time, I had screened thousands of potential boyfriends on Match.com, and of these, I'd corresponded with at least three hundred, eliminating men who sent emails like "My best friend is my hairless little dog" and "I can spot a Degas at twenty paces—can you?" I had met for coffee with about forty. Yet I'd only made it past a first date once, with an architect who treated his fork and plate as a percussion instrument.

Clearly, something was amiss. When my friends began suggesting that I take a look in the mirror, I could no longer avoid the issue, and I realized that factions were forming around full-blown theories.

The most popular was, in the words of my grandmother, "You're too picky." It was alternately known as "You're not open minded" and "Who do you think you are, Gwyneth Paltrow?"

Of course, the very people espousing this theory were the same ones setting me up on ludicrous blind dates. One date, billed by a friend as a "writer," turned out to be a motorcycle *rider* who'd recently filed for bankruptcy and was twenty-seven years older than I. My friend's excuse: "Hey, I met him in a bar. It was loud and dark and he was wearing a baseball cap."

Another friend tried to fix me up with a stockbroker whom she had never actually met. Our conversation:

Me: So, what's he like?

Sheila: Well, I know both of his parents and they are *very* good people.

Me: Is he athletic?

Sheila: Well, he must be—he's quite tall.

When I failed to shower these friends with gratitude, I was accused of being shortsighted and unappreciative, as if I were a homeless person refusing the offer of a warm bed unless the sheets were 300 thread count. I began to wonder: *Had my own friends put me in the category of the desperate? Did they really think my only dating criteria were a pulse and a penis?*

It's true that I was choosy. I wanted something more than sex. I wanted a guy who could utter the phrase "I feel" in a context other than "I feel like eating at Burger King." Still, I didn't have a trivial list of requirements, like a certain salary or a graduate degree. And I certainly wasn't as obnoxiously nitpicky as some of the men on Match.com, like the one who wrote: "Seeking a gorgeous, exotic woman who is my intellectual equal. No offense, but please do not reply if you weigh more than 120 pounds." When I dismissed a prospect, I felt sure that any reasonable woman would have done the same. I will confess that I did reject a few guys on the basis of looks alone, but only if they flunked the Newt Gingrich Test. (Would I rather have sex with this guy or Newt Gingrich?)

Still, my friends and family insisted I was to blame. Among the other theories explaining my drought: I was too assertive, I wasn't assertive enough, and I was looking for love in all the wrong places.

One friend insisted I join a Harley-Davidson club (never mind that I was deathly afraid of motorcycles). Another decided the problem was an energy imbalance in my apartment. "Hire a feng shui consultant," she insisted. In the spirit of hopefulness, I actually tried that theory out; my $400 feng shui consultation left me with a twenty-gallon fishless aquarium—but no sex.

Naturally, I did, from time to time, wonder whether my appearance might be the problem, usually after visits with my grandmother. "Have you gained weight?" she'd ask. "You look heavy.

Men don't like heavy." I didn't take this notion too seriously, though, since a week later she'd be back at it. "Have you lost weight? You're too skinny. Men like a girl with some meat on her bones."

Then there were the "get therapy" theorists. These friends insisted that, if only I'd seek counseling, I would give off the sort of vibes that would draw men to me like mosquitoes to a bug zapper. "Once you deal with your issues, a relationship will just 'happen,'" one friend maintained.

But I knew exactly what my issues were: I hadn't had sex in two years and it sucked.

Just how bad was it? Well, a friend once told me that when it comes to sex, women are like camels: "They can go long periods without any, but eventually they need to replenish or die." Though I was fairly certain I wasn't going to die from lack of sex, I can assure you that enduring a streak like mine was no picnic.

A good bit of the time I was consumed by lust. Sometimes I'd catch myself having thoughts that were, if not criminal, then at least totally inappropriate. For example: I'd be lifting weights at the gym and my eyes would focus on a tall, muscular guy doing squats. *Hmm,* I'd think, *that guy has a nice ass*—and then realize that in addition to having a nice ass, the guy probably had chemistry homework, since he looked to be in the sixth grade.

But even though I desperately wanted sex, I couldn't actually remember what sex with another person felt like. It was sort of like knowing I'd had to-die-for tiramisu that summer in Tuscany, but for the life of me not remembering how it tasted. Sometimes I worried that I'd forgotten *how* to have sex. What if, like a car that hasn't been started in several years, I wouldn't "turn over" when I finally got the opportunity?

It was maddening—and I was often a little mad about it, particularly when it came to people complaining about their own, less heroic dry spells.

Once, flipping through a magazine at a supermarket, I ran across an article titled "Could You Give up Sex for 40 Days?" The subhead: "Would you last a day? A week? A month? We asked five women to summon their willpower, fend off their partners, and take a vow of celibacy for 40 days." Forty days! Such fortitude! Such sacrifice! I fumed. What would next month's featured story be: "Could You Give up Shopping for 20 Minutes?"

I was especially impatient around married people who complained they "never" had sex with their spouse, by which, of course, they meant 1) they never had it as much as they wanted it, or 2) they never had it much as they used to have it, or 3) they never had it as much as they believed their single and Streak-less friends were having it. But "never" doesn't actually mean *never.* This is especially common among couples with infants. You do the math, and you'll see that even someone with an eight-month-old is still—worst-case scenario—well under the six-hundred-day mark.

While I was doing my best to plot an end to my streak, I was dealt an additional blow: My younger sister got engaged. The moment she and her fiancé made their announcement at a family gathering, my grandmother turned to me and shrieked across a room full of people, "*You* should be the one getting married! Why can't *you* find a man?"

It's at moments like these when you truly feel the impact of being single in your thirties.

In your twenties, you tend to look upon singleness—or a sexual dry spell—as a common and temporary condition, like the flu. But a decade later, it feels like something more serious, something chronic, painful, and obscure—like diverticulitis. Deep down you know you haven't done anything to cause your condition, but you know that other people suspect it's your fault, and in your worst moments you start to wonder if they're right.

Sure, I wondered, but never for long. During moments of doubt, I'd remind myself that all of the friends and family members who held me responsible happened to be coupled up. It seemed to me they were subconsciously examining my life through too harsh a lens. I knew from my own experience that couplehood comes with its own understandable self-satisfaction: When you've found another human being to stamp you with a seal of approval, all the insecurities that come with singleness quickly fade away. You become utterly convinced that if you could find somebody, then anybody can. So, for those of us who are "still single," only one explanation seems logical: We must be sabotaging ourselves.

Despite my occasional discouragement, I never lost hope. I went on with my life—I worked and traveled and took up competitive cycling—all the while figuring that eventually The Streak would end. But when? *When?!?*

Despite my best efforts, I reached the dreaded One Thousand Days—my own personal New Millennium. Something about this ignominious achievement put my predicament into sharper focus, and finally some answers began to emerge. I now saw that I had, inadvertently, grown protective of The Streak. At age thirty-four, I'd regressed to the virginal mindset of "saving myself"—a mindset that I didn't possess even as a virgin. It dawned on me that I really was holding out for Mr. Right or, at the very least, Mr. Significant Probability.

My streak had nothing to do with morality; it was a matter of practicality. I knew that whatever fleeting pleasure I might have felt from a fling would be a pale imitation of the real thing. Even in my libido-starved state, I knew there really are stronger urges than sexual desire, and one of them, at least in your thirties, is the urge to find true love and happiness.

I wouldn't wish 1,358 days of unintentional celibacy on any-one, but in my case, the wait was worth it. After nearly four years, I broke The Streak with a handsome, down-to-earth, redheaded marathon runner I met on Match.com.

Let's just say that sex with Paul, on our fourth date, was even better than I could have imagined. Afterward, I remember feeling so comfortable in his arms and realizing that all my worries had been unfounded. What I recall most vividly was Paul's reaction, a few hours later, when I told him about The Streak.

I'd wrestled with whether I should reveal my big secret, know-ing it was the sort of information that could send certain guys sprinting out the door. But I had so much confidence that Paul wasn't one of those guys that I took the chance. We were still in bed when I spilled the beans. He looked at me in shock, and it seemed like five minutes before he was able to speak again. "But . . . but . . . you're so *normal*. How could that be?"

I think it's the sweetest thing anyone has ever said to me.

The Wisdom of Men-o-pause

★

by WENDY MERRILL

L ast year, my three younger sisters all chipped in to give me a special gift for my forty-eighth birthday. I love getting presents, so when I received their box in the mail, I immediately sat down and ripped it open. Inside I found a tastefully wrapped basket containing a book, *The Wisdom of Menopause,* a certificate to join a popular dating service, and two jars of face cream, one for daytime use called Hope and the other, a night cream called When Hope Is Not Enough.

Also enclosed was a sympathy card expressing deep regret at the passing of my youth and a pretty, but *very* conservative, beige sweater set (you know, the kind you might see Barbara Bush wearing) several sizes too large.

Now, I know the basket was a joke. But since I am the oldest and my sisters are all more or less married, I couldn't help but hear, "You are getting old and fat and will die alone if you don't get moving—use it or lose it, sister!"

Thanks, girls! I said to myself, as I held the sweater set up to my chest, studied my reflection in a nearby mirror, and frowned. The only thing missing was a tasteful strand of pearls, I thought, and lightly touched my collarbones, remembering a time when getting a "pearl necklace" had a *completely* different meaning. Turning away from the mirror, I wondered why all of a sudden, getting another year older seemed so hard.

Granted, it is possible that I was a little overly sensitive about aging at the time, having been recently dumped by a younger man because, as he put it, "your eggs are no longer viable." Although my girlfriend Cameron pointed out that "when they start saying your *legs* are no longer viable, that's when you need to worry," I swear his comment threw me into early menopause. I had accepted the idea that I would never bear children, but I had never been rejected by a man because of my inability to conceive. I was starting to feel like I had been left on the shelf past my expiration date.

Hadn't this been the objective for most of my single life, to enjoy sex and not get pregnant? I had breezed through my thirtieth and fortieth birthdays, wondering what all the fuss was about. My biological clock may have been ticking all along, but I finally got alarmed. I may not want children, but I don't want to be rejected because I can't have them!

But menopause or not, I've never been a sweater-set girl, (and certainly did not want to be mistaken for a Republican), so I returned the sweaters to Macy's "Past Her Prime" department, exchanging them for sexy lingerie and a trendy lime-green skirt. I may be living in denial of my age, but as long as I can get away with wearing a thong, I will. Plus, being single again means that I can buy underwear with impunity, since it has been my experience that buying lingerie when I'm actually dating someone seems to be the kiss of death—a certain precursor to breaking up. (Also included in this superstitious category are leaving something that

I care about at his house, making long-term vacation plans, and shaving my underarms in front of him.) I don't, however, want to end up being fifty years old trying to look like I'm still twenty-five, so I have a trusted stylist friend who has promised to let me know if and when I cross that fine line and usher me into my age group.

As for the rest of the basket, I put the creams and dating-service certificate aside (for the time being) and sat down to read *The Wisdom of Menopause*. At first it seemed overwhelmingly negative and absolutely terrifying—horror-monal stories of weight gain, night sweats, and mood swings—but as I dug a little deeper, I found a chapter with a shred of hope. Apparently all of these symptoms are labor pains leading up to a birth—or a rebirth—of me. It seemed that the biggest promise of getting through "the change" was that my brain chemistry would change and I would finally have more access to my intuitive, higher self. Perhaps the sane, calm, and knowing woman who had appeared in my life only periodically would now become a regular, even as my periods become irregular. This saner version of me had previously been only a sidekick in my life—the dependable Ed McMahon to my chronically irreverent Johnny Carson, or the likeable Andy to my unpredictable Conan—and I was looking forward to her taking on a bigger part of the show.

Anyway, the idea that I would have more clarity and focus, and be able to use my intuition on a regular basis instead of constantly being at the mercy of my hormones, was appealing. Losing the elasticity of my skin and interest in sex was not.

A few months later, my up-and-coming intuitive cohost made an appearance in the form of a bad joke during sex. While clearly still at the mercy of my hormones, I was making love with Ken, yet another younger and inappropriate but sexy boyfriend. His penis was very hard and I stroked it teasingly. "Wow, did you take Viagra or are you just really glad to see me?" I asked.

Ken had always used the state of his penis as a barometer of his attraction for me, often taking my hand and pushing it against his crotch when we would meet to show me the effect I was having on him. He seemed inordinately proud of his erections, and sexual chemistry had been an important part of our equation, or so I thought.

He looked sort of shocked, then sheepish, and stammered, "Well, yes, I did. And I guess . . . I mean, I am glad to see you."

My hand stopped midstroke as I absorbed what he was saying. I was kidding about the Viagra; he was only forty years old!

I closed my eyes for a second. *This explains so much,* I thought. It was as though an important and elusive centerpiece of the jigsaw puzzle that was Ken had suddenly dropped into place, and a whole new version of our relationship emerged in my mind.

I remembered some talk-show psychologist warning that "in bed with someone's penis in your hand" was not the ideal place to discuss sexual dysfunction. But there I was, penis in hand, about to plunge into dangerous territory. My head was reeling with questions: Why had he taken it? Was it me? Did he take it to get a hard-on or keep one? I wasn't very well versed in Viagra and assumed that dating younger men meant that I wouldn't have to be for at least a few more years. (Thanks to my seventeen years in recovery from alcoholism, forced clean living, and my emotional immaturity, I seem younger then I am, and tend to attract younger men. I felt I had made some progress in discernment by ruling out anyone who called me "dude," wore chains on their belt, or overused expressions like "sweet!" to describe something they liked, but Ken had somehow slipped through the screening cracks.)

I opened my eyes and proceeded with caution. "Is this something that you take all the time?" I asked, not really sure I wanted to hear the answer, and even less sure what to do with my hand.

"Um, yes," he said, nervously.

"What, like every time we've made love?" I said, my mind racing back over the past few months.

"Pretty much," he replied.

"Why?" I asked, wondering if he had needed to take Viagra with Victoria, his beautiful ex-girlfriend.

"Ever since I got sober," he answered, "my equipment has been . . . unreliable. It doesn't matter who I'm with. Sometimes it works, but most of the time it doesn't. When I smoked pot I could fuck all night and not lose my erection, but without it, well, it's a problem."

Fuck.

Fortunately, I was seeing my therapist the next day, so I took my unanswered Viagra questions to Rita. Rita had been my therapist for about a year, and we had been working on how I could take the "me" out of men—no small feat. I had been in a series of codependent and inappropriate relationships, and I didn't want to continue to do the same thing over and over again, expecting different results.

"Viagra?! I know it's not all about me, but what about me?" I asked defensively, flopping down on the couch for our session, deciding that if it couldn't be all about me in therapy, where could it? As I described the Viagra incident in question, Rita grabbed her copy of the *Physician's Desk Reference* (something all good therapists and recovering drug addicts are familiar with), and together we reviewed the indications and side effects of the drug.

"Okay," she said, flipping through the heavy book to the Vs, "it says that men take Viagra about an hour before they want to have sex." She read a little more. "The gist of it seems to be that Viagra doesn't cause the penis to become erect, but keeps it in play once it's there."

"Good, so at least that means he's still probably attracted to me," I said. "But does it make it harder for him to come?"

Rita replied, "Yes, it's harder for him to come."

Well, that explains a few things, I thought, unconsciously rubbing the sore muscles in my jaw.

This may have been my first experience with Viagra, but it was certainly not my first experience with sexually dysfunctional men. I crossed and uncrossed my legs, gearing up to rationalize my choices.

"You know, he really took a chance telling me the truth. He could easily have lied," I said. "Maybe he's becoming the real *stand-up* guy that I'm looking for, who's finally *coming* around and taking a *hard* look at himself." As always, I called upon my trusty and battered pun shield to deflect any real feelings.

Rita looked at me with her loving, steady gaze, and smiling gently, said, "That reminds me, have you heard about the new Viagra eye drops that make you take a hard look at yourself? Why don't I write you a prescription?"

I sighed, wishing my healthier coping skills were as strong as my denial. "Good idea," I said. "Better make it an endless refill."

Driving home from my session, I reflected that maybe Ken's using Viagra to maintain his erection was not that much different from my faking the occasional orgasm. I mean, wasn't I sometimes faking it just to further excite my lover, equating his hard-on with my self-worth? Maybe erections are just as important to a woman's self-esteem as they are to a man's. If I were a man and had trouble maintaining an erection, what would I do, aside from everything I could possibly think of, including therapy, hypnotism, acupuncture, taking herbs like Ram Goat Dash Along or Horny Goat Weed, eating oysters, drinking tequila, watching porn, and dating twenty-five-year-olds? (Yikes, that was scary, I felt like I was inside of a man's head there for a minute!)

I have never told any of the men I've been with when I've staged an orgasm, and certainly no one has ever asked (apparently

I'm convincing). I mean, who asks a question that they really don't want answered (aside from me)? Sometimes I fake it because I don't want to inspire hurt feelings, or I'm tired and want to get it over with, or I'm just trying to "fake it until I make it." But other times, I'm just afraid—afraid to tell the truth, especially in the bedroom. How hard would it be to just say, "I'm sorry, I can't come right now. I'm tired, I feel emotionally detached from you, none of my backup fantasies are working, and just getting off with your penis is impossible right now, so can you please just finish up and let's get some sleep"?

God, no wonder men are using Viagra!

In the end, maybe relationships and menopause are like the labor pains of childbirth. Denial is key to getting into them and through them, and what keeps us going through all the pain and fear is a promise. The promise of a birth—of a child, a new love, or even a new me. Perhaps my denial about my age and the appropriateness of the men I choose to date is really just optimism, dressed in black, and all that really matters is how well I treat myself and other people in the process.

When I got home that evening, I listened to a message on my answering machine from my sister Vicki while dressing to go out on a date for dinner.

"Hey, Wen, if you liked what we got you for your birthday last year," she said, "you are going to love what we're planning for your forty-ninth. . . . " As she continued eluding to this year's evil surprise, I went to my closet, put on my birthday thong and trendy lime-green skirt, and sauntered over to the dresser, where I applied just a little Hope, and this time when I caught my reflection in the mirror, I smiled.

Thunder

★

by CHELSEA HANDLER

O ne of my girlfriends was getting married. This was becoming an annoying pattern. Sarah was my third girlfriend to get engaged within six months, and it was becoming clear to me that more and more people were going to go through with it. It's not the concept of marriage I have a problem with. I'd like to get married, too. A couple times. It's the actual wedding that pisses me off.

The problem is that everyone who gets married seems to think that they are the first person in the entire universe to do it, and that the year leading up to the event revolves entirely around them. You have to throw them showers, bachelorette weekends, buy a bridesmaid dress, and then buy a ticket to some godforsaken town wherever they decide to drag you. If you're really unlucky, they'll ask you to recite a poem at their wedding. That's just what I want to do—monitor my drinking until I'm done with my public service announcement. And what do we get out of it, you ask? A dry piece of chicken and a roll in the hay with their hillbilly cousin. I could get that at home, thanks.

Then they have the audacity to go shopping and *pick out their own gifts*. I want to know who the first person was who said this was okay. After spending all that money on a bachelorette weekend, a shower, and often a flight across the country, they expect you to go to Williams-Sonoma or Pottery Barn and do research? Then they send you a thank-you note applauding you for such a thoughtful gift. They're the ones who picked it out! I always want to remind the person that absolutely no thought went into typing in a name and having a salad bowl come up.

I prefer giving cash. When I get married, I'm gonna register at Bank of America. Both times. I'm a Jew. I don't mess around when it comes to money.

But it doesn't end after the wedding. Next they want you to come over and watch the wedding video. Like I really want to see footage of me passed out in a cake.

A wedding can really put a damper on a good friendship. Once people get married, they think they've got the whole world figured out. Immediately they think all their single friends are sad and pathetic.

"Oh, why don't you come over Friday? We're gonna have a bunch of people over and play some board games. Maybe you'll meet someone nice." What a hoot. My response is always the standard, "Unless you're playing Who's Hiding the Ecstacy?, I don't think I'm gonna be able to make it. I've got plans." Don't married people know that the last thing a single person wants to do on a Friday night is play a nutty game of Yahtzee? I'd rather take a bubble bath with my father.

And then there was Sarah's bachelorette party. Las Vegas and I have a special relationship. We never let each other down. Olympic Garden is touted as the best strip club in Vegas, and for good reason. Eight of us went there on the very first night, and I will never forget the look on all of our faces when we saw our man. They announced his name, THUNDER, and I thought, *Excellent.*

THUNDER was beautiful. This wasn't a *Playgirl* pinup type with long hair and a bow tie who could rival Fabio in a "Who's

Grosser?" competition. This guy was Dylan McDermott good-look-ing, with an ass that could double as a shelf—by far the most beau-tiful body any of us had ever laid eyes on.

All the girls were drooling and signing up for personal dances with him onstage. It quickly became clear what had to be done: I had to take one for the team.

I had never seen all my girlfriends go goo-goo over the same guy. Most of them were in relationships and two were already mar-ried. Each one of us was in her own personal fantasy of what could be done with a body like that, and I knew I had to be the one to act on it. Out of the corner of my eye I saw Lydia and Ivory start to drool and told them to step off. "He's mine."

Other than that, I didn't have much competition, except for every other girl in the club. Well, they could have him too—I just wanted a piece of the action. One of my friends bought me a dance with him, and I was called onstage. Now, I'm not a big fan of strip clubs to begin with. I like a little mystery, and it's my personal belief that men look better in clothes. I was wrong. I got my dance—and his ass in my face—but I managed to keep my cool. He had the most adorable face I had ever seen. Sweet baby-blue eyes, dark hair, and the cutest smile to hit that side of the Vegas strip.

While he was dancing around me onstage, he asked where I lived, and I told him L.A. He said he lived there too and just drove here on the weekends to work. A commuting stripper. Talk about dedication to your craft. I wrote down my number and bid him adieu. My work there was done.

The girls made me promise I'd go out with him.

"Go out with him? I'm not *going* anywhere with him. I will go to him and then I will have him."

Immediately I wondered how much weight I would need to lose to be acceptable to a stripper. All he saw were other girl strip-pers and their perfect bodies. Maybe I would just tone up. These thoughts took over my brain for the next few minutes until I found the limo and then the minibar.

THUNDER called me the next week. He tried to tell me his real name, but I quickly interrupted him. "I like THUNDER. Let's just stick with that for now."

"Okay, I guess, but no one really calls me that," his husky voice replied. This guy was giving me too many details.

"No matter," I said. "How was your drive back from Vegas?" I had to feign interest in all this nonsense until I could ask when I could come over and sit on his face. I didn't say that out loud, of course. I never say the things I really want to. If I did, I'd have no friends.

"Can I take you to dinner?" he asked.

"How about drinks?" I replied. I just wanted his address, but I didn't want to scare him.

We met at the Lava Lounge. I made sure it was somewhere close to his place. I told him I didn't want him driving too far after his drive back from Vegas.

He showed up in a flannel shirt and blue jeans. Nothing too revealing, kind of like a lumberjack. Kind of like on a men's calendar. I stared at his flannel shirt, wondering whether it was material I could actually rip with my own two hands. I decided that it was going to be very rough sex.

As I downed a couple of vodka collinses, I asked him questions about his life and what he planned on doing. "Well, I just turned thirty-seven" (that was a shocker—he didn't look a day over twenty-nine), "and now I want to start really focusing on my acting." Oh my god. I looked around to see if anyone else had heard him.

"An actor?" I said, trying to sound intrigued. "Wow, that's so . . . You have a great look, I'm sure it won't be a problem."

Who in his right mind decides to get into acting at the tender age of thirty-seven? Weight lifting, maybe, but acting? Was this guy serious? What had he been wasting his time with until then? Well, stripping, I guess. They say it's hard to walk away from that kind of money. THUNDER told me he made anywhere from three to four grand a weekend, which, compared to my $311 per week unemployment check, sounded like quite a handsome income. But forget taking this guy to Sarah's wedding; I'd never hear the end of it. I just smiled and thought, *Keep on talkin', you hot piece of ass.*

"So you're a comedian," he said. "Tell me something funny."

"Okay. The great thing about being an alcoholic is that when you're bored at a party, you can leave without saying goodbye, and people just think you blacked out."

"Are you an alcoholic?" he asked me.

"That's not really the point," I responded. "And I don't like the word 'alcoholic.' I like to think of myself as an advanced drinker."

"I'm confused," he said. It was pretty obvious that THUNDER spent a lot of his time being confused, so I switched the conversation back to his career.

There is only so much actor-talk one person can take, and I had reached my limit. We needed to wrap this little chitchat up now. I excused myself to the bathroom, hoping that would give him some time to finish his beer and we could move on to the action. In the restroom, I met two girls who were making fun of a guy one of them was talking to. Evidently, he had a pretty bad lisp. I told them that was nothing—if they really wanted to see funny, they should come and listen to THUNDER for a minute. "I'm not even sure this guy can read," I said and relayed the story of how we had met.

They got excited at the idea of meeting him, and the three of us all went back to the table together.

I made the introductions, explaining to THUNDER that I had run into some friends. They looked at each other and giggled. It was clear they were taken with his beauty. Who wasn't? Then one of the girls whispered to me, "Does he talk?"

I said, "Yes, he talks, he's not a chimp."

"Ask him a question," she persisted.

That's too mean, I thought. "What should I ask him?" I said with clenched teeth.

"Ask him to spell something," she shot back.

That crossed the line. I started to feel bad about mistreating THUNDER. Flashbacks of being harassed in high school by older girls flooded my conscience. I had never wanted to be mean like that to someone, and now here I was acting just as bad. Possibly even worse, since I was technically an adult and should know better. And at some point, he was going to catch on. He was a little slow, but he wasn't out-and-out brain-dead.

So we bid our adieus and jetted back to his pad. I told him I wanted to see his headshots.

Twenty minutes later I'm airborne and getting the bottom knocked out of me. This guy wasn't so stupid after all. He really knew his way around a woman. It was crazy, rough stuff. I couldn't get enough of him. He was flipping me around, pinning me this way and that. His skin was soft and he had a back you could just hold on to for dear life. His arms were solid muscle and he had this beautiful, perfect ass. Of course I had seen this all before when he was onstage, but now I was living out every girl and gay guy's fantasy. Soft lips too. Really good soft lips. I love men.

There's something truly wonderful about a man who knows how to take a woman. I thought maybe it was love. I even slept over. I knew I would be back for more. Who cares if he didn't know how to multiply? This guy was some sort of sign from God.

THUNDER and I started seeing each other on a regular basis. We got into the pattern of skipping the formalities of cocktails altogether, and I would just come over. The sex was amazing every time. I even enjoyed sleeping next to him. It felt like sleeping next to a rhinoceros. His body was so big, I felt petite next to him. I wanted to show him off to my friends, but I didn't want him to speak. I was torn.

I called him while he was driving back from Vegas one Sunday. He didn't seem happy to hear from me. I sensed something was wrong and that I would not be getting any action that night. He told me he was exhausted from driving and didn't know if he would be up for one of my visits. What? Too tired? I understood our Cirque du Soleil act required some stamina, but I felt it was well worth it. Then he laid it on me. He had met someone else whom he thought he wanted to get serious with.

"A girl?" I asked.

"Yes," he said. "You're a really great girl. And we've been having a blast, but I think we both know that this is not something that's going any further. I just don't see myself getting serious with you."

Oh my god. I couldn't believe I was getting dumped by THUN-DER. I couldn't believe I was getting dumped by someone whose real name I didn't even know. My time in heaven was up, and I was being told I wasn't the marrying kind by someone who undressed for a living. Was it because I wasn't flexible enough? Not serious enough? We were seeing each other at least two times a week. How much more serious could we get?

"Are you there?" he asked.

"Yeah."

"I'm really sorry."

"It's okay. I understand," I lied. "So, is there any way I could still just see you tonight?" I asked.

Silence.

"Goodbye, Chelsea. I wish you well." He hung up. Well, onward and upward. It's not that I hadn't had my heart broken before, but this was the first time I heard my little beaver cry a little. Talk about sad. She didn't leave the house for days.

A Work in Progress: Inside the Mind (and Bed) of a Single Sex Columnist

★

by RACHEL KRAMER BUSSEL

I feel like a failure when I'm not actively having sex. If I go more than a month without getting laid, more than a month with no partner other than my trusty Hitachi Magic Wand, a little voice starts to whisper louder and louder, "There's something wrong with you."

You could say it's an occupational hazard. No, I'm not a prostitute or porn star, but I do deal with sex constantly. In fact, I'm surrounded by it pretty much day and night: I work at a porn magazine, I write a sex column for a major alternative newspaper, I edit books of smut, pen steamy erotica stories, and at home, every conceivable sex manual seems to magically land in my mailbox whether I ask for it or not. My friends write sex blogs, and even the ones who don't are highly eager to share their latest sexual adventures with me (especially if they're the type who rarely has sexual adventures).

Car sex, foot fetishes, lap dances, public spankings, double fisting, bondage—you name it, I've heard about it.

Most of the time, I lap it right up, but sometimes I just want to clear my head of all things sex, so as not to remind myself of what my life is lacking. Granted, I have had my share of sexual adventures (a tryst with Betty Dodson's boyfriend in a sleazy motel, sex with a porn director, a date where all I did was get spanked and masturbate in front of my spanker). I've written about my love of blow jobs, breasts, threesomes, and kinky sex. I've even posed for nude photos and had people tell me they've jerked off to them.

Yet that's only a small part of my life. Mostly, I go to work, I go to comedy shows, I hang out with my friends, read, rent movies, go to the gym, and wander around New York City. I geek out over board games, babies, and cupcakes. I'm in daily touch with my parents and in weekly touch with my grandparents. And, like many other women, I stress out about being late, my student loans, and my weight.

Sex is vitally important to me and, as a subject, something I usually find endlessly fascinating. But despite the fact that many friends, and plenty of strangers, seem to think I'm bedding someone new every night, I'm much more of a voyeur than a participant. I love hearing about what turns other people on, especially if it's something particularly bizarre (shower-cap fetish, anyone?). Discovering what makes people tick sexually is a subject I (almost) never get tired of.

Yet when it becomes all-consuming, drowning out time to indulge my more G-rated interests, I sometimes freak out.

You see, I'm single, and have been for most of the ten years I've been living in New York. I've never lived with anyone, I've rarely had sex on a daily basis, and there have even been stretches, especially in the two years I've been writing my sex column, where I haven't so much as made out for months.

The discrepancies between what people *think* I'm doing, what I *am* doing, and what I *want* to be doing are sometimes so vast, I have no idea how to bridge the gaps.

I'm not claiming to be a saint; if I wanted to, I could be having sex with someone right now, instead of lying sprawled across my messy couch with a bottle of Diet Coke and a bunch of books with names like *Sperm are From Mars, Eggs are From Women; No More Christian Nice Guy;* and *The Debutante Divorcée* (I need some levity). But empty sex has often left me feeling worse than when I'm alone, showing me how hollowly some people treat the act. Except for rare occasions, I'm not interested in sleeping with someone just once. If I like you, I want to continue to share not just sex but all the attendant getting-to-know-you dorkiness, like what you dream about and what your childhood nicknames were and what you like to eat for breakfast.

Sex without the rest of that just doesn't suit me as it once did.

In the ten years I've been living in New York, I've had various flings, several ongoing hookups, and one semi-serious relationship, but the biggest shift hasn't been from single to coupled and back so much as from early twenties "I want it all" mode to early thirties "I want a baby" mode.

When a guy I was hooking up with in classic friends-with-benefits style dropped off the face of the earth to immerse himself in a local film fest, then resurfaced after two months, the old me would have crawled right back into his bed, in part because I missed him and in part because he has one of the most gorgeous cocks I've ever seen. But this time, I didn't. Not because his complete silence after our manic, must-flirt-and-fuck time together hurt me, but because I realized that if he chose work over me, he wouldn't make a good boyfriend or, eventually, a good father.

That being said, I can't help but admit that casual sex has occasionally saved my life. Okay, maybe that's a bit of an exaggeration, but for an overly long six-month period, I was obsessed with a particular guy. To call it a crush would be putting it mildly. I thought about him and visited his website multiple times a day, found excuses to see him as often as I could, and generally imagined us getting married and living happily ever after. The fact that he showed not even the slightest smidgen of interest in me beyond that of friendship didn't deter me in the least. In fact, I almost turned down what wound up being one of the hottest nights of my life because of my fixation.

When a guy I know propositioned me via email, I was startled yet intrigued. But I wrote back and said that while his come-on flattered me, I just wasn't in the right mindset; I was hung up on Crushboy.

"Maybe I could help you forget him . . . by spanking you," he wrote back. The audacity of his request both startled me *and* turned me on. If I'd been interested in a serious relationship with this guy, I never could have admitted to my feelings of confusion and depression over Crushboy. But instead of laughing at me, my friend let me explain what I was going through, offered some advice (sunlight and exercise every day for the depression), and then picked me up, did all sorts of amazing things to my body, and took me back home. It was a simple, yet healing, one-night stand that did wonders for my self-esteem.

I guess as I've grown older (and grown up), I've come to realize that being single is not simple. There's give and take in any relationship, including our relationships with ourselves. So while sometimes I wish I had someone I could curl up next to every night in bed, just as often I savor the room I have instead for my pillows, blankets, and books. Living alone has made me aware of how independent and, perhaps, set in my ways I am. I like things the way I like them—even if they might not even make sense to most people.

If you asked, I would probably tell you that I'm looking for a stable, monogamous relationship, but that doesn't change the fact that two nights ago I went to an underwear-only Shabbat dinner and wound up in a bed with six other people, being groped by and groping people I'd only just met, having an R-rated threesome (tops came off but panties stayed on), and enjoying it tremendously. Ideally, I want to combine that freedom for exploration with a partner, so instead of going to the orgy alone, I could take him or her along. I want to continue to have sexual adventures, but with someone by my side, someone who can experience them with me and enhance that experience, not someone who will "save me from myself."

Granted, I can't be "on" sexually 24/7, and I can't (and don't want to) fake it. But when I'm in the moment, I'm as horny, lusty, perverted, and kinky as you can get. I love it when I can let go of all my baggage and go completely wild in bed, letting myself be loud and ask for what I want. Often this means I'm not strong or powerful or any of the other qualities I want to be in the rest of my daily life. Often it means I literally have to let go of rational thought and just go by what feels right. This may mean giving a blow job in a cab or asking someone to tie me up or getting off on watching a couple have sex right in front of me. It may mean holding a paddle and making someone's ass turn the most gorgeous shade of red, or whimpering into the phone as my long-distance lover tells me he wants to put his cock and his finger inside me at the same time, or lusting after my straight friend and entertaining the most wicked fantasies about what we could do together. It may mean all these things and others I've yet to experience.

The best, and really the only, thing I can do for myself is make sure I'm deciding what to do as a single woman based on my own values, not someone else's. Exploring my fantasies and desires in print and in various beds has shown me what I both do and don't want, making it easier to make such decisions. I can choose when to simply indulge my hedonism, such as the recent orgy, and when I want to hold out for something more. Being single allows me the freedom to decide without having to worry about someone I care about judging me for those decisions, but it also means I lose out on having that kind of super-close confidante whose ear I can whisper into after (or during) sex, who is with me even when we're apart, who can perhaps know my mind better than I do.

That's what I miss about being in a relationship, although not having that has forced me to get to know myself in ways I don't always like, but can appreciate.

I've had to face my best and worst points, and see where total freedom can take me. Sometimes it means doing things that seem fun at the time but that I later regret, and I've spent countless nights beating myself up over stupid sexual choices and fostering anger at men who really did nothing to lead me on. Sometimes it means submitting to a fantasy in which I allow someone to swoop in and seemingly sweep all my problems under the rug, assuming that somehow our desire for each other will make the rest of my daily drama disappear.

Of course, once things go sour, I'm inevitably faced with the same overdue deadlines, filthy apartment, student loans, and other hassles as I was before, only now they've been exacerbated by my not facing them head on.

And that's when I step back to get my life in order before trying to find Mr. or Ms. Right.

Don't get me wrong, I don't have everything figured out quite yet. I'm still prone to extreme flattery when someone I respect or think is hot expresses any interest in me, and I'm all too ready to race to my favorite stores and rack up pricey bills in order to flaunt new dresses and high heels in an effort to make him or her like me even more. I sometimes have to restrain myself from tossing my plans to work late into the night in favor of heading off to flirt with someone who can make me forget my mountainous to-do list. And in the very back of my mind, I do sometimes have this idea that the perfect lover will rescue me from every single flaw I have, real or imagined.

But right now, I'm just working on figuring out how to make sex both my career and something special, private, and revelatory in my life, how to keep it sacred even when I'm covering it, how to keep it inspiring when sometimes it feels like I'll never be horny again. There's a risk to putting your sex life out there, all the time, and I am sometimes tempted to believe my own hype. Of course, it's flattering to have strangers act like I'm the answer to their dreams, and pulling back from that fantasy life and recognizing the reality—that dating is a struggle, though sometimes with a happy outcome—isn't always easy. I sometimes feel like there are two sides of me: the slutty, exhibitionistic side and the girlie, pink cupcake–loving one.

When a friend tells me she has a nice Jewish boy looking to get married whom she wants to set me up with, I panic. Not because, at heart, I'm not a nice Jewish girl, but I worry that I'm already tainted, one Google search away from being castigated into the world of sluts and whores. Maybe I've had too much sex, and written about most of it, to ever qualify as someone's dream wife. At the same time, I wouldn't feel comfortable pretending to be some almost-virginal lass, shoving my bisexuality or penchant for spanking under the rug along with my sex toys. Ultimately, I don't want to have to choose, to pick sex over romance or cock rings over cupcakes. I want it all, and even though it may take longer for me to get it on my terms, it'll be worth the wait, rather than having to hide some aspect of myself to try to fit in with what everyone else is doing. Merging my two selves is something I'm still figuring out how to do, and I don't ever want to stop learning, even when I (hopefully) really do settle down, with (hopefully) a mate and several babies to dote on.

For now, though, I'm a single, and sexual, work-in-progress, and I wouldn't have it any other way.

Next Is Now

★

by MICHAL REED

I'm fifty-two. Well, really I'm fifty-one, but I will be fifty-two at the end of summer. I round up my age every June so that by the time I am the older age, it feels familiar.

When I was in my twenties, older women warned me about sunning myself. If I kept it up, they told me, in my fifties I'd be old and wrinkled. Of course I wouldn't want *that*. But I figured by fifty I'd be old and wrinkled anyway. I loved the sun. Still do. Every Christmas I go south of the equator so that I can take in the warmth and light. Recently, one of my musician friends who rarely sees the light of day compared his smooth white arm with my textured brown one. Yes, old and wrinkled.

My husband left six years ago. My girlfriend and I split up nine months ago. I am old and wrinkled and single and supposedly invisible. I miss the touch and the desire of a lover, but I don't have time for one anyway. My thoughts and actions are now filled with endless house projects: the family-house-turned–B&B; a photo installation going up in a few weeks, a book that I am almost finished with; and a new project about hiking alone. I enjoy the hours I spend exploring my local mountains. Not needing to worry about breaking a partner's rhythm, I can stop whenever I want and write little notes of my observations. There is a peace within my aloneness that I never anticipated.

I teach. During the school year, I usually work out with my high school swim team students. But as soon as school is out, I shift to swimming laps in my own pool. I live alone at the end of a long driveway, surrounded by hills so barren in summer that the cattle disappear. By swimming here, I don't have to drive to work out and I don't have to wear a top. A few weeks ago, I was about fifteen minutes into my workout, the music of my MP3 goggles maintaining my pace while I was deep in thought, imagining conversations using my high school French and Spanish to keep my language skills up for travel, crafting phases about my new hiking project, when, as I turned my head to breathe, I noticed movement out of the corner of my eye. The pool guy was here! This wasn't his regular day!

After a lifetime of swimming naked in rivers and mountain lakes, I didn't really care if he saw my breasts, but I felt reflexively that I needed to feign embarrassment to assure the safety of my reputation. What? Where did that come from? Since when did I care about reputation? I covered my breasts with my arms—who knows where I had learned that maneuver—and asked him to throw me my top. I put it on.

"In three years of this job, nothing like this has ever happened," he said.

"I usually swim at school, but now it's summer break."

"I thought this was a vacation home. I never seen anybody here. You swim like that at school?"

"No, there I swim totally naked. My students love it."

He gasped.

"I'm being sarcastic. Of course I don't swim topless at school. I wear a one-piece Speedo, like the girls."

"This is such a fantasy."

"Not mine." I didn't want to be rude, but I didn't want to encourage him, either. I got out of the pool and wrapped my towel around me.

He pulled leaves out of the skimmer. "Really, three years and I've never seen nothing. My friends all ask me, 'Hey, you seen any college girls, any divorcées?'" He paused. "Are you married?" I found his honesty amusing.

"I'm divorced. But I'm fifty-two." That was supposed to break his fantasy. "How old are you?"

"Twenty-seven."

"Ah, my kids are twenty and twenty-three." I didn't want our interaction to be awkward or arousing, so I quickly moved to the safety of my mother role. As we talked, I looked at him. Nice body. Strong eyes. Edgy bone structure. Hmmm. He *could* be *my* fantasy . . . but I stayed maternal.

"You swim a lot?" He didn't stop working.

"A few hours a week. I hike and ride my bike, too." I moved over to the garden to pull weeds.

"Yeah, you look like you work out a lot. My partner works out. He puts the treadmill on 'Kilimanjaro.'"

"What?"

"Kilimanjaro. It's the hardest setting. It's the tallest mountain in Africa."

"I know. I'm planning on climbing it this Christmas."

"No kidding? Who are you going with?"

"I'm going on my own."

"No boyfriend?"

"I asked several friends, but those who have the time and money don't have the fitness, and those who have the fitness don't have the time or money. If I don't go now, when? I may not have the endurance even now."

"You look like you have the endurance."

I pulled weeds while we chatted. He told me about what a good student he had been in high school—after his probation officer motivated him—and how he should have gone to college. I encouraged him to start now. I had successfully desexualized our interactions, shifted our roles to mentor/student. He left the chemicals for me so that I could finish my swim.

As I continued swimming back and forth, I thought about how though the time may come when we might be free of husband, kids, and lovers, we can never escape the relationship we have with our community and our culture. I was alone. I had this great house and, within it, for the first time in twenty-six years, nobody else's feelings to consider. I liked both relationship sex and spontaneous, exciting new sex. Or at least I used to. I thought about the pool guy—Jason. He was clearly attracted to me. But I lived in a small community. I didn't talk, but others did. How safe would I be, living alone, if people knew I had had sex with the pool guy? What would be next? The gas-meter reader? The UPS guy? Here I was, fifty-two—okay, fifty-one—financially stable, world-traveled, accomplished, independent, and I had to worry about my reputation like a sixteen-year-old girl? Or did I? What was different now, from then? When did I become conservative? And was it a bad thing? When I used to ask a rhetorical question in therapy, my therapist would say, "Answer the question," and we'd fill the hour up from there. But my laps were finished and I wanted to get back to my writing.

The next two Tuesdays I made a point to swim in the morning. When I heard Jason's truck pull up I stayed at my computer and didn't go outside.

Even though I'm middle-aged and invisible, I still drive three hours to get my Beverly Hills haircut from a friend who services the stars, although I often don't bother to engage in the necessary drying and ironing that the cut requires. In the summer I regularly go out in public, shamelessly, with lumpy hair or a hat. Instead of contacts, I wear my five-year-old glasses. Clearly, I am not trying to attract a lover.

So I was surprised when the irrigation guy came on to me. What was going on? Another question to answer. I was fussing in the garden, cutting back the lavender and rosemary, when he arrived. I was wearing an old sports bra, baggy, below-the-knee corduroy shorts that my son had worn when he was in junior high, and dilapidated Birkenstocks. I had the aforementioned bad hair and glasses. Nate, the irrigation guy—cute in a commercial kind of way, fit, midthirties—had been fixing the sprinklers and drip lines every summer for the last few years. I treated him with a warm but aloof respect. After all, he was the irrigation guy, young and cute, and I was invisible. I tried to help him with his tasks just because I wanted to limit his boss's exorbitant hourly billing. In between turning the water on and off, I asked him about his kids. He told me about his unhappy marriage. I offered matronly support.

Because the weather had just begun its summer climb into the 100s, when it was time for Nate to leave I suggested that he use the pool. I told him I was going to go back into the house to work and he could swim without a suit, I didn't care, I'd get him a towel and leave. Matter of fact. Maternal.

"It's no fun swimming alone," he said.

I hesitated. What was he saying? "It's really hot out. A swim will lower your body temperature. You'll feel better on your other jobs if you take a moment to cool down."

"Swimming naked in your pool is not going to cool me down."

It took me a second to hear what he had said. I had been a polite middle-aged employer. I looked a mess. I thought I was invisible. I laughed. He was watching me. I laughed again. "I'll get a towel, and if you feel like swimming, feel free. I have work to do. Thanks for fixing the sprinklers."

"You sure you don't want to go for a swim with me?"

I paused, thinking about the pool guy. What was up? What kind of porn loop had I entered? I was going to have to start answering some of these questions.

"Thanks, but I have work I need to do." He looked at me directly, with a kind of intensity I had not thought him capable of. This beautiful man, who knew of my kindness, but not my brain, desired me. Invisible, middle-aged me. What *was* going on? "Thanks, Nate, really. But I am going to go back to work."

The third Tuesday, Jason knocked on my door, saying his cell phone didn't work and one of his trainees was trying to reach him. Could he borrow my phone? Sure. He made his call and then asked if I was still uncomfortable with our encounter.

"No. It's no big deal. Really. Did you tell your friends?"

"Nah, I didn't tell nobody. But I have been thinking about it over and over."

"What have you been thinking?" It was a reflexive response. I quickly hoped that I wasn't conjuring some kind of flirty, phone-sex type of interaction.

"Pervy thoughts."

"Pervy?" Uh oh.

"Well not *pervy,* but, you know, what it would be like to be with you." He sighed. "I'm really into older women."

Ha! There it was. One of those guys who doesn't avoid age but fetishizes wrinkles and the experience they represent.

"Yeah, older women know what they want, know how to ask for it. They have this power and this calm—they're really hot." I was being objectified, part of a "they" even as his bad grammar was slipping away. He moved toward me as carefully as my feral cat does when I put out her food. I could feel his sexual power, that overwhelming young-man energy that I experience within myself those few days before I ovulate. As if I were in a cheesy romance novel, I felt the cliché of my body tingling. He was right in front of me, offering himself, waiting for me to make the move. I wondered what I would do.

I stepped back. "But you are married." That was always an effective mood breaker.

"No. I have a kid but I'm not married."

"But you live with her?" There had to be an easy social way out of this.

"No. This is embarrassing, but I live with my mother. I wouldn't be able to ask you over or nothing if we got something going."

"I can't imagine us getting something going." Twenty-seven. He couldn't even conceptualize who I was, how I identified myself to myself. He had identified me in another way.

"Really, you can't see it?" He stepped forward again and the romance novel clichés continued: I felt his need. It sounds ridiculous, but he had this sexual energetic force that was pulling me in. Is this what being single is about? Being exposed to the weather of humanity's sexual desires? What kind of shelter had I been inside for all those coupled years? I made an effort to shift to a more nonsexual place and said, "Well, let me just give you a hug. Nothing else. Okay?"

His body was scaled to mine, small and solid. It had been a while since I had felt the warmth, the solidity, of another human. For years, my kids would fling their little bodies over mine while we were watching movies; even as teens they would sometimes stretch out with their feet in my lap. But now, without kids, without a lover, there weren't any forms of touch in my life, none of that aspect of being human that I had considered essential. How had this happened? His hands stroked my back, he pressed into me, and I could feel every contour of our bodies through our clothes. It would be so easy to take him into my house, to open to his touch. To feel my humanness. He felt the slipping of my guard, and when

I pulled back, he slipped the tips of his fingers into the waistband of my pants, tugging just a little, keeping me close. The exchange felt comfortable, familiar. I easily could have gone with it. I took his hand away as I stepped back.

"No. Not now. Let me think about it. In a week I might be really into it. But I'm not sure. I have to sort it all out. If you'd like, you could give me your number and I could call you."

"Okay. I hope you decide yes. I really hope you decide yes. This is going to be the longest week of my life."

I needed to go to L.A. to get the great haircut, see friends, look at art. I ran my pool-guy scenario past my gay haircutter.

"Is he cute?"

"Yeah."

"Then what's stopping you? You deserve some fun."

In the past, I wouldn't have hesitated to take advantage of this "fun." What *was* stopping me now? I thought about what my therapist would have said—answer the question.

During the three-hour drive home, I tried to do just that. This was the first summer in twenty-six years that I hadn't had a husband or kids or a lover to include in my activities and thoughts. I was really, really single, as in no witness to the trials and joys of my day, no one to tell when I went for a hike, no one to ask for help. Reflexively I had always been drawn to sex and relationships; I had made time for them. But now, I was making time to be with myself. I was in a genuine relationship with myself. And, as in the best relationships, it had come about gradually. We had just started hanging out more and more. Going for bike rides and hikes, watching movies. When I needed to express my day in words, I wrote in my journal. The depth of the relationship had snuck up on me, I realized in a silly, gushy way—I was infatuated. I didn't want anyone else.

After a lifetime of needing to be desirable, now, at this moment when I anticipated I would be invisible, it didn't matter to me. After many years of living with one person, and many shorter episodes of sparky interludes with others, I knew what it was to engage with another. Now I wanted to spend time doing and thinking on my own, with myself. I began to wonder if it would be best to be faithful, to give this relationship a chance before I sabotaged it with distractions.

I was deep in thought, having just spilled out of the Grapevine into the expansive flatness of the San Joaquin Valley, when Jason called.

"Have you thought about me?"

"Yes."

"I mean, have you thought about me when you were by yourself?"

Jesus. "Yes."

"I have, too. I have been thinking about nothing else."

"Jason, your sexual energy is very powerful and compelling, and at another time of my life I would have followed through without hesitation." I took a breath. "But not now."

"Hey, that's all right. I expected you to say that. It was too good to be true."

"I do appreciate how respectful you have been. I never felt pressured."

"I would never pressure a woman, but you have to know, I will be watching for another chance. Will you still come out and say hi sometimes?"

"Of course."

At fifty-two, I know I might not get another chance to experience the raw, objectifying excitement of a young man's sexual energy. But that experience is familiar to me, predictable, known. Long, uninterrupted expanses of time with myself, with my thoughts and adventures, are less familiar. Now I want to make time for those unknown possibilities.

Aware that I might be settling into the gravity of monogamy I wonder, Will this relationship go anywhere? What would it be like to marry myself? How would it be the same and how would it be different from marrying another? More questions to consider. I'll get to them sooner or later. But right now I want to indulge myself with this infatuation.

Sex Ed

★

by SARAH IVERSON

It is a large vibrator, the kind you plug in. The woman spreads her labia with two fingers so that we can see the lubrication, the swollen inner lips. We lean forward as she presses the vibrator between her legs and moves it in a tight circle. She arches her back. She cries out. Sitar music swells and the screen fades to black.

The dean wheels out a dry-erase board. "All right, ladies, let's make a list of the benefits of masturbation!"

After a moment of nervous silence, answers popcorn out:

"It helps you get to sleep?"

"Um, sometimes when I have a paper to write, I, you know, masturbate? And then I stop thinking about sex and I can write better."

"It feels good."

We giggle nervously. Brown University is different than I expected. It is less like an intellectual crucible and more like a state fair. There's food and prizes, I spend most of the time lost, and the whole thing is slightly surreal.

The dean holds up an enormous diagram of the clitoris. "It's like an iceberg," she says.

I am seventeen years old and have never really masturbated. I am attending this workshop out of morbid curiosity and a vague feeling that something is wrong with me.

The dean claims that when the whole iceberg is considered, the clitoris is larger than some penises. We cheer. But the news is not all good. We learn that the word "masturbate" comes from the Latin *mas* for "male" and *turbare* "to stir up." We brainstorm new feminist terms, such as "patting the bunny" and "Jilling off."

I somehow miss the most important message of the workshop, which is: Buy a vibrator.

I go back to my dorm room and pat the bunny, without effect. Knowing the etymology of the word *masturbate* is no help at all. I think Goethe summed it up the best: "Dear friend, all theory is gray, but green the golden tree of life."

What I don't realize is that I have never had an orgasm. The problem is not that I can't masturbate; the problem is that I can't come. I am still a virgin, but I have done everything else. I have had two devoted boyfriends—one of them an Eagle Scout—kneel between my legs and lick their jaws sore. I have been felt up and felt down, but I have never felt much.

As a child, most of my sexual education came from my cousins Melissa and Nikki, who were half-Latin and lived in New York City. They spoke in a kind of gnomic rhyme:

Kiss my applejack
My soda crack
My beep beep beep
On Sesame Street
Your ma
Your pa
Got a greasy ass
Got a hole in your pants

Got a big behind
Like Frankenstein
Cleopatra
Was a tittie snatcher
And old King Kong
Had a big ding dong

Whenever they taught me a new piece of filthy information, I would drag it back to my mother, like a dog with a dead bird.

At four years old: "Mom, Nikki and Melissa told me a boy puts his penis in a girl's vagina and that's how babies are made."

To my horror, my mother confirmed this theory.

At five years old: "Mom, what's this?" (Holding up a condom in its wrapper.)

My mother: "Adult medicine."

At seven: "Mom, Melissa told me to ask you what the word 'orgasm' means."

My mother: "It's the best feeling in the world."

This answer becomes one of two working definitions of 'orgasm' that I contemplate like Zen koans throughout my late teens. The second definition is from my seventh grade health textbook: "An orgasm is the accumulation of tension, followed by its release."

When I make out with boys, I keep watch for any sudden releases in tension. I convince myself that I feel them. I decide that my mother's definition was hyperbolic. At some point, I start telling my partners that I have come. I'm not really lying, I'm just trying to make everyone happy. If they lick my pussy for a long time or touch me particularly passionately, I tell them, "Ooh, I came a lot that time."

The summer after my freshman year in college, I go to Martha's Vineyard to work a nanny job I have accepted sight unseen. The family turns out to be a horrible hybrid of old-money WASPs and Pentecostal Christians. I suspect I see swastikas in the three-year-old's drawings.

Then I meet Nat. He is a carpenter who lives on the island year-round, and he is eleven years my senior. I go to his house for cocktails. His aged grandfather resembles a P. G. Wodehouse character. We sit at a table on the porch, drinking gin and tonics, eating cashews, watching the songbirds come and go. I have never felt so happy. When the nanny job ends, I move in with them for the month of August.

One sun-drunk day I lose my virginity. Nat is very sweet, and it only hurts a little.

I go back to school and we keep dating. I travel via bus and ferry to visit him: long trips over land and sea during which my body aches with desire. We have a lot of sex and yet I always want more. When we're done, he falls asleep and I stay awake, staring at the ceiling.

Richard Pryor does a bit about fucking a woman so well she falls right asleep. He crows, "I'm a macho *maaan*. I put your ass to sleep."

I wonder if Nat is not macho enough. He is six feet tall and works with power tools for a living. He has a long cock. He knows where my clitoris is and pays attention to it. But I never feel like I want to go to sleep after fucking him. I feel like I want to hump the furniture.

The porn star Annie Sprinkle comes to Brown to do a presentation on female ejaculation. I attend, along with everyone I know. Annie Sprinkle has the largest breasts I've ever seen. Her list of the benefits of orgasm is ambitious: "cures PMS," "cures the common cold," "promotes world peace."

Annie plays us a video in which she is spread-eagle on a table and serviced by a team of women in elf outfits. One fucks Annie with a dildo, one palpates her mammoth breasts, one rubs her clit with a gloved finger. Various permutations occur. Sometimes

Annie gets a finger in her pussy, sometimes a dildo, and—for one scary moment—a fist.

Superimposed over this is a line graph that represents Annie's level of arousal. This line mounts higher and higher, then spikes. Annie comes, with great howlings and thrashings. The elves murmur encouragement and redouble their efforts. Now the bar graph enters a plateau phase, and a clock appears in the corner of the screen, measuring the duration of orgasm. Annie sounds like a soprano doing bizarre vocal exercises. The clock hits one minute, then two. This has to be a world record. At some point, copious liquid shoots from her pussy.

"Now, I want to be very clear," she says. "That liquid is not urine. We have had it scientifically tested."

The lecture is warmly received. I am haunted. Was Annie just acting, or is pleasure on that scale possible? I want bliss like that. I want to feel what Annie felt, only without the fist.

That winter Nat visits me in Providence. I am subletting the attic of a biochemistry grad student, and the ceiling is so low Nat can't stand up. We make love on a mattress on the floor. Nat fucks me from behind and reaches around to play with my clit. Things are going pretty much the way they always do, when something very strange happens.

It feels like a massive release of tension. It leaves my heart thundering. It happens too fast to be certain, but I suspect *it is the best feeling in the world.*

"Stop," I tell him.

He pulls out. "What's the matter? Does it hurt?"

"No. I think I came."

It takes some time to convince Nat that this is my first orgasm. After all, I have been crying wolf for some time. Finally he gets it. The next morning we go out to Louie's Diner for bacon and eggs. Nat raises his glass of orange juice.

"Cheers," he whispers. "To your first orgasm."

After that, I do not have an orgasm during intercourse for a long time. But I do come from oral sex and from having my clit played with. I can neither anticipate nor control these orgasms. They are suddenly there, like vistas in hilly country.

My relationship with Nat begins going sour. My friends dislike him. He embarrasses me in public. His screenplay is mediocre.

To create space, I sign up for a semester abroad in Morocco. It is a bewildering, difficult experience. I get followed, groped, and called a whore in three languages. I live with a Muslim family. The eight-year-old boy barges in on me in the bathroom while I am straddling the bidet. The mother tells me they use it for pre-prayer ablutions.

Two good things come of the trip. I learn the beautiful, trans-formative power of marijuana, which changes the city of Rabat into Disney World. And—*el-hamdulillah!*—I learn to make myself come. The family has given me a private room and I make use of it, Jilling off like a fiend every evening.

Practice makes perfect. I soon learn to follow the line graph of my arousal. I learn to feel the climax coming, to slow down right before the spike, to make it last. I learn that pleasure is not all about Nat.

When I come home, I break up with him and buy a vibrator.

"You don't treat me well enough," I tell him.

He is sad and generous. "My dad told me the same thing," he says.

We part ways, and the last thing he says to me is either, "I'll have to find someone smarter than you, because I'll never find someone better in bed," or, "I'll have to find someone better in bed than you, because I'll never find someone smarter."

I can't remember which it was, because I recall knowing with Tiresias-like clarity that he would find neither.

Tiresias was a soothsayer from Greek mythology. While walking through a field one day, he thrust his staff between two mating serpents. They cursed him by turning him into a woman. In his new female form, he became a courtesan of great fame. Seven years later, he saw the same serpents, thrust his staff between them again, and changed back to a man.

He was later called on to resolve an argument between the god Zeus and his wife, Hera, about which gender gets more pleasure from sex. Hera argued for men, Zeus for women. Tiresias, in a unique position to know the answer, replied, "Out of ten parts of pleasure, women get nine and men only one." Hera was infuriated by this answer and struck poor Tiresias blind. Zeus, to lessen the blow, gave him the gift of prophesy.

I wonder about poor Hera. Why was she so mad to hear Tiresias's answer? She lost the argument, but didn't she win the war? Doesn't she want to have *nine times more pleasure* than a man?

The conclusion is clear, yet—bafflingly—has escaped classicists for years: Hera had never had an orgasm.

It explains her behavior throughout antiquity. Hera spends myth after myth pursuing and punishing the lovers of Zeus, mostly poor nymphs he has raped via devious methods, such as showers of gold. Why is Hera so aggressive and angry? Why does she blame the victim? Why is she even awake?

The fact is, it takes some of us longer than others to learn how to come. I was twenty years old when I had my first orgasm. I'm thirty-two now, and I'm still continuing to learn.

For a woman there are always two kinds of sexual education. There is the kind that happens in the classroom, bedroom, and back seat of the Nissan. And then there is the kind that happens in the veins and arteries, the slow thawing of the iceberg, the self-knowledge that makes goddesses of us all. This is the real education, for it requires full participation of the woman. Where there is nine times the pleasure, there is at least nine times the pursuit.

Fortunately for her, Hera was immortal. I'm sure she's figured it out by now.

Part 5

Unwed Mothers

Candy Cane: What time is it, Mr. Clock?

Mr. Clock: Two minutes to menopause.

—FROM "THE CANDY CANE SHOW" SKETCH, *IN LIVING COLOR,* 1993

Me and I

★

by RACHEL TOOR

I worked for three years in college admissions. During that time, I saw lots of what I came to think of as "pathological parenting"— people who didn't know where they stopped and their children began. "We're juniors," mothers would say to me at college fairs, "and we're applying to Duke." The kids would hang back while their mothers—or sometimes dads—would list their achievements and accomplishments. I was embarrassed for all of us.

When I meet parents who seem to have even a soupçon of objectivity about their own children—that little Buffy might not be a vampire slayer; that Albert, at age eighteen months, probably can't prove the Riemann hypothesis—I applaud them. But I don't expect it. I've come to expect not only to hear about how wonderful, brilliant, perfect, and well-behaved some of these spawn-of-the-devil kids are, but to endure long stories that delight the tellers and can ignite smoldering rage in me. Sometimes, I will admit, they're vaguely amusing. Little kids will occasionally do things that are laugh-out-loud funny. But I've built up so much resentment that it can be hard to give due credit to the humor of a three-year-old child walking around with his head in his hands, chanting, "We're doomed! We're doomed!"

My life, as a single person, revolves around me. I do what I want, when I want, and with whom. If I feel like it, I eat breakfast cereal for dinner. Or ice cream. I can go to sleep at eight at night or read until it gets light. I don't like background noise, so the television is rarely on. I get invited to do cool things—run a one-hundred-mile, five-day stage race in the Himalayas, do a marathon in Thailand—and I go. I can always just pick up and go. I like it like this.

But the cost of freedom can be unadorned narcissism: I'm selfish, self-centered, and self-involved. People with children don't have the luxuries I do to focus on their own lives, their own selves. I've learned to make space for my friends' offspring in our conversations and time together. I try to remember their names and to ask about them, though I've given up on birthdays. I will confess there's something wonderful about being recognized by a child, about being remembered. There's something amazing about seeing how children think and develop and grow. But still, not every kid is the messiah.

And here's the worst: It's not just that my brother talks about his daughter—who brings out in him a softness and sweetness I never knew him capable of—as if he wouldn't be surprised to see her part the Red Sea (she may, at some point, be able to do that, but right now, she can't even reach the faucet on the sink). It's that my mother talks about *me* in exactly the same ways. When I meet her friends—or, now, her doctors and nurses—and they say, *Oh, you're the one who* . . . I try not to get annoyed. I try to be a big girl. I am, after all, forty-four years old.

My mother was diagnosed with multiple myeloma two years ago, and since that time, I've talked to her on the phone more frequently and tried to be less grudging about sharing my accomplishments and achievements, since she is now more limited in how much she herself can do. One of the big things she has to talk about is me. I try to remember this, try to understand that it gives her pleasure to bore strangers with tales of my recent heroic exploits, like learning how to fry an egg.

I have never been a parent, but I do know a few things about unconditional love and the ways in which someone else can complete you. A few years ago, I lost my darling Hannah, a blond mutt of inordinate intelligence, wit, and wisdom who'd been my constant companion for eighteen years. I had to learn how to live alone for the first time in my adult life. People tried to convince me to get another pet, but I couldn't. I told myself that this way I had even more freedom—to travel, to stay out all night, to wear clothes not embroidered with pet hair. It was okay; eventually, I'd get another pet. But I wasn't ready.

Instead, I started dating Jim. Jim wanted to take care of me, to nurture, feed, and tend to me. It's not that I mind being tended to. It's just that I didn't love Jim, and I never would. He had bad breath, an unfortunate laugh, and rarely said anything that interested me. He was a nice guy, but nice wasn't enough.

What I realized, after a long dinner punctuated by too many uncomfortable silences, was that I needed someone to love. My winsome days and nights were fine, but one of the things children did for people was give them a reason to come home—it wasn't just Penelope waiting for Odysseus to finish his travels, it was also his son, Telemachus. And, well, Argos, his dog. After I lost Hannah, I hated coming home to an empty house, hated not having anyone to greet me at the end of a hard day or to look forward to seeing in the morning. When you live by yourself, you are a different person. Quieter. Less exuberant. I was less comfortable being at home. I was lonely.

Having a boyfriend seemed like a good idea, an anodyne for itchy solitude. And in many ways, Jim was a good boyfriend. But he made me aware of my own moods, because he interacted with me. The luxury of living alone is that sometimes you're not even aware of the fact that you may be in a bad mood. You just are. It's not a problem.

I was happy being single, but not happy alone. I needed someone to love and I was ready. But not ready enough for another dog. To his credit, Jim later said, "I knew my days were numbered when you got the rat."

Whenever I meet a vet, or a lab technician, or anyone who works with lots of different species of small animals, I ask which one is his or her favorite. I've come to expect the answer: rats. And it's always for the same reason: They're smart. But that's not all. Rats, the most reviled and dissed of all species (save spiders and snakes, whose bites can kill you), exhibit selfhood: They come when you call them by name. They are suffused with one of the qualities we cherish most about childhood: curiosity. They are affectionate and loving. A therapist friend once told me about raising children, "They want to love you. They're set up to love you." And so it is with rats.

I named her after I'd brought her home, set up her cage, and let her run around on the living room floor. When I glanced over at my bookshelves I saw the spine of a novel by Iris Murdoch, a woman of fierce intellect and wit. Only later, while reading the Homeric hymns, did I learn the origins of the name. In Greek mythology, Iris was the swift-footed messenger of the gods; she was the personification of the rainbow, stretching from earth to sky, linking us sad-sack mortals—we who are tethered to the world by the inevitability of the decline and failure of our physical bodies—with the undying ones.

Iris is a hooded rat. For the most part, she is white. But her head is a fawn color of exceptional richness and depth. She has a small, shocking-white blaze on her forehead and golden/gray/

brown splotches that run down her back. "You didn't tell me your rat was a paint," said my friend Dan, when I showed him a picture. People often don't know, even, that she is a rat. "But she's so cute," my other buddy Jason cooed when he first met her. "I wasn't expecting her to be cute."

Iris has a cage, of course. But when I am at home, she ranges freely. Like all of us with never-resting minds, she seeks out novelty. To her, the world is a benign and infinitely interesting place. She knows no fear. She searches, she learns, and then she moves on, always looking for the next new thing. She loves to play. If my hand is idle and she wants to play, Iris pulls at it with hers, nudges it with her nose. Then we engage. She rears up on her hind legs and boxes with my fingers. I poke her on the side and she twists, quick and sharp, does a gainer, and comes back around. Then she'll rush away, and rush right back. She always comes back. Then it's time to nap. She comes to me—climbs on my hand, my lap, my shoulder—curls up and goes to sleep.

When she wakes, she yawns, a big, hearty yawn, and then she stretches, reaching out like a ballet dancer with one arm, and then flicking her wrist down, like God reaching out to Adam in Michelangelo's *The Donnadio.* Iris does not have what you could call paws. She has hands, with tiny, delicate fingers that clutch and grasp and hold, and feet—pink, teenage-boy feet—that seem too big for her body.

Iris spends a lot of time exploring, but I'm never afraid that she is going to get away. She doesn't want to get away; she wants to explore, and then to be with me. When I call her, she comes. She follows me around the house like a little kid. I tell her she's my "Little I," my girl, my baby, my mini-me. "You complete me, mini-me," I tell her. "I love you, Little I," I say to my rat about 487 times a day. She perches on my shoulder, snuggles on my lap, grooms my hands, and we are a happy pair.

After I'd had her for about two months, I accused my friend Jeff of not liking her. "You hate Iris," I said to him.

"No," he said, with a big smirk, "I hate you. When you talk about Iris so much." I can, it seems, talk for hours about Iris.

My mother had also begun to tire of my pathological rat-parenting. Whenever we spoke on the phone, Iris was usually curled up on my lap, and I used a lot of minutes telling her just how adorable sleeping vermin could be. My mother has always loved my pets, but trying to develop affection for someone the size of a pickling cucumber who lives 2,500 miles away can be a stretch.

Because I teach at a university and had the summer off, I decided that I would spend it with my mother. And because the average life expectancy of a healthy rat is about a thousand days, I wasn't willing to pass an entire summer without Iris. My mother fussed a little about whether having a rat in the house would be good for her weakened immune system, but I called on some medically trained friends to reassure her that Iris was probably less contaminated with germs than my stepfather.

My mother is in constant pain. She lies on the couch—she can't stand or sit for long—and reads for much of each day. In the evenings, we make our way through DVD episodes of *The Gilmore Girls*. Iris pokes around the house, but she always has a final destination in mind. I watch her run along the top of the couch, make a pit stop on the end table to sample the eraser on a pencil or pull out a long length of dental floss, and then, before she leaps, I holler, *"Incoming!"* alerting my mother to the fact that her grandrat is about to pounce on her chest.

Iris is a gregarious, outgoing girl. She loves meeting new people. But she is crazy about my mother. She seeks her out. The other day I caught Iris lying on the bed, facing my mother, watching her while she worked her computer. She waits in my mother's place on the couch, and when my mother comes to lie down to read, she snuggles in, stretches out, places a tiny hand on my mother's arm. My mother turns the book pages carefully, so as not to disturb the rat.

My mother has begun pointing out to me how cute Iris looks when she is sleeping. She saves little pieces of food for her, especially scraps of flour tortilla (flour tortillas are like crack to rats). She comments on how adorable it is the way Iris holds her food in her hands. She giggles when Iris gets crazy and starts zooming around, wanting to play. From another room, I hear her talking to Iris. She tells her friends about the exploits of her "grandrat." I've also heard her call Iris "my healer."

Can animals sense illness? Do they have innate stores of empathy? I don't know. I just know that I came home for the summer to take care of my mother and it feels like Iris is doing the lion's share of that work.

At a time in my life when all was too quiet on the relationship front—I was worried about my mother, busy with work, and feeling harried and hassled—I got a rat. Like a planned pregnancy or a bureaucratically difficult adoption, I made a hard choice to become a mother, fully aware of the great responsibilities, as well as the fact that I was signing on to care for a member of a species not exactly known for its longevity.

Most children figure out, pretty early on, that they will likely outlive their parents; fear of desertion comes with the territory of loving someone. The Greeks understood this; their gods laughed at us. The one thing that we can count on is that we are going to get old and die. Becoming an adult is about accepting this process; we do it more or less gracefully. But we've all known haunted people—those who have lost a child often never recover. That's a different story. It is a perversion of the natural order. It is the essence of tragedy. The Greeks knew this, too.

I was living alone when my mother was diagnosed with an incurable cancer. The prospect of loss is a constant presence in my life. And yet, I got a rat. It diminishes the experience of (human) motherhood, not at all to say that I think of Iris as my child. She is a focus for me, a locus for my emotions, and someone who, even when I'm just watching her sleep, makes me ungodly happy.

Plus, Iris gives me something other than myself to brag about. I talk about Iris the way those irritating parents prattle on about their own rug rats. I know it's a bore, that my friends don't really want to see photos documenting her growth or hear stories about her cleverness. But you know what? Iris really is wonderful, brilliant, perfect, and well behaved. And some day, she may be able to part the Red Sea or prove Riemann's hypothesis. And if not, I'll just keep on loving her. And I'll relish watching my mother play with her grandrat for as long as I can.

The built-in temporality of loving a short-lived critter almost kept me from getting another pet. But I knew that was silly. I chose love over the inevitability of loss, just as we must do every day with our parents.

I choose love.

Doctor, Donor, Desperado

★

by MARGARET SMITH

I thought referring to Dr. Cornelius as my fertility doctor instead of by her proper title, infertility doctor, was a more positive approach to take. I needed a fertility doctor before I picked a donor. So I went to see Dr. Cornelius, who came highly recommended. Her success rate was unequaled by any other, except that doctor who was arrested for inseminating his patients with his own sperm. Talk about coming home from the office exhausted. He's now getting all the rest he needs in jail. And you know those mothers wouldn't have pressed charges had the good doctor looked like Brad Pitt. But it was his lot in life to look like, albeit with thick black hair, Larry "Bud" Melman. It's guys like him who are endowed with Olympian sperm. Their sperm is genetically coded to succeed. It has evolved to compensate for looks. In other words, it knows it's only getting one chance, so it could bounce off a wall onto a woman's thigh and still army-crawl its way to her vagina if it had to. Brad Pitt, on the other hand, doesn't even have to have sperm. Dust could puff out and he'd still do well. He could have a vagina.

Cornelius examined me and said, "Your levels look great. You're very young reproductively." I liked her immediately. She informed me of options for donors. She had specimens available right there in her office. Patients who had become pregnant and didn't need any more left their extra specimens in her care. It made sense that you couldn't return the stuff, what with all the product tampering that goes on today. This sperm had a successful track record. It was appealing, but I didn't like the fact that my child could be in the same school district with his/her biological sibling. They could meet, fall in love, then find out the awful truth. You've watched the Lifetime channel. The California Cryobank in Westwood sounded like the best idea. It wasn't far from my house. I could actually pick up the sperm, bring it to Cornelius's office myself, and save a few dollars. My mother would be so proud of me. She might even start to warm to the idea of my being inseminated if I could tell her I got a deal.

It was the end of my first office visit. Dr. Cornelius and I were saying goodbye. She was telling me how picking a donor is a crapshoot and joking about what her worst unknown donor nightmare would be, sperm with a Kevin Bacon nose. I said, "Too bad none of these places offer pictures." She said, "Oh, there is a place that's doing that now. They just sent me some literature. I think you pay a little more." Cherubs came from behind clouds with harps and sang songs. The universe was providing for me. I was elated. (I don't know why I say things like, "I was elated." It's not like I look elated or act elated when I'm elated.) Everyone I had talked to had told me a picture was impossible, that donors must remain anonymous, that they don't want you to know their names, let alone give you a picture. There were whisperings of a select few donors who would allow contact at the child's request when she/he turned eighteen. I was told there might be a contact clause in the event of a life-or-death medical emergency. Now it was all a bunch of bull, old information. Such is life in the fertility business. Cornelius handed me the brochure that made the cherubs sing and cautioned me, "It's in Georgia, so it's not as convenient as something local." *Yeah, yeah,* I thought, *by the time I get home that could be bull, too.* I left her office with folders under my arm, the world smiling on me, and the universe saying, "Cheese."

I called the firm in Augusta, Georgia, and requested their donor list. A few days later it arrived, five pages of Mr. Rights. At the top it read "Fall 1994 Donor Listing," and it had a donor number and nine columns of descriptions: race/ethnic origin, hair color, hair texture, eye color, skin tone, blood type, height/weight, occupation, and interests/religion. An asterisk next to the donor number meant the donor had washed sperm for intrauterine insemination, and a pound sign meant a photo was available. I scanned the list for pound signs. There was one, then another. They all had straight hair. I wanted curly. It read straight hair, straight hair, straight hair, and straight, thinning hair. I thought, *What is going on?* Then I saw it: a pound sign with brown, curly hair, blue eyes, fair skin, O-positive blood type, six foot one, 190 pounds, occupation, electric company. Okay, it's not exactly a career, but it is a job and he's probably perfectly happy at the electric company. He could be an engineer, or maybe he touched some bare wires and has a nice desk job now. Then I noticed the interests/religion column: fishing, hunting, baseball, and Church of God. I don't know about you, but I can't read the words "Church of God" without hearing it in a deep fire-and-brimstone voice: "CHURCH OF GOD!" My thought was, *No way am I putting redneck, Christian Right (or, as I call it, Christian Reich) sperm in my body.*

There was my lower self again. It takes very little trepidation to send me into a downward spiral. I have downward spirals all the time. This one went like this: "I can't believe I have to ask someone for sperm, let alone pay for it. They wanted two hundred bucks a pop. Was it cheaper in college or what? I was practically tripping over the stuff. Now look at me, calling out of state during peak rates for some and begging for a picture. I probably won't even be able to see what he looks like in the picture. He'll be wearing a white hood. I'm pathetic."

It's interesting trying to experience a person based on a few facts written on a piece of paper. That "just the facts, ma'am" approach was bringing out the worst in me. It's the same approach we use in our courts of law. The defendants have to sit there like a cardboard cutout—silent so they don't stir our juices and affect our judgment. What's in a personality anyway? Who is donor 666 without the distraction of a flirtatious comment or a crooked smile to animate his DNA? He is hidden in that reduced state of being recorded on a donor profile sheet. How many dates would it take to find out that the guy you're seeing goes to the Church of God? Not as many as it would take to find out he's in the militia.

"Hi, I'm calling about donor BFM 9059." I told myself BFM stood for "big fucking male." "That comes with a picture, doesn't it?" She said, "Well, let's see." I could hear her shuffling papers. *Probably the same ones I have in front of me,* I thought; *I'm one step ahead of her.* I said, "I have the list. It says he comes with a picture." I immediately had this fantasy of her saying back to me, *Well, if you put it that way, they all come with a picture, don't they? I think this one used* Playboy's *December centerfold. Yes, I remember, because it was around Christmas time.* But that's not what she said. What she said was, "We're out of BFM 9059."

I had never even considered the possibility of rejection. Here I was, all vulnerable, expressing a need, and *boom!* I hear a big fat "no." It was as though she had told me someone almost-but-not-quite close to me had died. I was filled with disbelief. "There's none left?" I said in my pathetic Kübler-Ross first-stage-of-grieving voice.

"Yes, it's been discontinued." Who has time to grieve on long distance during peak hours? I hurried into another Kübler-Ross stage, anger. "Let me get this straight. You're not getting any more?"

"That is correct."

I was now in the final stage of grieving, acceptance. Surrender always puts me in touch with my higher self. Now I wanted to be nice to her. Did we not both suffer? On some level I guess I thought we were in the same boat. I didn't have any sperm, and now I saw she was capable of running out, too. Compassion has a way of quieting the mind.

I was much more casual now, as I often am after a devastating loss. I said, "I have a couple of others circled that look interesting." I was on the rebound. The donors had become just "interesting." I would probably never get so attached to another one. "What about BGL 9276?"

"No, we're out of that."

"How about BGL 9220, thinning hair? You must have a barrel full of that."

"I'm afraid we're out of that, too." There wasn't a hint of regret in her voice.

"If you're out of everything," I asked, "why bother to answer the phone?"

Silence. "Will that be all?"

I hated her. You give some people a little power and they can't handle it.

I went to the wastebasket and took out a wadded-up piece of paper. I uncrumpled it and queried, "CFN 8848?" It was reminiscent of last call at the Auto Bar. I figured, what the hell; they're probably out of it anyway. It was a policeman. I picked him for the photo quality. From a kid's point of view, he'd look real important in the uniform. The unborn have never seen the Rodney King video or read about the Rampart corruption scandal. She said, "We may have some at our other location." Not bothering to cover the phone, she yelled to someone, "Bobby, do we have any CFN 8848 over in Emmit?" *That was a little unprofessional,* I thought. Then I figured, *What's one little red flag?* She said, "While he's checking, is there anything else you're interested in?" I told her, "Not really." The rest were pictureless or had brown eyes.

I waited. I hadn't realized there wasn't a pair of brown eyes in our entire family until my manager pointed it out to me at my family reunion. "Does your family have something against brown eyes? I'm the only one here with brown eyes." I had begged her to go with me. It was back when I couldn't face my family alone. I paid her handsomely and there she sat at the picnic table, aware that she had the only pair of brown eyes there. I forced myself to look at them. We're not big on eye contact. Not even the extended-family-in-law faction had a brown eye among them.

I heard a muffled "no" from Bobby on the other end of the phone. The receptionist relayed Bobby's "no" because she liked saying no. I wanted to have a blue-eyed baby but was willing to make one exception. I had a good feeling about one donor who happened to have brown eyes. My agent was right about casting calls. He said, "They don't know what they want." I said, "What about DFL 8801?" This brown-eyed donor was premed, English/Irish, and possessed a pound sign. She said, "We don't have any left in the regular, but there is some in the Blue Line Special."

I flipped through my pages. Had I missed something in my desperation? I didn't see anything about a special. How would I ever tell my mother that I had missed the special? "What's the Blue Line Special?" I asked. She said, "Well, a regular specimen has approximately fifty thousand spermatozoa. The Blue Line has over a hundred thousand. It is a bit more expensive, but you're getting twice the count." I knew from my drinking days that a double costs more than a single, and even if you never drank, any idiot who ever ventured into a Starbucks knows that a double costs more than single. I needed to hang up at that point. I didn't think I was ready to order the special, and no way was I prepared to say, "Give me the cheap stuff."

Choosing Single Parenthood and a Two-Roof Marriage

⭐

by MIKKI MORRISSETTE

P erhaps for the first time in my life, I'm trendy. In at least two ways.

As a single mother by choice, I'm "hot." We've come a long way since the TV character Murphy Brown got lambasted by Dan Quayle in 1992 for making fathers seem irrelevant. Since then, Rachel on *Friends,* Miranda on *Sex and the City,* Angelina Jolie, Sharon Stone, Meg Ryan, and many others have embraced single motherhood as a lifestyle choice without a loud national debate.

Personally, I know hundreds of us. And none of us are highly paid celebrities or TV characters. We are all quite real, quite normal single women who simply reached a point—generally around age thirty-five—when we realized that if we wanted to be mothers, it was simply up to us to do it.

To be even trendier, I've coined a new term for us: Choice Moms. It puts the emphasis where I think it belongs, on proactively *choosing* motherhood, rather than simply being single when a child falls from the heavens into our life.

My estimate is that fifty-thousand women in the United States make this decision each year.

How did I get this number? Basic guestimation math. The National Center for Health Statistics tells us that more than ninety-two-thousand unmarried American women over the age of thirty-five gave birth in 2004. Since roughly half were living with a partner, you can figure that about forty-six-thousand single women who were old enough to know how to use birth control ended up pregnant. And if that seems overly generous, factor in the detail that the number doesn't include single women who adopt.

And the second trendy aspect of my life?

I've been married, since my daughter was five and my son was ten months, to a man I don't live with. I understand from *The New York Times* that this makes me part of another new demographic category: the "living apart together" (or LAT) couple. More commitments like ours are being formed, the media tells me, in which living under two separate roofs is part of the "I do" pledge.

I was five months pregnant when I met my husband in 2003 and, until that moment, had no intentions of finding a life partner until my kids were grown. My greatest ambition was to finish writing my *Choosing Single Motherhood* book, have my second baby, and develop resources for women who choose this lifestyle.

He was a widower with a challenging special-needs daughter and a musically talented son two years shy of high school graduation. His greatest ambition when I met him was to someday be absolved of parental responsibilities and become a cabana boy on a quiet island.

Neither one of us could have predicted that we would be willing to make a commitment to each other.

To be honest, neither of us expected that when he proposed (a romantic surprise following a hot-air-balloon ride six months after we met) we'd remain thirty miles apart, even as husband and wife. But as the wedding drew closer, and our plans to merge my young-sters with his teenagers threatened to strain our relationship to the breaking point, we opted to live as two separate families rather than do something that would never work for any of us. I even understand that someday, maybe not too far off, he just might wan-der off to that secluded island after all.

Ours is an experiment in marriage that will take years to play out.

A sociologist quoted in *The New York Times* article equated LAT relationships to yet another form of selfishness.

"One of the challenges of marriage is to learn how to live with a person and integrate that person into your life," he said. "By liv-ing apart, you are losing the opportunity to gain that level of inti-macy and cooperation." His point was that marriage presents an opportunity to learn selflessness as well as giving and forgiving, whereas a long-term romantic arrangement that doesn't involve cohabitation "glorifies individual needs."

Selfishness seems to be the classic insult thrown at anyone who doesn't conform to the two-parent, one-roof paradigm.

In the view of many outsiders, it is selfish to raise kids on your own. It is selfish to live alone instead of with a partner. If you are infertile, it is selfish to conceive instead of adopt. If you are a single parent, it is selfish to date. If you and a partner have children, it is selfish to divorce. If you are part of a couple, it is even selfish (whis-pered in the recesses of the brain) to remain childless.

Many believe living as a single entity, instead of as a coupled unit, is the sign of a person who is unable and unwilling to make the sacrifices and compromises required of a normal, healthy life. Cer-tainly a woman who decides to become a parent before she finds a committed partner is often judged as "too picky" or "self-absorbed." I know several who have been told—by mothers, fathers, sisters—that if they lost weight, dressed nicer, worked harder at it, they'd be able to find a husband.

Being solo, the judgment goes, is an indication of something lacked, rather than of a deeper understanding of what we are capable of—or of how we need to correct our alignment.

I've largely given up trying to convince people who would like to think otherwise that the way I live *my* life does not threaten their *own* way of life. I try to remember that any judgments about my choices, especially from people who don't know me, are generally based on their weaknesses, not mine.

The easy response is to say that anyone who consciously becomes a parent, married or single, is doing it for "selfish" reasons. It's a choice based on wanting to nurture and love a child as part of their life's work. But I know that what most people really mean is that a woman who purposely raises a child on her own hasn't considered the consequences of her child being denied a father.

In reality, the "Is it fair to the child?" question is one of the biggest concerns women grapple with as they decide whether to raise a child alone. If they decide they can be strong enough parents to compensate for being one parent instead of two, and if they make the choice to add that child to their life, eventually they find that the "selfish" label no longer sticks.

It still hurts to be unable to give our children everything. But it also becomes obvious to us (and our children) how much we have their best interests at heart.

That is, in fact, why my husband and I don't live together. We are both single parents who knew that our children would suffer from being uprooted, or forced to blend, and we put their needs first.

I guess you could say we're doing nothing less than redefining the old family tree. And I'm very happy about that.

It starts in first grade. Our children come home with assignments to fill in their rudimentary family tree. And some families—donor conceived, adopted, multigenerational, foster care, raised by single parents—don't quite know what to do.

I talked to my seven-year-old daughter about this dilemma, and in her infinite childlike wisdom she came up with a solution. Essentially, each person is a flower, she reasoned, with roots and petals and veins and leaves. At every age and stage, the child is free to fill in his or her flower with the important people, family and friends of choice. And it will change year to year.

Simple. Basic. True.

We are all flowers. Individual daisies. And instead of feeling adrift because we don't have this branch or that branch, these roots or those roots, the goal is to concentrate instead on the people who have made us who we are.

The perfect metaphor for the single entity. Being comfortable with self doesn't mean we are cut off and detached from the world. Rather, it enables us, after we have surrounded ourselves with the nurturing influences and connections that make us strong, to grow bigger and brighter with every new stage.

Am I single? Yes and no. I consider myself single, even though I'm legally married. Even though my house is filled with people—my kids, two tenants, a college student who baby-sits my kids part-time. Even though I'm connected at my church, at my daughter's school, with old friends and new friends.

I got into trouble once by forgetting that for most people, "single" means the basic legal definition, "not married." I was being interviewed for a column about single female homeowners. I talked to the writer about the unusual communal living situation I had in my five-bedroom home with other single women—two of us moms—and she turned it into a profile about me and the Choice Motherhood lifestyle. After the column ran, a friend of my husband's called to tell her that I was, in fact, married but living apart. Boy, was the columnist pissed, thinking I'd purposely misled her about my legal status. Her next column focused on me again, negatively this time, including the comments of a reader who thought I was selfish for raising kids on my own.

Since then, I've thought a lot about what it means to "feel" single, even after I've pledged in front of friends and family to commit myself for life to one partner. And the irony of my particular pet peeve: that long-term homosexual couples are not allowed to legally be anything but single, even when they want to make the same commitment I have, to someone they actually live with.

To me, living together *with* a partner is *not* being single, despite legal status. Living *without* a partner in your home is.

Of course, it's legal status that grants or denies government or corporate benefits. Yet it does not define who we really are.

It's not legal status that determines the level of love and faithfulness I feel for my partner. It's not legal status that determines how emotionally fulfilled my children are, or determines whether I'm lonely.

In my first marriage, when I was in my twenties and trying to have the "normal" life, I felt more isolated than I did as the unmarried mother of two. Sitting alone on a rock in Ireland on a solo journey, I had never felt more connected with the universe.

Attending the fiftieth wedding anniversary of my husband's parents, I felt "out of my skin," serving church coffee and posing for pictures and chatting with people I didn't know. The celebration of fifty years with one partner was beautiful and poignant, but so foreign to my own experience that I felt like an interloper intruding on a Norman Rockwell painting. As if I were wearing pink hot pants, standing behind Grandma's floral-print apron in that classic Thanksgiving scene. Granted, nobody could see the hot pants but me—I was able to play the role of the traditional good wife—but at any moment I felt as if some kids would point at me and start sing-songing, "Which one of these things is not like the other?"

Twenty-four hours later, I was sharing a vacation house with three other single mothers and our seven children on Lake Superior. I didn't know the women well. Two of them had gotten out of abusive relationships with the fathers of their children. One of them had adopted a second child whose birth parents were thirteen when he was born. Although we came to parenthood in different ways, we were connected in identifying ourselves as single entities with immense responsibility for shaping the lives of our little ones. We sat with our boys, and my lone girl, on a rocky beach, watching small-town fireworks in yet another Norman Rockwell painting gone wild. The men missing not because they were off to war, but because they were not in the room when the artist began his work.

I know that I am alone in the universe, and yet I feel supremely connected and whole. To the people in front of me, and the people off canvas. To the people who were roots to my flower, and the people who were leaves or petals long since shed and replaced with fresher ones.

We all feel uncomfortable in certain situations. We all make mistakes. We all get lonely at times. But at our most glorious moments—dare I say, at our most spiritual—we find a way of shaking off and regenerating and reaching points, alone or with others, on a cliff top or in a church hall, when we realize how happy we are with the lives we have created for ourselves.

I share my happiness with others, and others contribute greatly to my sense of well-being. But nothing can match the peacefulness that comes from knowing that I am solely responsible for the life I create, and that with each passing year I seem to be closer to "getting it right"—even if that means becoming dreadfully "trendy."

Being a wife, being a mother, being an advocate and entrepreneur and writer who communicates with hundreds of single women about their lives—they are what I *do*. They are parts of who I am. But at the core, I am the single person I have always been, since I arrived solo from my mother's womb. And I am blessed to have a lifetime to get closer to that person.

Single Scapegoat Seeking . . .

★

by RACHEL SARAH

I t all began so harmlessly. An editor at *The Washington Post* invited me to be a guest blogger for their weekly "On Balance" column, to contribute four hundred words on how I've managed to balance single motherhood and dating.

I can't stand self-pity, so I went for the lighthearted, self-mocking tone.

"At first, the thought of dating again was unthinkable," I wrote. "It was tricky enough balancing hours of peekaboo and dirty diapers with editing and deadlines. Besides, trying to get over my ex had shut out the possibility of romance. Not to mention how exhausted I was. When I hit thirty, however, everything changed. I stopped nursing. I was ready to get out of domestic overdrive."

I gave readers a sneak peak at my Match.com profile—"Are you an honest, big-hearted man with no addictions, except coffee?" Then I explained how I'd organized "my men" in a thick three-ring binder. Of course, I touched on how I became a single mom in the first place, and how challenging it was at times. But in just one page, in four hundred words, you can't get too deep.

Minutes after my essay went up, readers started to respond. In fact, they came out of the woodwork in droves to respond.

"Rachel sounds like she still doesn't get it," wrote GetYourDates-Right. "After being irresponsible in the first place by getting pregnant by her bipolar, alcoholic boyfriend, she's still too focused on being single and 'getting the guy.' There's now a far more important person in her life: her daughter. Yet Rachel is spending way too much energy on finding a boyfriend. What is wrong with this woman?"

Apparently, the author felt he knew exactly what was wrong with me, because minutes later, he posted again:

"Rachel is obsessed with finding another man rather than focused on raising her daughter."

But GetYourDatesRight wasn't alone. MyThoughts felt I was "pathetic" and railed about the "plague of illegitimate children born in the USA today." Dating felt I was a "loser." AnotherView wanted to know, "How is getting knocked-up out of wedlock by a bipolar drunk a credential for giving Jewish people dating advice?"

At first, I was so caught off guard by their wrath that I couldn't believe they were addressing me. This Rachel, age thirty-three, is a Cancer and a mother-at-her-core. This Rachel, who breastfed her daughter for almost three years, could be accused of self-sacrifice. But "spending way too much energy on finding a boy-friend"? C'mon.

And they didn't stop there. BeenThere wrote: "Here's some advice that will benefit all readers . . . don't have sex with bipolar alcoholics. And if you do, and you end up pregnant, put the baby up for adoption."

Adoption? At that point, I probably should have taken cover. Unplugged the computer and gotten my butt straight back into bed. But I didn't.

It was the Fourth of July, and I was home in Berkeley, California, with my six-year-old after camp. She'd spent the day at our local Adventure Playground, a scrap-lumber yard where kids get to build sculptures with real hammers and nails (sounds dangerous, I know). Now she was hot and cranky. There were no more Scooby-Doo Mystery Popsicles left in our freezer, and she was sulking over my offer of ice water.

"Mom, we have to go to the store and get some more popsicles," she said. My girl always has the best ideas—and she always wants to do them *right now.* But I was in one of my frenzied house-cleaning moods—and I wanted her to help me pick up the remnants from her latest art project on the floor *right now.*

Besides, I didn't want to leave the house. My office was smack in the middle of the living room. I kept walking by my computer, and each time, the temptation was too strong. In a sick way it was almost fascinating to take quick peeks to see how these nutballs kept coming at me.

What drove their blind hatred, I wondered. *Was it a gender thing, a political thing, an age thing? Who, exactly, were these single-mom haters?*

The next time I logged on, a man who called himself Cal told me:

"You are obsessed—and yes, that's the word, deeply, weirdly obsessed—with finding another man rather than finding out why you were driven to not only have a relationship with a mentally ill addict, but have a kid with him. [This] demonstrates that your daughter's luck not only landed her with such a dad, but a sadly self-absorbed mother. I hope you have enough sense to keep whatever no-hopers you choose out of her life entirely and not, god forbid, introducing them as an 'uncle.'"

What if my partner had been in the Marines and had died in combat in Iraq? I wanted to ask Cal. What if he'd had a heart attack while running the marathon? Would Cal still have attacked me like this? What planet did guys like Cal live on? And why did there appear to be so many of them? What was it about single moms that made us such a popular target?

Fortunately, right around this time, my *Washington Post* editor emailed me:

"Rachel, I had no idea there was so much sexist vitriol out there! Does this rabid prejudice against single moms ring true for you? It is INSANE. This happens sometimes—a column touches a nerve and stirs up a lot of ugliness."

The thing was, "this rabid prejudice" didn't ring true for me at all. Maybe it was because I live on an island here in Berkeley, where every time you turn around, there's another example of a nontraditional family and people don't look kooky-eyed at you. Out here, we barely notice the two dads and their African American sons, or the single mom who used Latino donor sperm to make her beautiful baby girl. You name it, Berkeley has it, and people don't stare or point or judge. They're an all-accepting bunch of folks, and since moving here, I hadn't felt any stigma whatsoever about my little single-parent family.

I guess you could call me naive. Or sheltered. After all, I don't listen to radio hosts like Tom Leykis who say men should never date single moms because time with children reduces time in the bedroom. Googling the talk show host, I found that one of his radio courses, Leykis 101, was actually called, "We Don't Date Single Moms." In it, he teaches men not to waste time on women who are TMW (too much work).

Out of curiosity, I started surfing the Internet. Three clicks of my mouse and I was at a website that sold T-shirts and hats emblazoned with the statement SINGLE MOMS SUCK. "Tell those money-grubbing single moms just how you feel by wearing the always-fashionable Single Moms Suck gear," read its copy. Clicking back to the *Washington Post* website, I found still more anger.

"Abortion certainly would have been an option," suggested RegisteredVoter. "Not to mention . . . drum roll please . . . birth control! But then, that would have required effort and responsibility."

"Why do women hook up with losers who won't marry them and want to leave them with a child to raise?" wrote Patrick. "I have sympathy for the child but not for the loser mom. You made your bed, now lie in it."

Were these people truly concerned for the welfare of my child, or were they more concerned that my daughter would turn out just fine, that single moms like me were *too* competent? It was hard to say. What seemed obvious, though, is that they felt single moms should be punished, that we should somehow "pay for our sins."

One of my single-mom friends in New York City, who adopted her daughter from Guatemala in 2001, said that while she was ready for the sleep deprivation, "nothing prepared me for the other side of single motherhood, an under-the-radar, insidious variety of intolerance."

In New York City, I too had met "the other side of single motherhood" when I felt shunned by married moms at the playground. Needless to say, I was the one guilt-tripping myself. As a new single mom, you're prone to feeling at fault if your kid doesn't have a dad. Today, years later, I know that father figures come in all forms: My dad and stepdad, for instance, are genuine, loving men in my daughter's life.

But when society tries to punish you on top of whatever guilt you pile on yourself, it's hard to keep your head high.

Remember Nathaniel Hawthorne's *The Scarlet Letter,* in which Hester Prynne, a single mother, was assigned a scarlet letter to publically shame her? These readers apparently wanted to admonish me like Hester. And what was really frustrating was that no one felt compelled to call them out on it. Whenever you post a comment on the *Washington Post* blog, there's a set of rules you've got to read: "User reviews and comments that include profanity or personal attacks or other inappropriate comments or material will be removed from the site."

I couldn't help but wonder: Why didn't anyone step in and remove the inappropriate comments? Was it just universally accepted that single mothers should be publicly trashed?

And by whom? I began to picture the blog-posters, an angry army of forty-year-old guys living in the basements of their mothers' homes, each of them hunched over a computer, anonymously picking on the single mothers of the world while their own moms brought them beef stew.

Until I realized I was stereotyping them the same way they were stereotyping me. Fuming at them felt damn good, but *becoming* them wasn't the answer. The last thing I wanted was to go at them with the same senseless ammunition they used against me. After all, just as much as they didn't know me, I didn't know them.

As it turned out, due to the Fourth of July holiday, my blog post stayed up for two days, instead of the usual one, which meant I was open to another full twenty-four hours of attack.

But a funny thing started to happen on that second day—the tide began to turn. Once single moms across the country got wind of the rage against them on the site, they came out in full support.

"I think this illustrates a major stigma a lot of us carry against single mothers," wrote Spob. "Single mothers are expected to sacrifice everything (give up men, their sense of self) and be Wonder Women to raise their children in perfection."

Well said!

"The single moms I know raise some of the most considerate, empathetic kids out there," added Leslie. "The kids must see how much their mothers sacrifice for them. Never met a spoiled brat with a single mom. So go, Rachel!"

FairfaxWorkingMom wrote, "Rachel has taken responsibility for her daughter, for her past mistakes, and for her needs as an adult (not just a 'mommy'). . . . This community is rife with mean-spirited posters, and today is a particularly gruesome example. I will not post again."

"This article is way too short for anyone to jump to such horrid conclusions about the hows and whys," wrote CubFan. "The mom is just talking about dating and carving out a little time for herself. Maybe even meeting a great guy who can be an amazing influence on her daughter. Kudos to men and women who raise kids alone."

Reading that last post, I began to think about single men raising kids on their own and wondered how the negative letter-writers would do if they were in my shoes.

My daughter is a poised, healthy, strong-willed girl. Her kindergarten teacher described her as a silly, sweet kid who makes friends easily. Her grandpa definitely spoils her when they get together every Monday, but I think she's turning out just fine.

All of her friends have asked her, "Do you have a dad?" and I've listened from the other room to her matter-of-fact response: "I live with my mom." When prodded ("But where's your dad?"), she has said, "I have a birth father, and he lives very far away." She has come up with this birth-father story on her own, no doubt created by listening to the stories of other children of single moms who had donors.

She doesn't seem to have any anxiety about being dad-less. It's simply, "I live with my mom." Just the facts, ma'am, as if she were talking about the weather: "The sky is gray." There is no shame in her voice. In fact, living with her mom might be ideal. What child wouldn't want all of this one-on-one attention, day in and day out?

One day, our situation may change, may become something more traditional. And if or when that happens, I'll be thrilled. But I'm thrilled now, too.

As much as I've longed for a life partner over the past six years, I know that The Man isn't The Answer, despite what Cal or any of those other chowderheads think about my decision to become a Single Mom Seeking. . . . I've spent the past six years on myself—developing by leaps and bounds right alongside my daughter. I didn't ask for this life scenario called single motherhood, but I feel blessed to have it.

As for the bloggers, I leave the last word to my wise editor.

"From the posts on this forum today, it's pretty clear that there is a stigma for a single mother to date," she wrote, closing the door on the discussion. "I wonder if the posts would be so nasty if a single father were dating. I doubt it."

Part 6

I Married Adventure

[The transatlantic crossing was] so rough that the only thing I could keep on my stomach was the first mate.

— DOROTHY PARKER
MARION MEADE'S *DOROTHY PARKER: WHAT FRESH HELL IS THIS?*

Tangled Up in Wild Blue

★

by AMANDA CASTLEMAN

A ge eleven, I skidded around the ferry terminal. Sugar-propelled, I hummed and hopped, watching my reflection in the windows: a small, fierce, blond child superimposed on saltwater.

"That boat's going to Alaska," my father interjected.

My orbit stopped. Alaska. Land of the Midnight Sun. Dogsleds and kayaks. Wilderness areas the size of states. Even the ferry had a frontier-anarchy air with its gypsy patchwork of tents. *Alaska!*

The ship slid from the dock, my dreams churning in its wake. I wanted so very badly to go, go, go, get gone from the tulip fields, the silage and sleech of Skagit Valley.

Two decades later, I'm finally underway.

I cough myself awake on the MV *Columbia*. I haven't kicked the cold I acquired in Zimbabwe last week. Sleeping on deck isn't helping, but I refuse to wuss into a cabin.

No one said travel writing would be easy. But oh, the places you'll go.

In the glittering, greedy city of Hong Kong, I sipped gin and tonics at the Foreign Correspondents' Club and danced until dawn in a scarlet bob wig and pink aviator glasses despite my capitalist guilt. I refused a Bedouin sheik's proposal—to become wife number two—while veiled in a Jordanian desert camp. Last month I watched jackass penguins nesting in the dunes near Cape Town, South Africa. Next month I'll see puffins at Europe's northernmost point, Nordkapp, Norway. The dots connect in nearly a straight line: one degree of longitude, over 105 of latitude.

And all so, so far from the gooey mud of Skagit Valley.

Many people rank this career just below that of a rock star. Some of these enthusiasts take the travel writing courses I teach online. From a Taos hacienda or Croatian castle, wherever I've wandered, I edit their fledgling articles and dispense advice. But unlike certain colleagues—"Get paid to travel the world for free!"—I am honest.

I confess that my toilet rocks on its moorings in the garret back home. Tell them of my ink-stained secondhand clothes, of my crummy pension plan, of the four-o'clock-in-the-morning courage of self-employment.

I worry about the expense of kitty grit. And how to wrestle the twenty-pound sacks home without a car. But it can be done. And—Look, Ma! No hands!—it can even be done sans safety net: no partner, no day job, no trust fund.

Live by the pen, die by the pen.

The ferry heaves in Queen Charlotte Sound. The windows flash slug-gray sea, then sky, a slightly whiter shade of pale.

My temper matches the stormy weather.

Here's what I don't tell my students: Often I cry after a long trip. The house is empty except for Jake the Tabby and Molly Alley-cat, grown almost feral during my absence. My pet sitter's mother has alphabetized all the soup cans in yet another eerie, compulsive display. And the pages of memory resemble nothing so much as outstanding bills. . . .

I want someone there smiling. Preferably with a leafy green salad, a glass of pinot grigio, and nothing on except an apron.

Okay, scratch the apron. Boxer briefs would be acceptable. Preferable, even.

That slice of cake is too big, I'm told.

"Professional travelers can rarely have dogs, gardens, children, or any other variety of significant other," Susan Spano wrote in a 2005 *Los Angeles Times* column.

My thoughts swing back and forth like the prow. The MV *Columbia* is threading the Wrangell Narrows, forty-six switchbacks through shoals. Spruce and hemlock stand sentinel on the shore. Fishers' kids run alongside the ferry, waving so hard their bodies wiggle.

The home I've created is a happy one: two rescued cats, a porch full of potted herbs and tomatoes, a view of Mount Rainier's snow-shadowed cone from my desk. Friends draw close; they keep the gods and monsters at bay.

Except I crave more: the whole happy-family fantasy. Being part of something larger than myself. Sharing kisses at dawn and dryer lint. Memorizing the pressure points of another soul.

And I want to see the puppy-shimmy—joy made into motion—from a child of my own.

Edit that. Of *our* own; if only I knew the right companion for that long and winding road.

Once, I was married. Seven years, in fact, just like the itchy jokes.

I fell in love on the Rome–Bologna train. We'd dashed to the station, determined to hop the next service, wherever it might lead, for the long weekend. His knapsack contained only a tattered volume of Xenophon, two oranges, and a toothbrush.

And so we lived: ricocheting through England, Italy, Greece, Cyprus, Turkey. We rode our relationship hard and put it away wet. The glue factory was inevitable.

My ex has a mortgage now, two kids, a job he dreads. And I? I remarried adventure.

But I've always run straight at trouble like some woad-smudged berserker. "You have just two speeds," my friend and colleague Edward complains. "Inert and full throttle. If you don't figure out the middle gears, kid, you won't see forty."

But I fear the alternative, so ably expressed by Kent Nerburn in *Road Angels:* "I've watched the light go out of too many of my friends' eyes as their lives turned from a crazy garden of weeds and wildflowers to a well-manicured lawn. I'm not ready for that yet. I need 'bears behind trees'—surprises in life that are bigger than a plugged sewer line or an unexpected finance charge on my credit card. . . . If I don't have them, my life becomes just a long-term maintenance project."

Before dawn, I wake, twisting on the plastic lounge chair—my decktop bed these last three nights. Heat lamps grill overhead, sinister and ember-orange. In contrast, the landscape unfurls in gray-blue sheaves: sea shading to mountains, then clouds and beyond. The lightest tone is the color of my eyes, the darkest that of my dreams.

The scene echoes a thousand from my childhood on Samish Island, just south of the ferry's lower-48 terminal. Skagit Valley was chock-full of bubbas who scraped lowriders over speed bumps and blasted jacked-up trucks across cattle guards. The women adjusted their home perms over drip coffee: "That Castleman girl, why, she's grown real pretty for such a nerd. She doesn't even look like E.T. anymore!"

Back in the day, they gossiped about hayloft date rapes and drunks drowning in agricultural ditches, maybe the odd passion crime in them thar hills. Then Interstate 5 brought gangbangers and artisan cheese-makers to northwest Washington. Kinda made everyone miss the stink of pea silage, to be honest.

I am not a true daughter of this earth. But I moved here young enough to bear its brand. I've raced 100 mph over the salt flats. I've climbed glaciers in the same county where I primped for my junior prom. I've seen my reflection fragmented by blackberry brambles in flooded fields. The scent of this coast signals home to me, more clearly than any channel buoy.

No matter how far I run, Skagit Valley shadows my side. I can't escape saltwater and cedars, any more than I can escape my impulsive self.

Nor would I want to, it seems.

Humpback whales spy-hop alongside the MV *Columbia*. I watch their spray blossom like wildflowers upon the waves.

The Marine Highway—the world's longest ferry service—has lessons for me, I realize. Its wisdom is slow and majestic, just like our procession up the Inside Passage.

Someday, somewhere, I'll find a partner, perhaps. A man to adventure along beside me or at least comb my hair when I stumble home sick. And reassure me that the loneliness, the long hours, the financial Russian roulette are worth all these weak words.

Or—harder yet—maybe I'll learn to hold myself safe. Content in *this* moment, not reaching greedily for the next, not always going, going, going simply to get gone.

Mountains rear ever higher above the fjord. As I gaze into the wake—churned the milky sage of glacial melt—the MV *Columbia* bellies up to the Skagway dock.

Twenty years after my journey to Alaska begins, I finally arrive.

Postcard from the Edge

★

by HEATHER MCKINNON

I am not a good hostess. I can function for an hour or two; a weekend, possibly, depending on the guest. And then things start to go south. I read somewhere that guests and fish go bad after three days. When the catch of the day is my mother, our happy long-distance phone relationship is threatened by the specter of "quality time."

It's not that we don't love each other. We do. But she pushes my buttons, especially the "I just want you to be happy" button. I wanted that button to light up and deliver a big smile for Mom, but lately it appeared to be out of order. I was slowly recovering from a gut-twisting breakup followed by a wrenching rebound, the kind of situation that makes you write embarrassingly bad diary entries, drop fifteen pounds, and smoke Marlboro Lights.

My mother (along with my friends, therapist, and dog) thought I should be long past it all by now, and I was, for the most part. But I still preferred solitude over my "leave no thought unvoiced" mother.

It didn't help that her visit was prefaced by this terrifying exchange.

"So when are you coming?"

"I have a ticket for the fifteenth."

"And when are you going back?"

"I don't know, I'll see how I feel after the second week."

I knew I couldn't feign happiness for that long. My solution? Escape. Not just me, but both of us, together. Mom loves a B&B; I love getting out in the wild. We decided to drive across Florida to Everglades City.

Though I knew a weekend getaway would remind me of romantic trips past, I was willing to risk a little depression to give us something new to talk about. Besides, I might get eaten by a gator and then wouldn't have to worry about the ex *or* my mother "visiting" until the end of time.

The journey began as all my trips of more than ten miles do: with doughnuts and coffee. Then we were off. Two wild and crazy chicks on Alligator Alley.

"We're like Thelma and Louise," Mom chirped.

"Did you see *Thelma and Louise?*" I asked.

"No. Didn't they have fun?"

"They drove off a cliff," I told her. *(They also picked up Brad Pitt beside the road and took him to a motel,* I told myself.)

As the strip malls of Fort Lauderdale faded into saw grass and egrets, our spirits rose. Mom stared hopefully at each remnant of truck tire and slime-covered log on this ill-named corridor. In six years of traversing the state, I have yet to see an alligator on Alligator Alley.

"Wait until we get there," I assured her. "We'll see tons of gators."

"Can we go out on one of those big hovercrafts?" she asked.

"Yes!" came my cheerful reply. Good, a conversation-free afternoon already planned. Airboats to the rescue.

We arrived in Everglades City in less than two hours. Located on the Gulf, between Naples and Flamingo, the town gives fishermen and tourists access to the Everglades and the Ten Thousand Islands, and it gives ten million mosquitoes access to fishermen and tourists. Winter months are best for avoiding the attack.

At the Ivey House, a "nice young man" (according to Mom) took our bags and gave us the tour. The house was built in 1923 as a recreation hall for Tamiami Trail workers and had been restored without much of the lace and frills that frighten many men away from B&Bs. The living room contained books on local history, games, and cozy couches. Mom was pleased.

We were led down a wide, cool hallway into the dining area, where our host pointed out the town on a wall map, described the activities that awaited two single women who don't fish, and gave us the inside scoop on the thriving airboat industry.

Airboats, we learned, fall into two categories: big, fast, and deafening and small, fast, and deafening. We chose small and walked out the back door and across a gravel lot to Speedy's Fun Cruise.

Our pilot gave us ear protection before revving up and zooming off. I clutched the seat in front of me, balancing backpack, camera, and bird book on my lap. I needn't have bothered with the book: No bird worth his seed is going to pose obligingly on his nest while what sounds like a biker gang roars past. The driver did slow down long enough to teach us Everglades 101, covering everything from how mangroves form into islands to what alligators eat. And after poking around a bit, he did roust one gator. It looked real. Real annoyed. Though exciting in a Disney-ride sort of way, this probably wasn't the best way to observe life in the Glades.

For the remainder of the afternoon we rode bikes around town. Our stomachs steered us to Susie's Station, which advertised SUSIE'S WORLD FAMOUS KEY LIME PIE (regular or deluxe), STONE CRABS FRESH DAILY, and CLAM CHOWDER.

Our waitress was a gray, tired woman who betrayed an uncertain attitude about chatty, windblown tourists. "Chowder's good when we got it but we ain't. Stone crabs are good but we can't find none nowhere. Deluxe pie, ya pay extra for a little glob of stuff on it but it ain't no different, really."

The pie, sans glob, was wonderful—smooth and tart with none of those annoying little rinds and things Miami people put in it.

Satisfied, we moved on, following the Barron River past old Florida cottages in orange, blue, and gray. A fat yellow dog rested in the shade of a raised house, dismissing us with a tired glance.

After spending a full day with my mother, I was starting to feel a lot like that dog. My mother is seventy-one, looks fifty, and acts thirty-five; she never stops. She kept exploring while I made dinner reservations and took a nap. I was eager to dine at the Rod & Gun Lodge, the area's first home, built in 1864.

The old house was purchased by Barron G. Collier in 1922, along with the rest of southwest Florida. He operated it as a private club, hosting presidents and dignitaries; John Wayne, Ernest Hemingway, and Mick Jagger have smoked cigars in the trophy room and sipped scotch on the wraparound porch. Though not at the same time.

As I dressed for a trip back to a more glamorous time, my suitcase yielded only depressed-single-girl wear: hiking boots (smelling suspiciously as if my cat had taken a dislike to them), jeans, and a wrinkled shirt. Mom looked and smelled better. If we saw any dignitaries or movie stars, she would have the upper hand.

We drove the half mile or so down the dark river road and got a table on the screened porch to avoid mosquitoes; we ate an excellent meal of fresh grouper and wine, followed by Key lime pie, this time with glob. As I stared out at the reflections in the black water and the cottage lights across the river, life seemed pretty good. It got even better when four attractive men clomped across the porch and into the bar. I used honesty to convince Mom we needed a brandy.

"Let's have a drink and check out those guys," I said.

"I'm right behind you!" Maybe the wine was talking.

We strolled down a hallway papered with news stories, including such inglorious local events as President Nixon falling out of a fishing boat—twice on the same trip. In the trophy room, ex-critters of various kinds stared us down from oak-paneled walls. Katharine Hepburn could have walked in and not looked out of place.

We spotted the guys shooting pool. I waited until one drifted away from the herd and, coming up behind him, asked wittily, "Are you playing pool?" My only explanation is that it's difficult being coquettish when smelling of cat pee. And perhaps I was a bit out of practice; it had been a long time since I'd had the desire or the need to flirt. Looking to my mother—who can talk to anyone, anytime—for support, I found her gazing dreamily at a tarpon high on the wall while making casting motions with her arm. It was time to leave.

I had signed us up for a boat trip the following day. The Ivey House specializes in outfitting kayakers and canoeists, sending them off to wander the Ten Thousand Islands with maps and camping gear. The powerboat/shelling/lunch option sounded more like Mom's style.

We joined two other guests: Cicely, an English expatriate potter, and her husband, Arnie, a retired film editor now trying to write books. I couldn't guess their ages; they were gray and wiry, and life was their happy shared adventure. I envied them. Here was the couple I wanted to be half of in thirty years.

Our guide, David, complemented the mix. Few puns, no spiel, just pleasant conversation and interesting information. It felt more like visiting with friends than taking a tour. A dolphin chased us as we headed for the islands. White pelicans flew, dove, floated, and turned, always in perfect synchronization.

We waited at a cut in the mangroves where David knew a pair of roseate spoonbills had been seen. Arnie, who earlier had dismissed Cicely's interest in birding as "an English disease," leaped to his feet.

"There! I see them! I see them!" His happy enthusiasm caught me. Until then I hadn't thought it particularly important that I see these rare creatures, but it was now. I had become a birder. After making sure we all got a glimpse (though I think my mother was just pretending), David moved on. I sat in the bow of the small craft, reveling in the wind and sun, catching snatches of Mom's conversation.

"My daughter has a very important job at a newspaper, but she still cheats at Scrabble." At least she wasn't asking if they had any eligible sons she could point my way.

We dropped anchor and waded ashore at Pavilion Key, named for an incident when pirates kidnapped a woman and then left her on the island after she became too ill to entertain them. Pleasant fellows at heart, they gave her a pavilion for shade and promised to return. I guessed I didn't have it so bad.

Shells crunched as we walked: conchs, whelks, oysters, scallops in countless variety. David supplied answers to all our questions, gently warning us to take only a few prize finds.

Our next stop yielded more treasure. Calusa Indian pottery can still be found on Mormon Key after seven thousand years. The abstract designs on these shards gave more information on this advanced civilization than local references about the "crafty and savage" race that massacred Spanish settlers. We were not permitted to pocket these relics, but I did find a small glass bottle of an interesting shape. Cicely pronounced it "old" and I chose to believe her.

The afternoon ended with a picnic lunch at a shaded chickee hut built on stilts in the shallow water, safe from the islands' ubiquitous mosquitoes. We ate and talked of nothing in particular, enjoying the cool breeze and good company. No one seemed in a hurry to return.

I smiled at my mother, her feet dangling like a child's over the dark water. She smiled back. We were actually enjoying a visit for once. I hadn't made her cry. She hadn't made me swear. I felt for the glass bottle in the pocket of my shorts, promising to keep it on a shelf and remember this trip every time I dusted. That wouldn't be as often as my mother liked, of course, but whenever I did, there would be our trip, man-free and worth every minute.

Coda: Ten years later, that bottle still sits behind glass on my barrister bookcase, and I do a lot of weekend trips with my husband. And I still can't keep up with my mom.

Out of Africa, in Karen Blixen's Footsteps

★

by JILLIAN ROBINSON

E ver since reading *Out of Africa, Shadows on the Grass,* and *Letters from Africa,* Karen Blixen has been a hero to me. Isak Dinesen, she called herself. I fancied that she chose this name not so much to disguise her sex as to reveal her approach to life. *Isak* in Hebrew means "the one who laughs."

I was attracted to Blixen for many reasons. She was a voyager, a pioneer, a woman who bucked convention. She owned a farm in Kenya, rode a mare named Rouge, and journeyed on long safaris in the bush. Wild animals did not fear her; they wandered into her home as if it were their own.

She managed the daily business of a coffee plantation. When adversity came, she dug her hands in the soil and tilled crops. She served dinners in her home on fine china with wines decanted in crystal. She was adept with medical supplies. After mending a native boy's diseased leg, he became her cook. And in the kitchen, they shared the silent kinship of cooking.

Karen lived in harmony with the indigenous people. They came to her when they were bitten by a snake or accidentally wounded by a gunshot. She went to them when she needed to remember the abundance of risk in life, the inevitability of loss, or the regret of routine.

Blixen feared little. She led an ox caravan to usher supplies to British soldiers during the first world war. She camped in canvas tents near a group of Masai warriors. At night she listened to lions growl in the tall grass under a full moon.

Blixen dared to be different. Biographer Judith Thurman said that, even as a child, Blixen "had a precocious confidence in her own singularity."

In Africa, she cultivated this lack of convention. She and her lover, Denys Finch Hatton, never married, but led what Blixen called "parallel lives." And Blixen never bore children, at a time when society clearly expected a woman would. Africa provided the space, freedom, and splendor that Blixen had longed for in her Danish homeland. She discovered her soul-home there. As she once wrote: "I have become what I was meant to be here."

I yearned to journey to Blixen's Africa—to discover whatever I was to learn from my longtime hero. But this yearning was nothing new.

Ever since my first trip to Europe as a teenager, travel had become a consuming passion for me. It was what kept me reading, and dreaming at night, and what stirred me in the morning. It led me to research and produce television documentaries in various parts of the world, and to adventure solo during my vacations: black-water rafting through caves in New Zealand, trekking in the Andes, driving cattle in Wyoming. All of these experiences shaped me, but one extended odyssey changed me more than any other.

I had begun traveling in the footsteps of my favorite writers to some of their chosen places, and in doing so often found myself no longer studying the life of the writer I admired, but rather living it.

As I prepared to depart for Karen Blixen's Kenya, I was just coming out of a cul-de-sac infatuation that had preoccupied me for more than a year. Divorced for seven years, I had begun to wonder whether I would ever meet a man with whom I could share my life, and whether this was even vital to me. I didn't know what I would find in my hero's path, but somehow I sensed that I would discover important lessons for my life.

I followed Karen's footsteps to Kenya's Loita Hills, home to the most traditional-living Masai, where I camped and walked for three days with the Masai through their land.

"How many kids you have?" Murianga, a once-Masai warrior, asked me the day after we met. Murianga did not display his long, pierced lobes—a Masai sign of beauty—but rather curled them around his ear, like little piglet tails. He grinned broadly and often, unconcerned about his missing front teeth.

"None," I told him, and felt awkward. Children and cattle were the most prized possessions in Masai culture. I knew I was something of an anomaly here—and perhaps even at home.

Throughout my African journey, I'd ruminated over this dilemma, one that many thirtysomething women faced. *Did I want to have children? If I never married again, would I consider having a child on my own? Would I be happy trading the pleasures of travel and freedom for the promised joys of motherhood? And if I did not have children, would I feel selfish? Suffer regret later on?*

And I remembered Karen. She had once written in a letter, "I have always believed that one could not expect to get too much out of life if one were not able to clarify for oneself what is 'essential' for one, and that when this demanded it of one to let everything else go."

She also said, "It had become quite clear to me that I did not want to have a child." And later revealed, "I prize my freedom above everything else that I possess."

Did I, too, prize my freedom above all else? If not, was child-bearing my "essential" element? What I would choose if I had to "let everything else go"?

For the next few days, I walked through the savannah with the Masai, threw their spears, hurled their clubs, sat with them in the grasses as they crafted their bows. I watched a bloodletting ceremony where a prized heifer was poked in the jugular, was offered a taste of the sacred blood-milk.

I received glimpses into a new world that I would wish to experience, time and again.

On my final day, I visited Murianga's village and home. He sat inside his *boma* with one of his two wives and three of his children. The kids surrounded their father. Robert, a Masai man who spoke English well, sat beside them.

The *boma's* interior had one room. In the center, a fire provided warmth and light. The roof was low and smoke permeated the thatched walls. I joined the others on the dirt floor.

Robert began talking about *boma* life. I surveyed the two bedrooms from my seat; a taut cowhide bed filled each. Wooden poles adjoined the *boma's* main area with the animal den, where goat kids and newborn calves jostled and cried.

Murianga's children started to fidget and wander off. Murianga called them back. They reassembled around him. The son who bore his father's broad smile stood by his side. As Robert continued talking, the boy placed his small hand on his dad's shoulder. Murianga lifted him, turned him upside down and kissed him, heartily, on his cheek, as if no one else were there.

In that moment, I realized that children and cattle were the Masai's most prized possessions, yet suddenly, I felt satisfied even though I possessed none of my own. I understood that we all had gaps or "shortages" in our lives; it was how we filled them that mattered.

I could discover beauty in the face of an African child I'd just met; joy in joining a Masai man as he crafted a bow in the late-afternoon lemon light. I realized the riches I already had—parents, siblings, pets—and the ones that I would continue to amass: friends who would become like sisters—constant companions on the path of life, and the kindred spirits I would forever meet along the long, open road.

I didn't have one or two children of my own, but instead, felt as if I had dozens, spread throughout Africa, Peru, Mexico, the Czech Republic, Thailand. Children I had met and held, photographed and nurtured, even if only for a short while. My memories of them—and of the children I would meet on future journeys, some of whom I might even be able to help in some way—would always fill my heart with love.

Murianga and I, perhaps even all of traditional society and I, still shared these common joys; we just traveled different paths to obtain them.

Karen Blixen's Kenya had taught me I could always create—and keep—rich, memorable moments that in the end would add up to an abundant life, at least *for me*.

Karen Blixen's Kenya had taught me what I needed to know.

Me Make Fire for Lynn

★

by LYNN HARRIS

During what turns out to be my last summer as a single person, I fly to Idaho for a weeklong camping and horseback-riding trip through the 2.4-million acre Frank Church Wilderness, miles from the middle of nowhere. Through a freak scheduling accident, it turns out I'm the only person on the trip. Just me, two horses, four pack mules, and—oh my!—my guide: Justin, a twenty-year-old with a baby face and Wrangler jeans. Yes, just the two of us in the largest wilderness in the lower 48, accessible only by foot, horseback, or teeny plane. It's like *Blind Date* meets *Survivor* meets *Who Wants to Marry a Horse Whisperer?*

When we arrive at our first night's camp, Justin sets about gathering wood, saying, "Me make fire for Lynn."

We are going to get along fine.

We sit up and talk, looking at the stars and thinking, *Holy shit, I am alone in the wilderness with a not-unattractive member of the opposite sex.* I learn that Justin and I have different skill sets. He can hunt, fish, shoot, track, build, farm, break a horse, castrate a calf, dissect an elk. I can read Hebrew?

When the fire goes out, I go to my tent. Justin sleeps outside. I don't dare, yet. Fear of being swallowed by the pitchest of dark, fear of being tempted by the stupidest of moves. Sure, Justin could fashion a condom out of a squirrel bladder, but neither that—nor the fact that I'm twelve years older—is the issue. You don't want to hook up with your lifeline. In the wilderness, it's not like you can avoid him the next day.

But really: What is it about cowboys? Why do I love them so? As far as the guys I actually dated went, most were more Muppet than Marlboro Man; my type may be strong, sure, but he's not silent. I adore country music and collect shit-kicker boots, but I can do that by myself. I've never seen a single John Wayne movie, and I remain firm in my belief that *Little House on the Prairie* jumped the shark when they brought in Almanzo. Maybe it's just my frustration with some of the higher-maintenance New York men, who are less likely to say things like, "Well, little lady, I will name you all the stars in the night sky and then fry you up that elk I felled with my crossbow." And more likely to say things like, "Sure, I can totally meet you for a Gardenburger after my facial. Oh no, wait, I have yogilates."

Still, drifting off, I think more seriously every sleepy second about becoming a frontier wife and filing my articles by pony. Really, how badly would I miss gefilte fish?

For the next few days, Justin and I ride morning to dusk, through forest, over meadows, along creeks, over fire-scarred mountaintops spiked with sooty skeletons of pine. I learn to tell deer tracks from elk, moose poop from bear. I learn to plot a course three moves ahead, over pick-up sticks of fallen trees, wide enough so the mules can follow. We talk about our first times; we go hours in silence. We talk about our religious differences, so vast there's not much to say. We sing Merle Haggard. We lie in a miniature meadow of tiny red berries, letting them pop in our mouths like caviar.

One afternoon, riding along a ridge, we spot a giant bear shooing her cubs up a tree. Shortly thereafter, a smaller—but big enough—bear steps onto the trail fifty yards ahead of us. Jumping off his horse, Justin hands me her bridle and the mule line. The danger is that the animals will spook, which is one thing in a barn, quite another on a ridge. I hold tight, watching Justin run toward the bear. Not a typo: *toward* the bear. He yells and throws small rocks at it until it shrugs and lumbers away. This is the coolest, and hottest, thing anyone has ever done in my presence.

That night, Justin shows me his .357 Magnum. It looks like a prop.

"You never even seen one, have you?" he asks, having seen me take an inadvertent step back.

"I don't know anyone who owns one," I say.

"I don't know anyone who doesn't," he says.

I really know no one? I ask myself again. Nope. No hunters, no collectors, no post-9/11 rewriters of the rules of self-defense. Not even my Georgia granddaddy, though he'd been outlaw enough to make moonshine on the back stoop of a dry home. No one.

"I'll let you shoot it if you want," Justin offers. Oh, I want. To impress Justin. In truth, I am petrified.

He shows me the safety, the chamber, the feather-light action of the trigger.

"Why am I so scared?" I ask.

"You *should* be scared," he says.

Justin fires first, to prepare me for how loud it would be.

Beyond loud. The sound bores into my chest, through my gut, out my toes, and back into the trees. Justin makes me paper-towel earplugs and hands me the pistol. It feels heavy and out of place in my hands. He shows me how to aim at the tobacco tin he'd leaned against a tree. I half listen, focusing mainly on his instructions not to touch the trigger until I am about to fire. I also imagine the scenario: my finger slipping, the gun flipping, how a bullet would feel in my neck, how Justin would feel having to call my mother.

Justin waits. I eventually choose a moment from nowhere and move my finger. There is another noise and I am done.

"I'm proud of you!" Justin grins. The tobacco tin lies untouched.

We celebrate my initiation with chicken-fried steak. Justin also digs up a bottle of vodka, which, it turns out, mixes perfectly with Country Time lemonade. We tear at the steaks and talk with our mouths full, fingers slick with grease, chase it down with sweet pink drinks.

Then we dance. Justin picks my plate off my lap, stands me up from my log, and leads me in a humming two-step around the fire. I *knew* my country-dancing lessons would give me survival skills! Suddenly, he's flipping me over his shoulder like the fancy people on the country cable channels. I am over the moon, over the bright crescent moon that no one else can see for hundreds of miles.

Another day Justin tells me about growing up on a dairy farm, about branding and castrating time for the calves. "When we cut off their balls, we fry 'em right quick on the branding iron and eat 'em right there," he says, grinning.

"No you do not," I say. This has become a game of ours, trying to get the other to believe something insane about our foreign-to-each-other lifestyles. I'd made him fall for some tall tale about fighting off Rollerblading muggers, which wasn't that difficult; he'd seen *The Warriors*.

"Yes, we do," he says. "I'm totally serious."

"Shut the fuck up," I say. Of course, I know people eat cow testicles—excuse me, "Rocky Mountain Oysters"—which is what makes Justin's fib brilliant, I think. It's based on fact, naturally, but what he's invented is the fabulous, positively cowboy-gothic, fry-'em-up-on-the-iron detail. Genius.

"Lynn, I'm not kidding. I swear to god."

Holy moly, he *is* serious. Earlier, when I rubbed my aching back and made some crack about humans "not being meant to walk upright," he said something like, "You don't really believe that shit, do you?" Meaning evolution. Meaning that when this young man swears to god about something, he is not whistling Dixie.

So, okay. Fresh, branding iron–seared cow testicles. "They're delicious," Justin says. "Too bad they didn't pack us any."

I retaliate with talk of sushi.

On our last day we see salmon swimming upstream after laying their eggs, turning ashy white and fleshless as they die. They'll soon be like the skin of molted snakes, only without a new body in which to glide away. But what makes nature so cruel as to make them swim, going nowhere, on the way? Justin doesn't find this scene as heartbreaking as I do. He shrugs. We ride.

What is it, indeed, about cowboys? I am starting to get it. It's not that they're all macho and save you from bears—or, at least, not *just* that. They're both hard as horseshoes *and* soft as flannel, see. They're not unfeeling, I suppose—more like just used to pain. Life cycle, food chain: They see it all, closer up than we do. They may not "share" so much, but cowboys write poetry. And listen to good, thinking, feeling music. And dance.

When we ride into base camp we find the two other guides, Jared and Shane, making us margaritas in the cook tent. We all sit together in the outdoor hot tub. Not a typo: We all sit together in the outdoor hot tub. Drinking margaritas. (Wearing bathing suits.) My first thought: *Dear* Penthouse *Forum, I never thought these letters were real. . . .* I imagine the porn movie we could make: *Laura Ingalls Just Got Wilder.* But I just listen to the guys bullshit, proud that Justin could tell them the city slicker could handle her horse, her rare steak, her two-step, and her liquor, not to mention his gun. And I am glad that firing Justin's gun turns out to be a metaphor for what never happens between us—not even that last night when Jared and Shane turn in, not even after Justin coaxes me into jumping with him out of the hot tub, into the freezing brook, and back into the tub. We hold hands and say, "Go!" and the sudden, gulping cold-then-hot takes my breath away. God knows when I got this mature, but I figure sometimes it's better to wish you had than to wish you hadn't. I unroll my sleeping bag on some horse blankets, under the stars, next to Justin, who is next to his gun. And I sleep.

Part 7

HOME
SWEET
HOME

Live Alone and Like It

Singlehood is no longer a state to be

overcome as soon as possible.

—STEPHANIE COONTZ, SOCIAL HISTORIAN AND AUTHOR OF
MARRIAGE, A HISTORY AND *THE WAY WE NEVER WERE*

The Speech

★

by LAURIE NOTARO

Relationships suck.

They suck hard.

Sometimes, in the middle of the night, when my bedroom is as black as death and the sheets on half the bed are as cold as a five-day-old corpse, I think:

All I ever wanted to be was someone's Old Lady.

I want to be the ball and chain.

I need to be somebody's squeeze.

I float in this for a minute, in this bed that is too big for me, and feel a little bit lonely, when all of a sudden the wheezing, flopping noise from my lungs wakes me up and shocks me back into Relationship Reality, and I realize

The empty side of the bed does not fart in its sleep.

The empty side of the bed does not attempt to sodomize me while I am sleeping.

The empty side of the bed does not make me look at the turd as big as my leg grounded in the toilet and then ask aloud, "Dude, do you think it will go down in one flush?"

The empty side of the bed does not wrestle me to the floor, pin me, and then straddle me, in order to do the Spit Torture, dripping saliva out of its mouth over my face, then sucking it back up; dribbling it out, then sucking it back up; dribbling it out then letting it fall right near my mouth.

The empty side of the bed IS NOT, I repeat, IS NOT, a MAN. And for that, I am thankful.

I want a man as nice as my retarded dog, but one that doesn't crap on the floor. I want a man who will only cheat on me a little and who will call me once a week. I want a man who will buy his own drinks and who will hold back my hair when I puke. I want a man who is unconfused regarding his sexual identity. I want a man who has never heard of or practiced the Speech.

I will never find him. He has never been born.

The last time I got my walking papers, it was over the phone. "It" had lasted about five months, the longest-standing Relationship Record I had held in this decade. Well, it wasn't even a "relationship." I called it the "thing." He didn't call it anything. He thought I wanted to get married tomorrow, have seventeen kids, buy an Isuzu Trooper, and then staple his scrotum to the living-room couch. All I really wanted was one phone call per solstice.

Anyway, the conversation was off to a running start when he cleared his throat and said

"I am not ready and will not be ready to actively get involved with anyone for at least three to five years."

"Why?" I asked. "Are you going to prison?"

"No. What I am saying is that I'm not ready to commit to anything, either way."

"Either way? You mean you can or cannot commit to committing or not committing?" I said, growing suspicious and confused. "Are you giving me the Speech?"

"I think we should concentrate more on the 'Friends' part of our—well, you know."

Suspicions confirmed, I gasped.

"You ARE giving me the Speech! You just gave me the Speech! That was the Speech!" I cried.

So I got the Speech, which automatically drops you to the lowest point in life; it's like throwing the self-esteem balloon on a cactus. You become such a small specimen of existence that you could probably mate with yourself, which would actually be such a terrific advantage.

I guess I took it well. I didn't set anything on fire, practice any voodoo, or listen to sad songs. No, this time I just sat at the bar and drank, sneering and growling at all of the men except my friend Dave.

"How's it going?" he asked.

"Well, I got the Speech today," I said.

"Oh no. Not the Speech," he said. "Did he use the 'F' word?"

I nodded.

"Oh god," Dave sighed. "The 'F' word is low. Low down."

"Yep," I said. *"Friends.* He said, 'We're just *Friends.'"*

I don't understand the Speech and how men learned about it. Was it part of boys' eighth-grade PE class? Did the gym teacher make them say it to one another over and over in the showers so they would be good at it?

"Okay, now how does it go?"

"It goes, 'You're a cool girl, and I like hanging out with you, but I'm not ready to make a—um, that big word—commitment to one person, and I think we need to be . . . we need to be . . . '"

"Man, this is the most important part! The 'F' word, man! The 'F' word!"

"Oh, yeah! You tell the chick you want to be Friends! But you don't mean it, do you?"

"No. A chick won't let you nail her if she knows she's not even a Friend."

Or maybe the Speech is some kind of computer chip that gets implanted in every baby boy's dingle as soon as he's born.

"There are things running around out there with uteruses, son. You're going to need this."

Could it be a hormonal gift package with an added-feature thing, where women get PMS with estrogen, and men get the Speech with testosterone? I don't understand it.

I do understand one thing: I am pissed off at God for making me heterosexual, and I swore that the next time I heard the Speech, I was going to fix that. I have enough Friends, so I'm going to try really hard this time to be a lesbian. The only problem with this is that all men are fascinated by lesbians, lesbians are delicacies to men, and once they find out you are one, they want you back again.

But maybe it's just my destiny to remain alone, eating single-people food like Soup for One, collecting Precious Moments figurines, and thinking that my dog can talk back to me. Oh god. With any luck, I'll wind up living in a trailer park as a bitter, celibate alcoholic with a heart full of hate. I'd much rather be alone and make myself miserable than give someone else the pleasure. I'll die a graceful and glowing death when my cigarette plunges into the shag carpet as I pass out after my final date with Jack Daniel's, who will be resting very comfortably and very drained on the pillow of the empty side of the bed.

Home Alone

★

by RACHEL EVE RADWAY

W hen I was twenty-two and out of college a little more than a
year, I moved from New York City, where I'd grown up, to
San Francisco, where I was born but had never spent much time—
consciously, anyway. I found a charming, cozy studio apartment in
the Marina and paid what my friends with roommates considered
an insanely high rent—$650 a month—to live on my own.

It didn't seem strange to me. I'd managed to get single rooms
through four years of college (you just have to know which dorms
to ask for) and loved the independence of living alone. I was never
more than a few feet away from study groups, parties, advice, and
company, but I never had to deal with someone else's snoring, dirty
laundry, homesick phone calls at 2:00 AM, or loud sex in the single
bed on the other side of the room.

I'd always had roommates at summer camp; first dozens of
them, and then just three as we got older and earned four-to-a-bunk
status. And I'd also had numerous housemates when I traveled
and lived abroad, which I did intermittently in my late teens and
early twenties. I'd lived with quiet males and loud females, filthy
slobs and neat freaks, friendly sorts who showed me their home-
towns and introduced me to their families and hermits who rarely

emerged from their dens. There was a Kiwi rugby player who ate microwaved tinned beans with ketchup over toast every single day and never washed his dishes, a woman in Leningrad whose religion dictated (so she said) that she chant loudly every morning at five o'clock in the precise center of the tiny room. And there were many others—the couple who broke up because of me (more accurately, because she learned from me that being independent might be easier than putting up with her worm of a boyfriend); the sweet, slightly odd older man who introduced me to Cointreau; the high school seniors who held pot parties downstairs every night when I had to get up at the crack of dawn every morning for work.

Needless to say, by the time I moved to San Francisco, privacy and peace of mind were worth far more than $650 a month.

The week I moved into my studio, a friend of my mother's offered to help me with errands, since I didn't have a car and didn't know my way around. I wanted to find a good hardware store where I could pick up a few things. The apartment had two huge walk-in closets, but the top shelves were very high. My mother's friend said—slightly tongue in cheek but mostly serious—"That's what you need a man for!"

The truth was, I really only wanted a stepladder.

I love living alone. I love the freedom to get dressed or not, put on makeup or not, turn on the radio or not, as I choose. To keep the foods I like in the house, or not do any grocery shopping at all for weeks. To watch my favorite TV shows or have some quiet time. To go to bed early or stay up late; to sleep in or get up without disturbing anyone else. To decorate the way I want to and buy new stuff for the apartment when I choose to.

A few years after I'd moved to San Francisco, my boyfriend of a year and a half casually asked me to move in with him. But I couldn't do it. We had vastly different tastes—in food, in furniture, in clothes, in lifestyle—and I just couldn't imagine trying to blend all those together and really make it work. More than that, the thought of living with someone was just too far from my mind. I liked my autonomy.

When I bought my first place (a small townhouse in Seattle) years later, I couldn't wait to start making it mine—to choose paint colors and window treatments and pick out new linens. I commissioned an artist friend to make custom lightswitch plates for every room, and hung paintings and pieces from other local artists on the walls, right next to those done by my great-aunt and great-grandmother. I was incredibly proud of my home; I had bought it on my own and made it beautiful.

Not that there weren't times when it might have been handy to have someone else around.

The first week in my lovely new townhouse, I found an uninvited guest in my bedroom—a large, nasty-looking spider, about the size of my open palm (a friend later told me that it was probably a brown wolf spider). Whatever it was, I didn't want it there. I had no problem with little spiders or other insect visitors; I left them alone as long as they showed me the same courtesy. But this thing looked like it could take on a poodle.

When I saw it, I'll admit my first thought was, *Where's a big, brave man when you need one?* But I didn't have one handy. So I called my mother. Also single, my mother lives in a townhouse in Vermont with its own share of wildlife, both inside and out.

Mom told me to suck it up—literally, with a vacuum cleaner. Unfortunately, my bedroom had extra-high, coved ceilings, and even my trusty stepladder couldn't get me and my vacuum hose close enough. My mother and I laughed ourselves silly over my predicament, then I decided to go for it. Dragging my stepladder to the site of the ambush, I climbed up—broom in one hand, vacuum in the other—and batted in the general direction of the beast. After a few errant swipes, I knocked it off the ceiling—at which point it made a mad dash out the bedroom door and down the hallway. I scurried after it, still armed with my vacuum and broom.

I must have looked like a Merry Maid on speed, but I somehow managed to dispose of it (I won't go into details—let's just say I did what had to be done), proving to myself that I could handle anything, even a single woman's worst nightmare.

And I don't just battle wolf spiders. I've caulked and puttied, fixed toilet flushers and replaced showerheads, hung complicated blinds and put up more than my share of shelves. I own my own set of tools—I can talk socket wrenches and laser levels with the best of 'em—as well as a dog-eared copy of *Dare to Repair: A Do-It-Herself Guide to Fixing (Almost) Anything in the Home* (a housewarming gift from Mom). I'm also a champion furniture assembler: I once built a four-drawer, wooden, vertical file cabinet with iron hardware from scratch (well, almost from scratch; the instructions—in a language pretending to be English—pretty much left me on my own). What's more, I've mastered the fine art of unpacking an entire household full of stuff—putting everything in its place, storing the boxes, and hanging all my artwork—within three days following a move.

A questionable talent, I know. But something I've had to put to use quite a lot lately (in what can only be described as a bizarre streak of luck, I've had four different "permanent" jobs—in four different cities—in the past fourteen months). I know how to find a new place, even long distance; break a lease if necessary; get estimates, hire movers, and pack up all my worldly possessions—all without going into an emotional meltdown.

The truth: I hate moving. I hate packing, and I might possibly hate unpacking even more. It's not fun, and it would be a lot easier if I didn't have to do it all myself (and I'm not talking about hired muscle here). But there are so many positives about it. For one thing, as corny as it sounds, I'm in control of my destiny. If I need to move, I do it. I decide where I want to live—the city, the neighborhood, the building. I decide what goes into it—no arguing about hardwood floors versus carpeting, sleek modern versus quaint older construction. I can live where I like—even if it's in a hundred-year-old purple Victorian with a friendly house cat and flowers painted on the hallway walls.

I suppose some people might consider this a control issue. But to me, it's not about control but rather confidence in knowing I can take care of myself, knowing I can do what needs to be done.

I have a friend who's stayed with her husband for about fifteen years, although they've been on the verge of separating a number of times. She once told me (when we were both in our midthirties) that she hoped that if they did separate, it would happen soon. She didn't want to have to be single at forty. She didn't know how.

I'm lucky. I was raised by a single working mother who's always been a bit unconventional. Having been through a few marriages and divorces herself, she's never pressured me to get married. In fact, she once revealed that she'd actually promised herself when I was born that she'd happily finance any and all affairs I wanted to have if I didn't get married before I was thirty (a confession that nearly caused her book club to collectively faint).

Granted, I sometimes wish that my dating dance card were a bit more full. But I really do love being on my own. I have friends who say they'd be mortified to go to a movie solo—let alone eat at a restaurant at a table for one. But I love seeing movies alone, sometimes even more than going with people who can't stop fidgeting or talking or tearing a movie to shreds afterward. And yes, dining alone at a restaurant can be intimidating, but it can also be a good way to meet people or just enjoy a moment. I still remember eating at an Indian restaurant in Bath, England, where a kind maître d' not only gave me a table with a beautiful view of the river, but also presented me with a flower and coffee and dessert on the house. I'm pretty sure the women dining with their boyfriends and husbands didn't get any special attention from the staff.

I don't particularly want to be alone forever. It might be nice to have someone around to help me battle gargantuan insects or assemble furniture or (if he's well behaved) join me at the movies on occasion. But finding him is not my ultimate goal in life (and if I do, let me tell you, we're gonna have to live in a *big* house).

I'm perfectly happy being home alone. I have a wonderful house, a great job, and a warm and caring family and friends. And I have my stepladder—to help me get things down from high shelves and give me the perspective to see that I don't have to worry about knowing how to be single at forty—or at any age, for that matter.

Single All the Way

★

by BELLA DEPAULO

In December of 1992, I clipped an article from the Charlottesville *Daily Progress,* put it in a new manila folder, and wrote the number "1" in red Magic Marker on the tab. The story was from the "Senior Exchange" column about the upcoming holidays. I had underlined just one sentence: "Remember that one is a whole number."

What was I thinking? I was thirty-nine at the time, and surely did not consider myself a senior. I had never been alone for the holidays, and the coming season would be no different.

Maybe I was thinking about my mother. Her forty-two-year marriage had ended the previous fall, when my father's undetected abdominal aneurism ruptured and he died, seemingly in an instant. But she had never spent a holiday alone either, and, as it turned out, she never would.

Charlottesville, Virginia, was where I landed in 1979 to begin my first job as a professor of psychology. By the time I clipped the 1992 story, I had a cadre of friends. We practiced dyadic lunching; four or five times a week, two of us would pair up and head for a favorite restaurant. We often went out to dinner, too, especially in the warm weather when we could sit at the outdoor tables at the downtown mall. Many a Sunday evening, a small group of us would gather in my living room, for small talk, big talk, chocolate, and an hour of bad television. I was single and surrounded.

I was also single and settled. I had tenure and had carved out my area of professional expertise in the social psychology of deceiving and detecting deceit. I also had a home that I owned in a town that felt comfortable and familiar. I thought I might stay right there for the rest of my career—or even for the rest of my life.

Singlehood suited me. I loved waking up every day in a quiet place where I was the sole inhabitant. Whenever I heard important news, whether delightful or devastating, I preferred to hear it alone, turning it over in my mind and in my heart, figuring out what it meant to me. At social events, I often felt sorry for the couples. When they left the party, they still have another human stuck to them, while I, in contrast, could enjoy my time spent socializing and then savor my solitude once I got home.

There were, though, some aspects of my life that bothered me. I thought they *might* have something to do with my status as a single person in a workplace in which so many of my colleagues were coupled, but I wasn't sure. For example, when job candidates came to visit, my coupled colleagues would sometimes lay claim to the more desirable meeting times (say, dinner at a trendy restaurant on a Saturday night, tab picked up by the department) and just assume I could cover the leftovers. When we socialized among ourselves, the couples welcomed me to the kid-friendly events but rarely included me in their dinner and movie plans—those were for couples only. Come to think of it, since my father had died, my mother was no longer invited so regularly to join the couples she had thought of as close friends.

At my university, there were lab groups studying marital interaction and family dynamics. There was a Center for Children, Families, and the Law. In the fields of sociology and psychology, there were journals and conferences on marriage and family.

Single people comprised more than 40 percent of the American adult population—why weren't they on the map?

I kept a mental inventory of questions like these. For years, though, I kept them to myself.

Then, one balmy spring evening in 1998, as I was standing on the rolling green hillside that was my colleague's back yard, I turned to the stranger next to me and asked her, rather tentatively, if she ever got the impression that single people were treated as less fully adult or less important than coupled people. She did. I learned that she was a law professor and asked if there was any special area of legal studies pertaining to the interests of people who are single. Not that she knew of. Someone else sauntered by and joined our conversation. Then a few more people became interested. And then two or three others. Everyone, it seemed, had their own personal examples of what I would come to call "singlism." Even the coupled people knew what the rest of us were talking about.

Some singles complained of intrusive queries ("So why aren't you married?") posed by perfect strangers. Others seethed at the pity piled upon them by "concerned" relatives, some of whom were multiply divorced. Many described their shifting status in the world of the coupled. One, for example, recalled a conditional invitation she received: "When you find someone, call us and we can have dinner." Another shared the four words she most despised: "Per person double occupancy." There were stories from the workplace and the marketplace, restaurants and hardware stores. Movie plots and advertisements were recounted with outrage and indignation, and quite a few laughs ensued.

Afterward, I went home, pulled out a notebook, and started writing. All of those mental notes I had been taking during my years of singlehood came tumbling out onto the pages. After a few hours, I put my pen down. But from that day forward, I never stopped writing about contemporary American society's uneasy relationship with people who are single.

I gathered books and journal articles and television transcripts. I clipped magazine and newspaper stories and added my own personal annotations. When Angelina Jolie told *People* magazine in 2000 that she scared people off easily, the reporter mused about whether Jolie had just explained why she was currently single. On *Nightline,* a recruiter for a meat-packing plant was asked about the characteristics he was seeking in potential employees. "I want someone who is married," he replied (and *Nightline* didn't seem to think there was anything wrong with that). Even some of my junk mail became meaningful, such as the envelope that told me before I even opened it that I could "save up to $6,910 per couple" if I booked my trip right away.

Soon, my "1" folder overflowed into more folders, then into boxes, then into entire rooms.

When it was my turn for a sabbatical in the summer of 2000, I packed up my entire singles collection and moved to Santa Barbara. It was an odd choice, in a way, since I had never lived on the West Coast and there was no one in the area I knew very well. But I love warm weather and it was only for a year, so why not?

In the funky little town of Summerland, I rented a beach house with a magnificent ocean view. Sliding glass doors led out to a sprawling deck. From there, I could walk down the hill and in ten minutes have both feet in the Pacific Ocean. Or I could follow hiking trails through mountains and valleys and fields. Or drive a short distance and be at a farmers market, buying yellow cucumbers, green tomatoes, and red basil. I was in love. I never wanted to leave.

Within days, I learned that there was going to be a job opening at my level, in my area, at the university I was visiting (UCSB). I think I gasped when I first heard the news; already, I was smitten with the school and its scholars, with a campus that stretched to the sand and the sea. I quickly put together my job application.

Months later, the phone rang and I was delighted to hear the voice of one of my new colleagues. He was also the chair of the search committee. We chatted for a few moments, then he began to tell me about the passel of distinguished social psychologists who had applied for the position, and about how much all of the committee members respected me. Suddenly, I realized I was not going to be interviewed for the job.

Which meant I'd have to leave the place I so loved when my sabbatical ended. Unless I could think of something else. A friend suggested that I ask the university officials back East if I could extend my sabbatical for another year. They agreed, but understandably, they weren't about to pay for it. I got in touch with an acquaintance who had previously asked me to consult on a research project about deception. Any chance I could reconsider my answer? I could.

I'd also had an invitation to teach a graduate seminar at UCSB on the topic of my choice. I floated the idea of offering a course on singles but was cautioned against it. "I don't think anyone will sign up," said a colleague, "and you will get your feelings hurt." *Okay, then, I'll teach a course on deception,* I thought. *I'll do some consulting on deception, and I'll pay my bills. The rest of the time will be for reading, writing, talking, and thinking about singles.*

And since no offer was made to either of the two social psychologists who had interviewed for the UCSB job, perhaps I could try again. There would be another round of interviews the next year.

I put my Charlottesville home on the market, and it sold in a few days. Then I returned to pack up the last of my accumulated belongings, say goodbye to students and friends, and sign the papers that made my home sale official. It was the end of a double-decade era of my life.

The next day, back in Santa Barbara, I met a friend from UCSB at the Montecito Cafe. The beautifully plated seafood special had just been placed before me when she asked if anyone had ever told me why I had not been interviewed for the UCSB job. I never thought I needed an explanation—the two people they interviewed were superb scholars. I was disappointed, but not offended.

"They don't like your singles work," she explained. But, she added, she thought I could have a "real shot" at the position in the coming year if I rewrote my cover letter and expunged from my vita any mention of my interest in singles. She continued talking, unfurling one idea after another about how I could make this work. I knew she was putting herself out for me and I was grateful for that, but I was also devastated. They had rejected me because of my singles work. That was about the same as saying that they rejected me because of me. A moment before, the curried bay scallops had seemed delectable; now they looked like dead fish.

That night, I slept for a very long time. When I got up, I knew what I was going to do. I was in the forty-eighth year of my life. I had always liked my work, but this singles work, I *loved.* I had found my passion. I wasn't about to renounce it.

I realized something important that day. If a colleague and friend could think that the study of singlehood was a topic of so little substance that it could be flicked away from my person like a bit of lint, then I was not making my case very convincingly. I needed to learn how to write, and not just for academics.

I was introduced to the term "query letter," wrote one, and found an agent for a proposed book: *Singled Out: How Singles are Stereotyped, Stigmatized, and Ignored, and Still Live Happily Ever After.* In late November 2001, he wrote a cover letter in which he proclaimed that *Singled Out* had "breakthrough possibilities, both

in terms of sales and in the way it could change the way we think."
He compared it to books such as Susan Faludi's *Backlash* and
Deborah Tannen's *You Just Don't Understand*. He sent the letter
and my proposal to six of the most acclaimed editors at the most
prestigious publishing houses.

I began to fantasize about the advance. In a definitive book on
serious nonfiction (authored by an editor with experience at some
of those same big-time publishing houses), I found this statement:
"Most works of serious nonfiction sold to commercial publishers
sell in the range of $20,000 to $400,000." There it was. I could count
on $20,000. By then, I also subscribed to *Publishers Lunch,* a sort of
"inside baseball" of the book world. My favorite feature was the list
of new book deals, sometimes accompanied by a hint of how much
money each deal had fetched. Around the time of my advance fantasies, a biography of a circus elephant had garnered six figures.
That's not peanuts.

The last of the six rejections came at the end of January 2002.
"She's a smart cookie," the esteemed editor said of me. "But for
the life of me, I could not find the readership for [her proposed
book]."

Now I had two things to figure out: how to rewrite my proposal
to make it more convincing, and how to support myself. I had lots
of ideas for treading the financial waters—I could write a singles
grant or find a place on the speakers' circuit. I went to work on both
and, in the meantime, thought about my proposal revisions all the
time, whether I intended to or not.

In July 2002, my agent called. He had just read my revised
proposal. "I was really looking forward to reading it," he said. "I
expected to love it."

It would be nearly a year before I sent him another version. By then, though, I was confident. My professional interest in the study of singles had become well known. In addition to the informal talks I'd been giving to small groups of social psychologists or relationships researchers or patrons of the Women's Center, I was now invited to address large audiences at regional and national psychology conventions.

I'd given many major addresses on deception, so I knew the drill. If I ran into someone in the hallway right after my talk, they would say, "Enjoyed your talk," whether they did or not. After my singles talks, though, it was different. People would stop me, look at me, and say, "Thank you." Then the email messages would arrive. "Your talk was truly inspiring, and I could not take notes fast enough." Sentiments like those were my inspiration, and as long as they kept coming, no stack of rejections, no matter how high, could dissuade me from pursuing my work on singles.

By January 2004, I finally had a proposal that both I and my agent liked. He sent it out to six more editors, and I hit the reset button on my advance fantasies. A social psychologist far less experienced than I, and without my track record, had just landed a "good" deal. "Good," according to the *Publishers Lunch* key, meant that he got somewhere between $100,000 and $250,000. Another book with the proposed title *Urban Tribes of the Never-Married* was feted with a "significant" deal: That's somewhere between a quarter-million and a half-million dollars.

My sister Lisa, a successful magazine writer, warned me that the reporting in *Publishers Lunch* was selective: It's not as if people are going to call in all of their rejections. My agent suggested I think about what it might mean that many of the deals were reported without any dollar amounts attached to them. Still, that circus animal story really did get six figures. Elephants don't lie.

Three days later, the first rejection arrived. "Most single women who are actively interested in their marital status are actively interested in changing it," said the editor. Another came a few weeks later, delivered to my agent in a phone conversation. The editor said that she and her husband had sat down and made a list of their single friends and concluded that none of them were happily single. Therefore, I was "dead wrong" and she was not going to buy my book.

The next letter seemed promising. It began: "This proposal made me look at the world in a new way—something I love for a book to do." But, the editor continued, her own style was "softly-softly," and mine decidedly was not.

After rejection number twenty, I stopped counting. I didn't have a book contract, I didn't have a singles grant, and no one was interested in hiring me as a guest speaker (though a few were happy to have me show up for free). And the publishing world, I was discovering, was brimming with "matrimaniacs," each looking to peddle the puffed-up marital myths I was trying so determinedly to puncture.

Actual single people, however, had their own take on my message. After I lectured an undergraduate class in the spring of 2004, one of the students emailed me. "There have been so many times I have convinced myself to be unhappy because I wasn't with someone," he said. "I have a sudden sense of a weight being lifted off my shoulders." Word of my singles work was making its way into the press, too, and emails began appearing in my box with increasing regularity. "Thank you, thank you, thank you!" said one. "Finally someone gets it!!!!" A clinical psychologist offered this valentine: "I feel like I've just been given a gift for my practice and my work with my clients." A seventy-three-year-old commented, "I wish I had learned the value of being single at a younger age," and encouraged me to keep on writing.

Meanwhile, the rejections continued to roll in. Until, one day in May, when something unusual happened. An editor from St. Martin's Press loved my proposal. A flurry of phone calls ensued, then she met with her colleagues and came back to me with still more questions. Did I have a video of any of my media appearances? Were there any more stories about my singles work in the media? Did I have any connections to professional societies or other groups that could prove useful in promoting the book? No matter what she asked, the answer was yes.

The St. Martin's editor met with her colleagues one more time, and called my agent with their offer: $10,000. It was stunningly insulting, but it was a book contract. After a bit of negotiation, I accepted it.

I continued writing (I had never really stopped) and, fifteen months later, turned in my book manuscript.

Then came all the other fun parts of the publishing process. At social events, I told people I was publishing a book on singlehood. "Yeah, a lot of people have that problem," offered an otherwise brilliant man. Sometimes I would ask for people's suggestions for cover art. One woman, a respected professor, suggested a picture of a broken ring. A man I was meeting for the first time had an idea for an author photo: How about if I sit in one chair, with an empty chair right next to me?

As I write this, *Singled Out* is still in its production stages. Five days ago, I returned the page proofs; in four months, the book will be out in the stores. That means I can't tie up my story with a neat verbal bow. Much as I'd like to say, "Nyah, nyah" to all the editors who rejected *Singled Out,* I can't. Their predictions of dismal sales may still prove true.

Even if the book does get noticed, I can't predict what kind of reaction it will stir. I know there will be points I wish I had added or clarified, and points that I will wish I had written some other way, or not written at all—I just don't know which ones they will turn out to be. I like to think of *Singled Out* as a myth-busting, consciousness-raising, totally unapologetic take on singlehood. And that is jarringly at odds with the reigning cultural conviction that singles are pitiful selfish immature children or sex-obsessed crazed mate-seekers who ought to be duly defensive about their sad state. Who will get mangled when these two worldviews collide? I suspect that I will, as those who dislike my message take aim at the messenger.

But as I reread what I've written, and as I look back on my last few years, I feel proud. Writing this book is exactly what I wanted to do with my life, and now I've done it.

I'm sure any reputable financial adviser would have warned me against the way I spent these last several years. I should have been saving for retirement, building equity on a home. I should have taken the $60,000 profit on my home in Virginia and put it toward a place in the California sun. Instead, I used it to pay the rent. I used some of my savings, too. Six years after leaving Charlottesville, I have no regular paycheck, and no home to call my own. Dinner out is no longer the routine event it once was; sometimes, when I merely consider the possibility, I hear the gurgling sounds of my dwindling dollars circling the drain. With holidays permanently blacked out of my airfare awards programs and my family on the other end of the continent, I have, at times, spent Thanksgiving or Christmas alone.

But one is a whole number. And I have never been happier.

Single Blessedness

★

by ABIGAIL GROTKE

O ld maid. Spinster. Crazy cat lady. If you're single, it's perfectly natural to cringe at these commonly used terms. Throughout the ages, women have been bombarded with messages implying that a single woman = a freak of nature. As a collector of more than one-thousand classic advice books dating from the 1820s to the 1970s, I've certainly seen my share of books that assume that a young woman will date, fall in love, and get married, and that if she doesn't, she's destined to be a depressed, sad, and lonely (but possibly successful!) career gal. The horror!

You know the sort of advice I'm talking about. Like this, from Clifford R. Adams and Vance O. Packard's 1946 book *How to Pick a Mate: The Guide to a Happy Marriage*: "Psychiatrists agree that except in exceptional cases women who live alone will become neurotic and frustrated." Or this gem, from *Sexual Problems of Today*, written by William J. Robinson in 1921: "Thousands and thousands of women [who remain single] are ruining their health, destroying their beauty, stifling their desires, renouncing the greatest joy and pleasure of life, the companionship and embraces of the opposite sex."

Despite what these (ahem) insightful authors say, what you've read in advice columns, and what you can glean from book titles like *You Can Be the Wife of a Happy Husband* by Darien B. Cooper (1974), and Robert C. and Frances William Binkley's *What Is Right with Marriage* (1934), advice for single women throughout the ages isn't *all* bad.

One of my favorite books devoted to the topic is Marjorie Hillis's *Live Alone and Like It!* Written in 1936, and based on an unscientific survey of my crowded bookshelves, it's one of the earliest "it's okay to be single" (at least until marriage) advice books. Another early one is Jean Van Evera's *How to be Happy While Single*, from 1949. The 1950s weren't so hot for the pro-single advice book movement, but with the publication of Helen Gurley Brown's *Sex and the Single Girl* in 1962, things picked up again. What followed were a number of other "Sex-and-the's" for women and men. Helen wrote two more: *Sex and the Office* (1964) and *Sex and the New Single Girl* (1970); in 1964 Gael Greene's tell-all *Sex and the College Girl* was published.

The late 1960s were also a good time for single women, for instance: Rebecca Greer's *Why Isn't a Nice Girl Like You Married? Or, How to Get the Most Out of Life While You're Single* (1969); *The Single Girl Goes to Town* by Jean Baer (1968); and *The Single Girl's Guide to Living in the City* (1968) by Gwen Cummings.

Not yet convinced? Encouraging words for singles really *are* in the classic advice books. They're sometimes buried, but definitely there. Some examples:

ISO Mentally Insipid SWM

There are many reasons why single women don't immediately jump into matrimony—some good, some bad. Perhaps we've gotten pickier through the years, but even in 1912 there was a recognition that it might be wise to wait for the right man to come along before tying the knot.

"Many cultured women, quite capable of profound passions, refrain from marriage today, because their admirers are mentally insipid, or without capacity for intellectual conversation," wrote Walter Gallichan in *The Great Unmarried*. In 1923, Bernarr Macfadden summed it up in his *Womanhood and Marriage:* "She has remained unmarried because no man came into her circle of friends who possessed enough attractions to woo her from a life of 'single blessedness.'"

Vastly Happier in Her Lot

Feeling a little bitter about all the sickeningly sweet married couples around you? Cheer up, buttercup! Here are a few excerpts to remind you what exactly you're spared by remaining blissfully solo.

In 1886, author J. H. Kellogg published a book called *Plain Facts for Old and Young: Embracing the Natural History and Hygiene of Organic Life*. "If you find that you are overlooked," Kellogg wrote, "do not begin to bemoan your lot, but be glad and thankful that you are not the wife of an encumbrance, and be sure that in all probability, if you were not single, you would be in that unhappy predicament." Mr. Kellogg is pretty adamant:

> It is unquestionably true that the average 'old maid' is vastly happier in her lot, and more useful to the world, than quite a large proportion of wives. Certainly there is a vast deal of useful work which can be better accomplished by those who can give their undivided attention to the work in hand, than by those whose minds and energies are necessarily devoted to husband, children, and do-

mestic cares. We doubt not that the world would be vastly better off if there were a much larger number of useful old maids, and a less number of helpless, good-for-nothing, sickly wives.

Feel better? I do!

Satisfactions of the Career Girl

A common theme in advice books from earlier times is one that describes the single girl as a career gal. Not surprising. The girl who is not dating, planning a wedding, or raising wee ones has got to do *something* with all that free time. The successful single woman "puts everyone into good humor, and is always desired," wrote E. J. Hardy in his 1901 book *Concerning Marriage*. "She is not soured by celibacy, but can only think of and plan for the happiness of others. She is gentle, ready, helpful, and firm withal, in sickness or any other emergency."

Macfadden's *Womanhood and Marriage* optimistically describes the "bachelor girl" of 1923 as "an unmarried woman . . . who has gone out into the world of business and is leading her own independent, and generally very efficient, life. She carries with her no suggestion of failure. No one could ever think of her as a remnant on life's bargain counter."

In 1936, Joseph Tenenbaum got creative with expressing the benefits of work in *The Riddle of Woman: A Study in the Social Psychology of Sex*. "The rhythm of work is an echo of the rhythm of sex. Next to sex, work is the nearest channel for freeing excess energy. Both are effectual means of depleting tension and deflating the urge. Consequently there is no better compensation for sex frustration than hard labor."

You'll never turn down overtime again!

He continues by comparing labor pains to the "pains of labor." "The spinster, knowing no labor pains, becomes a marvel at physical and mental labor. She is careful to a fault, immaculate, fastidious, and overzealous. She has a phenomenal faculty for mastering details and, but for occasional loss of temper, would be an ideal worker. Many of the ablest executives among women are spinsters. Some of our greatest women, internationally recognized as leaders of great causes, are single women."

Ultimate Freedom

Forget successful careers. There is much, much more to living in single bliss. "Think of the things that you, all alone, don't have to do," author Marjorie Hillis describes in *Live Alone and Like It: A Guide for the Extra Woman* (1936). "You don't have to turn out your light when you want to read, because somebody else wants to sleep. You don't have to have the light on when you want to sleep, because somebody else wants to read. You don't have to get up in the night to fix somebody else's hot-water bottle, or lie awake listening to snores, or be vivacious when you're tired, or cheerful when you're blue, or sympathetic when you're bored. You probably have your bathroom all to yourself, too, which is unquestionably one of Life's Great Blessings."

Perhaps the real benefit of flying solo is the freedom to live life the way that *you* want to live it. "There are many allurements in the single life," writes Macfadden in 1923. "There is, for example, the greater freedom which comes to one who has no one's needs or desires to consider but her own. She can live her own life, which is what so many of us clamor for in the early years of adolescence. She is free to let her ambitions have full sway, and she may, therefore, achieve success."

Finesse, Grace, Gaiety, and Gusto

We've all listened to the concerned voices of family members wondering when we last had a date or spent time as a third wheel at social occasions. So it seems fitting to sum up with this upbeat excerpt from Jean Van Evera's *How to Be Happy While Single* (1949): "The life that is lived with finesse, grace, gayety, and gusto is sure to be a good one. The single woman who manages this kind of a life for herself derives a special satisfaction from having achieved her goal against the admitted odds which society has placed in her path."

So go forth, singles. Banish the negative old maid and spinster thoughts, those "admitted odds" (and oddballs) that have been routinely placed in your path. Be proud of your lot! Enjoy that single blessedness! Live alone and like it!

House Without a Spouse

★

by MICHELLE GOODMAN

The response was the same every time: "But what about your boyfriend? Where's *he* planning to live?"

"In his house, the same place he's lived since we met," I'd explain to whatever perplexed friend I happened to be with. Then I'd return to perusing the menu at the pizzeria, IHOP, or ice cream parlor we were in, while she'd lose herself in toddler-speak or triple-checking the high-chair safety belt.

From her blank reaction, you'd have thought I'd just told her I was having a polyamorous affair with a handful of Scientologists, not that I'd just purchased my first home—by myself. So went Baby Tour 2004, my long-overdue trip to the Tri-State Area to meet the umpteen kids collectively hatched by a cadre of childhood friends. During my two-week visit, I had this conversation on a daily basis, usually in the presence of shrieking infants and short-tempered spouses.

"So how long have you two been dating?" Childhood Friend A or B or C would inquire, while wiping off the spit-covered crayons or plastic utensils her spawn had thrown onto the restaurant floor.

"About two years."

"So, um, no plans to shack up together?"

"Not at this time." To put things in a context they could fathom, I'd sometimes add that my boyfriend and I just "weren't there" yet.

"And how far away from each other will you be living now—you said your place is outside the city, right?"

Relentless.

In a world where everyone was in a rush to get the picket fence and 2.673 kids, I stood out a like an unmown, dandelion-riddled lawn with a rusted-out muscle car on cinder blocks smack dab in the middle. Because I've never gotten engaged or hitched within three weeks of meeting someone, friends called me immature, commitment-phobic, a late bloomer, a player, a childhood-divorce casualty, or sometimes "a total freaking guy."

All that, I'd gotten used to. I wasn't the joined-at-the-hip type; others were. So be it. To each her own. Viva la perkytogethers. Long live quirkyalones. But the fact that some people still saw female homeowners as a big stinking deal in this day and age was a new one on me. I mean, it wasn't like I'd awoken in 1952 and made the shocking announcement that I was going to work outside the home. As a drug lord.

A thirtysomething female with a home of her own is hardly an anomaly. Single women buy one in five homes in this country (twice as many as single men), and I count my mom, my real estate agent, and several of my Seattle friends among them. But in more traditional circles, a single home-buying female with a monogamous boyfriend (especially one she considers a keeper) was a virtual freak show.

Part of me didn't get why the concept of two people being in love but not living under the same roof was so hard to grasp. Mia and Woody did it for years. Frida and Diego lived next door to each other and had an adjoining bridge. Katharine Hepburn, too, said she thought spouses would have an easier time just being neighbors who occasionally visit one another. The media even has a name for these couples: living apart togethers (a.k.a. LATs).

Perhaps I was being oversensitive to my friends' queries because I was the odd girl out. After all, these were legitimate questions from women who were like family to me, no matter how alien our respective lifestyles. I'd known most of them since my neon-clad, Clearasil-slathered days; surely, they were just genuinely concerned about how my life was shaping up.

Still, I couldn't help but feel like they were trying to shoehorn me into a timeline I didn't write. Never mind that several of them were miserable with their own life-altering decisions. What was it about people that made them drive others to follow the same path they'd taken—for better or worse? Did misery truly love company? Or did they know something I didn't know?

Truth be told, I wasn't always okay with the idea of buying solo. For years, I was a house divided. In fact, back in my savings account–challenged twenties, I had yet to stumble upon the notion that I didn't need to move in with someone I was screwing to get my hands on that golden mortgage-coupon book.

Of course, the family pressure didn't help. Like many women who came of age in the 1980s, I was blessed with a battalion of well-meaning grandparents, aunts, and older cousins who, from the moment I could walk, invoked the "find a rich husband" mantra. Somehow, I managed to defy them and grow into a—wonder of wonders!—self-sufficient woman who runs her own business, revels in her kid-free lifestyle, and questions whether having a guy and his dirty sock piles at arm's length is all that.

But I must have swallowed a few sips of the conjugal Kool-Aid at some point, because I assumed that owning a home would only happen if and when I bit the cohabitation bullet. I didn't see any other way.

All that changed one afternoon in my early thirties.

I was working from home, the tube tuned to one of those local talk shows that incessantly profiles self-help gurus and weight-loss success stories. A women's money coach, Barbara Stanny, was on, promoting her book *Prince Charming Isn't Coming.* Suffice it to say, the book's title alone—I never actually read the thing—knocked me on my ass. To me, the message was loud and clear: *Wake up, girl, and get a fucking grip on your financial life, because no one's going to do it for you.*

Fast-forward to my midthirties. As housing costs skyrocketed and even the sketchy neighborhoods of Seattle began to creep out of financial reach, my residential clock started to tick. A couple of leaky roofs, mentally ill landlords, and rats in the kitchen later, the tick had become a deafening gong. So for the first time in my life, I began to scrimp and save, determined to put my tenant days behind me. Thanks to some hefty corporate clients and a heap of overtime, I managed to slap together enough cash for a down payment.

And thus my journey home began.

Like many single buyers before me, I immediately came down with a bad case of DINK envy. With the power of their joint checking account, these childless, dual-incomed duos could swoop in and snatch my dream shack out from under me faster than I could smash a cockroach on the kitchen counter of my first New York apartment. My real estate agent warned me that sellers saw DINKs as a safer bet than their single-income counterparts. And in a seller's market, moneyed DINKs had no qualms bidding $20,000, $30,000, even $50,000 above a home's asking price.

I began to see the same fleece-clad, BlackBerried DINKs at the open houses I'd race to each Sunday. And began—I'll admit it— to entertain shameful fantasies about their demise: I'd will them to relocate, lose their jobs, call off their wedding, anything to whittle down the competition for what I saw as *my* house.

And then a strange thing happened. After a few fruitless months of searching and seething, grief unexpectedly moved in.

I'd lie in bed at night willing myself to fall asleep, sometimes beside my boyfriend, other times alone with the crickets, keenly aware that some long-buried dream of cohabitation was crumbling apart, like the rotting porch rails on the cozy fixers I'd lost to higher bidders. A single thought echoed in my head: *I always thought I'd be doing this* with *someone.* It was a dream I hadn't entirely realized I'd been clinging to. And I wasn't even sure it was *my* dream, or one that I'd adopted from my well-meaning relatives, my best friend back in the sixth grade, or my favorite episode of *Little House on the Prairie.*

Could it be I wasn't the Maureen Dowd of homeownership after all? Or was I just mildly hung over from the conjugal Kool-Aid I'd been force-fed since my diaper days?

For several weeks, my blue mood was acute, all encompassing, a leaky faucet I couldn't ignore. Suddenly I'd become the sad, single home-buying female portrayed in the media's "See Jane Remodel" trend pieces (circa 2002), more wistful for what she didn't have—someone to squabble with over paint colors, light fixtures, or the position of the toilet seat—than excited about the roots she was planting for herself.

But what was I really grieving for? I wondered. Some prepubescent fantasy of me and Shaun Cassidy in our Malibu (Barbie-esque) cliffside mansion with our nineteen babies? That a legitimate part of me had bought into the outmoded social equation that Adulthood = Coupledom = Mortgage Ever After? That had I only been willing to handle a shack-up of convenience, I wouldn't be looking at purchasing a 500- to 700-square-foot lean-to in the boonies and instead would have a shot at owning a kitchen that didn't double as a laundry room and/or bathroom?

If you asked me today, I'd have to put my money on all three.

When I eventually found The One—a hot little number with mint-green aluminum siding, more wood paneling than the *Brady Bunch* place, and linoleum so ugly it gave you vertigo—my blue mood dissipated, just as suddenly as it had arrived. Sure, my happy new home was a hole in the wall, but it was *my* little hole in the wall. As for the grief, I never told anyone about it, not even my boyfriend. Too ashamed, I simply swept that secret under the rust-colored shag rug and focused on the momentous move ahead of me.

As I packed, I began to have visions of becoming one of those wrench-wielding mamas who knows how to fix everything from a leaky toilet to a downed power line. And the more I listened to homeowning couples whine at dinner parties about their "brutal" DIY bathroom remodels, the more I fantasized about spackling, sawing, and soldering circles around them.

So did I start to strip, sand, and re-floor all 730 square feet of my house the moment I moved in? Did friends of both sexes routinely call me for home-repair advice? Did I become so dang handy that Home Depot asked me to teach their latest "Do-It-Herself" drywalling clinic?

In a word, no. My dirty little feminist secret is that when things go awry in my house, I either pay someone to make the problem disappear (bee guy, rat guy, broken-furnace guy), pump the Home Depot customer service desk for free advice, or—*gasp!*—enlist the help of my boyfriend.

Since I don't want to become an utter home-improvement ignoramus, I do insist on being the one to turn the screwdriver or hold the drill while the boyfriend looks up what to do in his fix-it books and relays the directions to me in home-improvement-ignoramus-speak. But basically, my home repairs usually go something like this:

Bathroom tub and sink clog. Simultaneously. With my mother due to arrive for an overnight stay in twenty-four hours. I try a plunger, then Drano, then finally call the boyfriend (whose tool-box eclipses mine), then order a large pepperoni pizza. Boyfriend attacks the tub with a plumbing snake while instructing me on how to remove the U-pipe under the sink. I get it off without a hitch, at which time fifty years of sludgy rust shoots into and out of the tiny Tupperware container I've placed beneath the opening, splattering onto the walls and floor, not to mention my arms and face. At which time my inner five-year-old girl takes the wheel and the only words I can muster for the next fifteen minutes are, "Ew, ew, ew! Oh my god, that's not sewage, is it? Oh my god. Oh my god. Ewwwwwww . . . " At which point the pizza arrives.

I'd like to tell you I make up for this with a green thumb, a sparkling bathtub, or hand-stitched curtains with matching throw pillows, but I can't. Instead, as I enter my second year of homeown-ership, the walls of my place are the same god-awful Pepto-Bismol pink and '70s-appliance gold (a hue more bile than bling) as when I moved in. Ditto for the hideous, hundred-pound burlap drapes (no doubt purchased during the Nixon administration). Domesti-cally, I'm more dimwit than diva. But I love my goofy little house just the same.

Naturally, my Baby Tour friends all have impeccable homes, so I don't dare admit my domestic shortcomings to them. Instead, when they call to see "how the new place is shaping up," I steer the conversation to my long-range plans, such as converting the unat-tached, unfinished garage into an office—which, I reveal, would push the total square footage of my homestead dangerously close to one thousand. The number seems to sit well with this crowd, all of whom gasped upon learning the modest size of my new dwell-ing. In fact, when I talk to them now, I can almost hear their shoul-ders unclenching.

That is, until, like clockwork, the conversation boomerangs back to the boyfriend I don't live with:

"Oh, so there would be more room for your boyfriend, like, if he wanted to move in?"

Yes, I'll explain, but more importantly, I'll be able to turn the garage into that freestanding writing studio I've always wanted, complete with skylights, French doors, Persian rugs, jade plants, big worktables, and a tricked-out stereo system.

But I lose them every time, I suspect after "yes."

Contrary to what my childhood pals might believe, there was no Miranda Hobbes "Oh my god, I have to check the Single box— kill me now" moment when I signed my mortgage papers. Granted, I may have been a house of secrets (particularly when it came to my DINK envy, and my unexpected grief over buying solo), but I was no longer a house divided. All I felt was pride. I'd purchased my first piece of property all by my lonesome—no cosigner, no roommate, no breadwinning guy as a financial crutch. After two decades in the rental trenches, it was a crowning achievement.

One that I celebrate every time a new salesperson stops by my door to hawk anything from window treatments to the New Testament.

"Can I speak to the owner of the house?" they always ask, and I must admit, I never tire of the question.

Instead I just smile and say, "Yes, that would be me."

Life After Death

★

by GENEVIEVE DAVIS GINSBURG

My grandmother, long dead, once said she thanked heaven that adolescence hadn't been invented when she was bringing up her children. I was reminded of that when I was searching the library shelves in the small Northwestern town where I spend my summers, looking for a book about widows—or widowhood, as it is called in these times of equal opportunity.

Remarkably, in front of me there were three full shelves on adolescence, while widowhood, older than all our grandmothers put together, was covered by just a handful of books: one on money management, a few inspirational volumes by widows telling how they overcame, and a sprinkling of pop-psychology bestsellers on how to overcome.

As a seasoned widow with a vested interest in the subject, I was looking for something beyond coping, beyond overcoming, and beyond the generic collection on death, dying, letting go, and saying goodbye to your pet. I was searching for something that would acknowledge widowhood as a bona fide life stage with uncharted potential—more particularly, a stage where the quest is not limited to replacing one partner with another, or to remaining a wife without a husband forever after. An affirmation, really, for the stage—in many ways as painful and full of change as adolescence—that could be described as living happily *without* a man after you've lived happily *with* one. It's the kind of pointless reassurance I often look for in a recipe for an already-cooked stew.

By now I know the ingredients. They are familiar enough. After ten years, the appellation "widow" is no longer part of my description of myself. I check off "single" in those boxes. But away from home base and the niches I've carved for myself, the ghost of an earlier identity—a woman without a man—rises. Each summer when I journey from my urban setting to my rural one, I can almost feel the stereotype closing in and the new stage slipping away.

At restaurant stops along the way, I must once again become accustomed to an ungraceful wait while the hostess and I clarify that I am not waiting for my husband to park the car. "Oh, I didn't realize you were alone," she accuses. And sure enough, as I look around, I seem to be the lone post–middle age female diner in this off-ramp microcosm of America. I leave a double tip in expiation.

As I continue on my two-day journey, fellow travelers seek me out at viewing points, motel swimming pools, and gas stations to award unsolicited gold stars and points. "Traveling alone? My, you're a brave little lady." "Going to visit your children, are you?" I nod yes because at this point I am already reaching for normalcy, as well as the senior discount. It wouldn't do to tell them how much I have come to enjoy driving alone with my own thoughts and a book on tape as my only passengers.

The inflection rises noticeably when motel desk clerks repeat, "One?" When I am solicitously offered a ground-floor room near the office and recommended (slowly and loudly) a restaurant with nice, plain food, I do feel lacking and wish I had brought along another widow, or at least a small poodle. By the time I reach my summer cabin in Idaho, I am what they think I am or, more accurately, not what I thought I was.

Once there, in a place where nobody blinks when women chop wood, hunt deer, or change the oil in the old pickup, my image takes another bashing. Neither coupled nor looking to be (measured by Saturday-night attendance at the local bar), nor the matriarchal head of a visiting clan, nor the surviving wife of an erstwhile fly fisherman waiting to sell, I am something of a curiosity. My neighbors have wondered aloud why this person (by this time it's "old lady") would choose to buy a cabin to live in *alone*.

Have you noticed the word "alone" keeps coming up? Bald eagles flying overhead, moose wading in the river, fresh pine in the air notwithstanding, my good neighbors—and they really are good—have also been heard to wonder, "What does she *do* in there all alone?" Once, following the departure of a weekend guest (female), I heard someone speculate, "She's too old to be a lesbian, isn't she?"

Certainly, I am not the only independent widow who enjoys her freedom, her solitude, her open-ended lifestyle, who does not especially care about sharing her life with a man. I think we—the hundred or so I've met—are weary over the confusion between being alone and loneliness. I'll probably go to my grave hearing, "You can't tell, maybe someday . . . "

From the moment my husband died, people thought to comfort me with the assurance that I would one day remarry. "You're young and attractive, you'll see." (I was in my middle fifties, a perfect statistical model.) Anxiously, as the years went by and I remained single, I began to feel as deficient as a sorority girl without a Saturday-night date. And, true to the repeated warnings of friends, family, and friends' husbands, put rather basically by an eighteen-year-old niece as "using it or losing it," I lost it. I was as celibate as a nun.

It was some time before I came out of the closet—if there is a closet for celibate, over-sixty women—and knew in heart and mind that I preferred the memories of a bonny companion and a good sex life to what was out there. Which in my case were cavalier men who offered, gratuitously, to service me.

There was even one old high school boyfriend who, as predicted in the widow's favorite fantasy, turned up serendipitously. This one, however, was quite deaf and snored—right in the armchair while watching television. Mostly, I met those men who had survived strictly on their ability to bore someone else to death.

Widowhood needs to be reinvented, for both those who live it and those who fear it. Let's bestow on it the status of a real stage of life, not that of a way station. We have been conned by movies, television, country music, getaway vacation ads, and other profit-making operations into believing that happiness marches two by two and anything less is loneliness. Daughters are not taught to be widows, love songs never hymn the quest for self. Where are the songs of love for the life we love and the joy of achieving single-handedly?

I was dragged by my heels into this so-called passage, but now that I'm here I've come to appreciate the opportunity to find the person buried under so many layers of daughter, wife, mother.

Frankly, it's been my stage for discovering that there are worse things than sleeping in the middle of the bed and not knowing whether you snore. That saying adieu to sex does not make your cheeks fall in and your hair fall out. That it's the best time for making new friends—friends in foreign places, go-for-a-hike friends, dinner friends, season-ticket friends, I-need-to-talk friends, and others I might not have tolerated when I had my one best friend. Most unexpectedly rewarding, though, has been discovering solitude and having the time for it.

Acknowledgments

A s usual, a number of individuals and institutions are responsible for the creation of this book. Thanks are due to Debbie
Stoller, editor of *BUST* magazine, who first suggested I write on
the topic of singles; to Bella DePaulo for her feisty and unflagging
defense of the singles life; to the writers of *Salon*'s Broadsheet for
their stellar coverage of contemporary women's issues.

I'm also extremely grateful to writers Rachel Kramer Bussel, Jane Ganahl, Michelle Goodman, and Judy McGuire for their
contributor suggestions. And of course, there wouldn't be a *Single
State of the Union* without the thirty-seven talented writers who
crafted the wise and witty essays included within these pages—a
toast to you all.

Thanks are due to the Seattle Public Library, Abebooks.com,
the Internet Movie Database, and the extraordinary Seattle used
bookstores Arundel Books, Epilogue Books, and Twice Sold Tales
for their research assistance. I'd also like to express my appreciation to Beacon Press, the South Florida *Sun-Sentinel, Venus, The
New York Times*, the *San Francisco Chronicle, Skirt!*, Paul Ginsburg, Phil Bevis, and Nicole Sarrocco for their gracious assistance.
A special nod of appreciation also goes to Veronica Markey, author
of the poem "Cinderella." And to Brian Curry and the entire staff
of 10 Mercer, my office away from the office.

As always, I'm eternally grateful to my sisters (Gloria, Mary, Frances, and Peggy) and to my mom (Viva Ruth), who raised us all single-handedly and instilled in us the confidence and wherewithal to go it alone in this world (i.e., "Learn a skill so you can get a good job and not have to rely on a man!"). Thanks also go to my dear friends (Angelo, Alan, Alex, Ashley, Caitlin, Chris, Claire, Dave, Emily, Heather, Jarratt, John, Jon, Judith, Laura, Leita, Leslie, Margaret, Michelle, Nick, Renate, Stesha, Steve, and Young Mike), who have always been there with support, patience, counsel, kindness, bad jokes, income tax assistance, a dry martini, and/or the occasional tale from the singles trenches, many of which acted as standard bearers for this book. Finally, I'd like extend my utmost gratitude to Jill Rothenberg of Seal Press for her vision, her support, her humor, her integrity, and most especially, her staunch belief that I was the single most qualified person for this project. This book's for you, Jill.

About the Contributors

Rachel Kramer Bussel writes the "Lusty Lady" column for *The Village Voice,* hosts the In The Flesh Reading Series, and serves as senior editor at *Penthouse Variations.* She's edited nine books of erotica, including *Naughty Spanking Stories from A to Z* 1 and 2, *Ultimate Undies, Sexiest Soles, Glamour Girls: Femme/Femme Erotica,* and *Caught Looking: Erotic Tales of Voyeurs and Exhibitionists,* with more on the way. Her writing has been published in more than eighty anthologies, including *Best American Erotica* 2004 and 2006, as well as *AVN, BUST, Curve, Diva, Girlfriends, Gothamist,* Mediabistro.com, the *New York Post,* Oxygen.com, *Penthouse, Playgirl,* the *San Francisco Chronicle, Time Out New York, Velvetpark,* and *Zink.* Her website is www.rachelkramerbussel.com.

Sasha Cagen is the author of the cult hit *Quirkyalone: A Manifesto for Uncompromising Romantics* and the founder of International Quirkyalone Day, a growing alternative to Valentine's Day that celebrates all forms of love on February 14. *Quirkyalone* has been optioned to be developed as a television show. Her forthcoming book, *To-Do List,* based on her popular magazine and blog (www.todolistblog.com), provides an interactive look at list-making and what our lists say about us. Cagen lives in San Francisco.

Freelance journalist **Amanda Castleman** has lived in England, Italy, Greece, Cyprus, and America. She larks around the globe on assignment, which does nothing for her romantic prospects. But she's headstrong enough to try marriage again, if the right mood and man ever strike. When not mocking her muddy roots, Castleman's contributed to the *International Herald Tribune,* MSNBC.com, *Wired,* and *Salon,* plus the BBC, *The Guardian,* and *The Mail on Sunday.* Her book credits include Frommer's, Michelin, Time Out, Rough Guides, *Adventure Guide to Rome & Its Surroundings,* and *Greece, A Love Story.* She teaches through Writers.com. Her website is www.amandacastleman.com; she egocasts further at http://roadremedies.blogspot.com.

Margaret Cho is one of America's most successful comedians, as well as one of the nation's leading political and civil rights activists. She has received awards from the American Civil Liberties Union, the National Organization for Women, the National Gay and Lesbian Task Force, the Gay & Lesbian Alliance Against Defamation, Lambda Legal, and the Asian American Legal Defense and Education Fund for making a significant difference in promoting equal rights for all, regardless of race, sexual orientation, or gender identity. Her essay "I Am Getting Married" is from her second book, *I Have Chosen to Stay and Fight.*

Suzanne Cope is an author and professor living in the Boston area. She has written essays on food, travel, and popular culture that have been published in various newspapers and journals, as well as two nonfiction books for children. A recent graduate of Lesley University's MFA program, Cope is finishing a family memoir about her childhood spent at her grandparents' airport entitled *Wingwalking: Growing Up on the Other Side of the Runway.*

Bella DePaulo is a scholar of singlehood and the author of *Singled Out: How Singles are Stereotyped, Stigmatized, and Ignored, and Still Live Happily Ever After.* Her essays have appeared in *The New York Times* and *Newsday,* and online at *AlterNet* and *The Huffington Post.* She began her career as an academic social psychologist (PhD,

Harvard, 1979) studying liars and their lies. She lives in Summerland, California, and has been single all her life. Her website is www.belladepaulo.com.

Litsa Dremousis wrote, directed, and produced the plays *If I Wake Before I Die* and *9:00 in the Afternoon*. Her work appears in *The Believer, BlackBook, The Black Table, McSweeney's, Monkeybicycle, MovieMaker, Nylon, Paper, Paste, Poets & Writers* magazine, *Seattle Sound, Seattle Weekly, and Swivel,* and on NPR. Among others, she has interviewed Sherman Alexie, Augusten Burroughs, Death Cab for Cutie, Demetri Martin, Colin Meloy, Sean Nelson, Tim Blake Nelson, John Roderick, Wanda Sykes, and John Vanderslice. She is a winner of *BlackBook*'s Hemingway Short Story Contest. Her short story "The Cousinfucker" appears in *Monkeybicycle's* upcoming comedy anthology.

Jane Ganahl is a columnist and author who wrote for San Francisco newspapers for twenty-four years; a version of her essay "Faux Boyfriends" originally appeared in the *San Francisco Chronicle*. Ganahl is also the cofounder of Litquake, a Bay Area literary festival. In 2005, she edited the anthology *Single Woman of a Certain Age* and has contributed to two other collections, including *Roar Softly and Carry a Great Lipstick* and *The Secret Lives of Lawfully Wedded Wives*. Her novelized memoir, *Naked on the Page: The Misadventures of my Unmarried Midlife,* was released in February 2007. She thinks being single rocks.

Susan Jane Gilman is the author of the best-selling book *Hypocrite in a Pouffy White Dress,* as well as *Kiss My Tiara,* from which her essay "Marriage Ain't Prozac" is taken. She has written commentary for *The New York Times, Ms., US, Real Simple,* and the *Los Angeles Times,* among others, and has won several literary awards for her fiction and essays. Although she is currently living in Geneva, Switzerland, she remains, eternally, a child of New York.

Genevieve Davis Ginsburg was a licensed counselor and author, best known for founding Widowed to Widowed, a Tucson-based advocacy group that went on to help thousands of people survive the death of a spouse. The author of *Widow to Widow: Thoughtful, Practical Ideas for Rebuilding Your Life*, she was also a recipient of the 1981 Jefferson Award for public service and community leadership and the Arizona Governor's Award for her social service. She died in 1996, surviving her husband by twenty-one years. Her essay, "Life After Death," originally appeared in *The New York Times Magazine*.

Michelle Goodman is author of *The Anti 9-to-5 Guide: Practical Career Advice for Women Who Think Outside the Cube*. Her writing has appeared in *The Bark, Bitch, BUST, Salon,* and *The Seattle Times*. She lives in Seattle with Buddy, her eighty-pound lapdog, and has yet to take down the Nixon-era drapes in her wood-paneled living room. Visit her blog at www.anti9to5guide.com.

Abigail Grotke has been collecting classic advice books for almost twenty years. She has combined selections of advice from her one-thousand-plus books with witty commentary to create her award-winning website, Miss Abigail's Time Warp Advice (www.missabigail.com), and book, *Miss Abigail's Guide to Dating, Mating, and Marriage*. During the day, Grotke is a digital projects coordinator at the Library of Congress. She lives in Takoma Park, Maryland, with her dog, Felix, and an amazing collection of ice crushers.

Chelsea Handler is an accomplished stand-up comic and can be seen regularly on the Chelsea Handler Show (on the E! Television Network) and on the Oxygen network show *Girls Behaving Badly,*

Handler's essay "THUNDER" is from her first book, *My Horizontal Life: A Collection of One-Night Stands,* published in 2005.

Lynn Harris is author of the forthcoming comic novel *Death By Chick Lit,* as well as its prequel, *Miss Media,* and several humorous nonfiction books, including *Breakup Girl to the Rescue!* An award-winning journalist, she writes for *Glamour, Salon, Nerve, The New York Times, The Washington Post,* and many others. She is cocreator, with Chris Kalb, of the award-winning website BreakupGirl.net. Harris lives in Brooklyn, where everyone is a "local author."

Jane Hodges is a Seattle-based journalist and writer. Her fiction has appeared in the *Brooklyn Review,* and her journalistic work has appeared in *The Wall Street Journal, The New York Times,* the *Seattle Times, Fortune,* and other publications. She is addicted to coffee and reads a mean tarot. Her favorite coming-of-age book is Florence King's *Confessions of a Failed Southern Lady,* and she is working on a fiction manuscript involving women, guns, and cars.

Amy Hudock, PhD, a single mom, teaches English at a private college preparatory school in South Carolina, where she lives with her daughter. She is the editor in chief of *Literary Mama* and coeditor of *Literary Mama: Reading for the Maternally Inclined.* Her work has appeared in *ePregnancy,* Pregnancyandbaby.com, *Skirt!,* LiteraryMama.com, and other parenting publications.

Sarah Iverson was born in Brenham, Texas, a town famous for ice cream and miniature horses (www.bluebell.com and www.monasteryminiaturehorses.com). She holds a BA from Brown University in comparative literature. She has worked as a pastry chef, yoga teacher, hedge fund recruiter, sperm lab technician, personal trainer, calculus tutor, and wine importer, and she was a New York City Golden Gloves boxing champion. She writes children's novels under a different name and has a special interest in mythology. She lives in Brooklyn, New York.

Columnist **Judy McGuire** has worked a number of very odd jobs in her life, including stints as an auto-parts delivery person, a heroin ethnographer, and managing editor of the well-known stoner journal *High Times*. Having long ago cast aside drugs in favor of love, she currently writes "Dategirl," a sex and love advice column, for the *Seattle Weekly*. Alternate versions of the column also enjoyed long runs in the *New York Press, Men's Fitness,* and the *Eugene Weekly*. When she's not writing about herself in the third person, she's updating her blog, which can be found at http://badadvice .typepad.com.

Heather McKinnon is an artist at *The Seattle Times*. Her writings and illustrations have appeared in newspapers across the country, including the South Florida *Sun-Sentinel,* where a version of her essay "Postcard from the Edge" was originally published. She lives on Vashon Island in Puget Sound, Washington, with her husband, two cats, and four dogs. When she's not picking up poo and cleaning litter boxes, she escapes to her art studio, where she recycles found objects into creepy dioramas. Nothing satisfies her more than chopping off Barbie-doll heads with a hacksaw. If you ever visit, don't look in the freezer.

Wendy Merrill has been conducting undercover operations in the arena of dating and mating for many years, earning her several advanced degrees. Her unique "catch and release" program has provided a rich body of data, and she's currently compiling her research for a collection of essays entitled *Falling into Manholes.*

Wendy has an essay in the recent anthology *Single Woman of a Certain Age,* which *Publishers Weekly* called out as one of the funniest. Merrill the entrepreneur founded WAM Marketing Group, a unique marketing communications company based in Sausalito, California, where she currently lives.

Mikki Morrissette is the author of *Choosing Single Motherhood: The Thinking Woman's Guide.* She speaks about issues and concerns with Choice Mothers in person through her www .ChoosingSingleMotherhood.com website and in an online discussion group for Choice Moms.

Under the cover of night, **Laurie Notaro** ran away from her former home in Phoenix and is now holed up in Eugene, Oregon, a town so nice it took her a remarkable three whole months to build up enough anger to flip someone off in traffic. She loves ghost stories and seeing models cry, and is under the impression that she looks cute in hats (sadly, this is not true). Her essay "The Speech" is taken from her *New York Times* best-selling first book, *The Idiot Girls' Action-Adventure Club: True Tales from a Magnificent and Clumsy Life.*

Rachel Eve Radway is a writer, editor, traveler, and lapsed artist. Other published pieces include "Car Story 2: The Tale of the Missing Gearshift, and Other Adventures of a Later Learner," available at http://thebluehammer.com/articles/car.html. Rachel has lived and traveled around the world, collecting roommates and stories. She now lives alone in a beautiful apartment that she decorated herself in Sausalito, California, and is planning her next big home projects.

Michal Reed has an MFA in art and critical writing from CalArts. She has taught university classes in writing, art theory, and the history of feminist theory. Most of her writing credits have been art reviews. Currently, she teaches English and art at a rural Californian high school. Without urban social interactions, in addition to occasionally showing her photography, she is able to easily integrate hiking, biking, swimming, skiing, and reflection into her daily life—though of course not all at the same time. She has just finished a memoir about climbing all of California's mountains that are over fourteen thousand feet and has begun a new writing and photo project about walking.

Jillian Robinson is an award-winning television producer whose programs have aired on PBS and the Discovery Channel and in more than forty-five countries worldwide. Robinson, who has traveled to thirty-three countries as well as lived in Italy and England (where she managed a TV production company), speaks about travel's power to enrich and change our everyday lives. Her essay "Out of Africa, in Karen Blixen's Footsteps" is an adaptation from her new book, *Change Your Life Through Travel*.

Dana Rozier received her MFA in Writing from Vermont College in January 2007. She is the author of *Whatcom County with Kids: Places to Go and Things to Do*. Rozier lives in Washington State with her two children, Elizabeth and David. After writing the essay that appears in this publication, she has purchased several pairs of cute underwear, and her life has become a lot more fun.

Rachel Sarah is the author of the recently released *Single Mom Seeking: Play Dates, Blind Dates, and Other Dispatches from the Dating World*. She's also the award-winning romance columnist for San Francisco's *j. the Jewish News Weekly of Northern California*. Her writing has appeared in *Family Circle, Parenting, Tango, Ms.*, and *The Christian Science Monitor*. Visit her website at www.singlemom seeking.com.

Suzanne Schlosberg is the author of *The Curse of the Singles Table: A True Story of 1001 Nights Without Sex.* She married her Streakbreaker, Paul Spencer, and they now live in Bend, Oregon. The Streak isn't the only feat of endurance Suzanne has managed to parlay into a writing gig. She is the women's record holder in the Great American Sack Race, a competition that required her to run five miles carrying a fifty-pound sack of chicken feed. She chronicled her unexpected victory in *Sand in My Bra: Funny Women Write from the Road.* Suzanne's latest test of stamina is an infertility streak that has exceeded seven hundred days. Her most recent book is *The Essential Fertility Log.*

Susan Shapiro is a New York–based journalist whose work has appeared in *The New York Times, The Washington Post,* the *Los Angeles Times, The Village Voice, Cosmopolitan, Glamour, Jane,* and *Salon.* She's the coeditor of the anthology *Food for the Soul* and author of *Lighting Up, Secrets of a Fix-Up Fanatic* and *Five Men Who Broke My Heart,* recently optioned for a movie by Paramount Pictures. Shapiro's book *Only as Good as Your Word* will be available in fall 2007. She teaches writing at New York University, The New School, and Media bistro.com and can be visited at her website www.susanshapiro.net.

April Sinclair is the author of three novels, including the critically acclaimed bestseller *Coffee Will Make You Black,* for which she received the Carl Sandburg Award from the Friends of the Chicago Public Library, as well as the 1994 Book of the Year (Young Adult Fiction category) award from The American Library Association. Sinclair has an essay in *Single Woman of a Certain Age,* edited by Jane Ganahl, and has been a fellow at the Ragdale, MacDowell, Yaddo, and Djeressi artist colonies. She lives in the San Francisco Bay Area and is working on a collection of personal essays.

Adele Slaughter is a freelance writer and teacher. She has covered environmental and personal health for USAToday.com. She has written for *Ms., Written By,* Modestyle.com, and *CoDe.* In 2003, she was awarded a national journalism prize for her coverage of multiple sclerosis. In 1993, the White House Commission on Presidential Scholars named her a distinguished teacher. She received her MFA in poetry from Columbia University. Slaughter's book of poems, *What the Body Remembers,* was published in 1994. She is the coauthor of *Art That Pays: The Emerging Artist's Guide to Making a Living.*

Margaret Smith is a two-time Emmy award winner for comedy writing and has won the Funniest Female Stand-Up Comedy Award. She has been a regular guest on *The Tonight Show* with Jay Leno and *The Late Show* with David Letterman and has done guest spots on *Oprah,* HBO, and CNN and starred on *That Eighties Show.* A writer for *The Ellen Show,* she is also the author of *What Was I Thinking? How Being a Stand Up Did Nothing to Prepare Me to Become a Single Mother,* from which her essay "Donor, Doctor, Desperado" is taken. Smith lives in Southern California with her sons.

In addition to penning the "Sweet Freak" column for *Metro* newspaper, **Amy Thomas** has covered fashion designers, perfumers, chocolatiers, wedding planners, and furniture makers for publications such as *Lucky, BUST, Time Out New York, The Knot,* and *CITY* magazine. She is the founder of the nontraditional wedding website Modgirl.com and the coauthor of the upcoming interior design book *Convertible Houses.* When not indulging her wanderlust, Thomas is happy to be home in New York City.

Rachel Toor, assistant professor of creative writing at the Inland Northwest Center for Writers, Eastern Washington University, is the author of *The Pig and I: How I Learned to Love Men (Almost) As Much As I Love My Pets* and *Admissions Confidential: An Insider's Account of the Elite College Selection Process.* She has also written for *Glamour, Reader's Digest,* and *The Chronicle of Higher Education* and is a staff writer for *Running Times* magazine. She runs many, many, many miles and is in love with a hooded rat. Visit her website at www.racheltoor.com.

Sociologist **E. Kay Trimberger** is the author of *The New Single Woman.* Parts of her essay are excerpted from the book. She is an ever-single woman and single mother, living in Berkeley, California. The author of two other scholarly books and numerous academic articles, Trimberger has published op-ed pieces in the *San Francisco Chronicle,* the *San Jose Mercury News, In These Times,* and the *Santa Rosa Press Democrat.* She is professor emeritus of women's and gender studies at Sonoma State University and a visiting scholar at the Institute for the Study of Social Change at UC Berkeley. You can access her website at www.kaytrimberger.com.

Jessica Valenti, twenty-eight, is the founder and executive editor of Feministing.com. She has a master's degree in women's and gender studies from Rutgers University and has worked with numerous national and international women's organizations. Jessica is also a cofounder of the REAL Hot 100, a campaign that aims to change the perception of younger women in the media, and the blogger for NARAL Pro-Choice America. Her writing has appeared in *AlterNet, Salon, Guernica* magazine, and *The Guardian.* Valenti's book, *Full Frontal Feminism,* will be available in spring 2007.

M. Susan Wilson was born single and has been that way ever since. A Florida native, she made her way in the mid-1990s to Seattle—the city she now calls home—via Madison, Wisconsin, New York City, and Pusan, South Korea, where she spent a year teaching English as a second language. A lawyer by training, she's spent most of her adult life working as an editor and a writer. She's served as managing editor of *Spa* magazine, *Seattle* magazine, and—the irony abounds—*Seattle Bride*. When not working, Susan enjoys traveling on the cheap, indulging in marathon sessions of *Buffy the Vampire Slayer* reruns, and riding horses (she is, albeit tentatively, learning to jump).

About the Editor

Diane Mapes is the author of *How to Date in a Post-Dating World* (Sasquatch, 2006), a funny journalistic take on the traditional dating manual. Her satire and reported essays on dating, singles' rights, television, travel, freak magnets, naked sushi, swingers, and more have appeared in *BUST, The Christian Science Monitor, Health, Los Angeles Times,* MSNBC.com, *Seattle* magazine, the *Seattle Times,* and *The Washington Post.* Happily single, she lives in Seattle.

Selected Titles from Seal Press

Single Mom Seeking by Rachel Sarah. $14.95, 1-58005-166-9. A single mom who knows the difference between "going to bed" and "putting to bed" shares her heartfelt and hilarious take on the challenges of balancing motherhood with dating.

No Touch Monkey! by Ayun Halliday. $14.95, 1-58005-097-2. A self-admittedly bumbling tourist, Halliday shares—with razor-sharp wit and to hilarious effect—the travel stories most are too self-conscious to tell.

Full Frontal Feminism by Jessica Valenti. $14.95, 1-58005-201-0. A sassy and in-your-face look at contemporary feminism for women of all ages.

Women Who Win by Lisa Taggart. $14.95, 1-58005-200-2. Bypassing the usual routine of sound bites and training regimes, Taggart delves into what really inspires each professional woman in her individual sport and reveals what makes her tick.

Intimate Politics: How I Grew Up Red, Fought for Free Speech, and Became a Feminist Rebel by Bettina F. Aptheker. $16.95, 1-58005-160-X. A courageous and uncompromising account of one woman's personal and political transformation, and a fascinating portrayal of a key chapter in our nation's history.